Glob

Mission Without Conquest

Langham

GLOBAL LIBRARY

Mission Without Conquest

An Alternative Missionary Practice

Willis Horst
Ute & Frank Paul

© 2015 by Willis Horst, Ute Paul and Frank Paul

Published in arrangement with Ediciones Kairos, Buenos Aires, Argentina

Published 2015 by Langham Global Library
an imprint of Langham Creative Projects

Langham Partnership
PO Box 296, Carlisle, Cumbria CA3 9WZ, UK
www.langham.org

Published in Spanish by Ediciones Kairós (9789871355266) and in German by Neufeld Verlag (9783937896953). This edition (9781783689149) is published in partnership with the Mennonite Mission Network.

ISBNs:
978-1-78368-916-3 Print
978-1-78368-914-9 Mobi
978-1-78368-915-6 ePub
978-1-78368-967-5 PDF

British Library Cataloguing in Publication Data

Horst, Willis, author.
 Mission without conquest : an alternative missionary practice.
 1. Mennonites--Missions--Argentina--Chaco--History--
 20th century. 2. Chaco (Argentina)--Religion.
 3. Missions--Biblical teaching.
 I. Title II. Paul, Frank, author. III. Paul, Ute, author.
 266.9'78234-dc23

 ISBN-13: 9781783689163

Cover & Book Design: projectluz.com

"We don't need to conquer souls,
just take spiritual food to others;
then they will come to church of their own choice,
to seek more from God."[1]

---

1. Quote of an unidentified Toba Qom speaker at indigenous church service of the Foursquare Gospel Church, Lote 15 (*El Matadero*) near the town of *Presidencia Roca*, Chaco Province, Argentina, known in Toba Qom as *Qochiiñi' Lai'* (place of many wild turkeys) annotated in Frank Paul's travel diary, January 10, 1999.

Contents

Foreword

"Every time we read your prayer letters and ministry reports," they told us, "we are reminded how much your work in West Africa resembles ours in Argentina."

The year was 1981. My wife, Jeanette, and I had just completed our first term serving with the Harrist Church, an African-initiated movement in Ivory Coast, West Africa. The comments directed to us came from Albert and Lois Buckwalter, long-term Mennonite mission workers with over thirty years of ministry among indigenous peoples in the Chaco region of Argentina.

I remember initially being somewhat surprised by the Buckwalters' remarks. Our contexts of ministry seemed far more contrasting than similar in nature. Situated on two vastly different continents separated by 4,500 miles and shaped by politico-religious and cultural histories sharing little in common, it was not immediately obvious to me how and why comparisons were being drawn between the Buckwalters' work and our own.

With time, however, I learned to appreciate that what held these two stories together was not their *context* of ministry, but their *posture* of ministry – a shift in approach occasioned and inspired in many ways by the remarkable seven-decade long story recounted in this book.

It might simply be called "the Chaco experiment" – the dramatic and intentional decision, made by Mennonite workers and administrators in the mid-1950s, to abandon the classical mission compound approach they had been employing for over a decade, and embrace a creative but uncharted strategy of accompanying and empowering the fledgling indigenous gospel movement gaining momentum throughout the region at that time.

In so doing, the mission found itself rediscovering some of the fundamental principles set forth by Jesus himself in his commissioning instructions to the disciples recorded in Luke 10:

- **Go local.** Visit every town and village. Don't expect people to come to you. Hang out with folk. Accept their hospitality. Eat whatever food they put on the table. And spend the night in whatever sleeping conditions they offer you.
- **Go light.** Forget the extra trunks and containers. "Carry no purse, no bag, and no sandals." Keep it simple. Don't rely on your own stuff. Stay vulnerable. Take the bush taxi. Place yourself

in the hands of local hosts. Be accountable. Never forget your guest status.

- **Go looking.** Know that God has preceded you in whatever location you might chance to visit. Find out what God has been up to in that place before you arrived on the scene. Get with *God's* program; don't import and impose your own. Build on local wisdom, gifts and resources. Be as gracious with your hosts as they are with you. Greet them with a "peace blessing." Then, seek out and nurture deepened relationships with anyone responding positively to your gesture of goodwill.

- **Go learning.** Marinate yourself in local ways of thinking, being, and doing. Know that only plants with indigenous roots will produce long-lasting, healthy fruit. Expect to be blessed, nourished, strengthened, and healed by hosts who extend their tables and offer you hospitality. Think "sharing circle," not "bully pulpit." Have the mind of Christ. Set aside privilege. Walk the path of humble obedience, remembering that "the servant is never greater than his Lord."

The lessons from the "Chaco experiment" are in some ways more about *posture* than *program*. Yet they do remind us at the same time that *message* and *medium* are more inseparably linked than generally perceived or imagined.

I believe that the course-altering decisions made in the early Chaco ministry have been foundational and direction-setting for much of our Mennonite mission effort in subsequent years – in partnering with grassroots African-initiated churches; in encouraging the growth of home-grown messianic faith communities in Israel; in nurturing locally-inspired Anabaptist networks in the UK, South Korea, Australia, New Zealand, and South Africa; and in developing North American urban programs in which participants are challenged to "see the face of God in the city," rather than importing their own personal passions, purposes, or programs.

It is my hope that the remarkable story recounted in the following pages might inspire followers of Jesus far beyond the Mennonite community to examine in new ways what it means to partner with others in God's reconciling mission "until we all reach unity in the faith . . . and become mature, attaining the full measure of perfection found in Christ" (Eph. 4:13, NIV).

James R. Krabill
Mennonite Mission Network, Elkhart, Indiana
March 18, 2015

Prologue

The title of this work synthetically expresses not only its content but also a new way to approach the missionary task of the church. A way that is more harmonious with the gospel of Jesus Christ. A way that makes of Jesus Christ's mission – the Word made flesh that dwelt among us – the paradigm for the Christian mission until the end of the age.

It must be clarified that the novelty of this missionary approach does not mean that its essential characteristics have been totally absent from the ways to do mission in the past. The novelty consists in that the authors of this book have rediscovered a way to do mission that is in sharp contrast with another way that was so common that the Christian mission became closely associated with the political and economic power of the empires beginning with Constantine.

In fact, the history of modern foreign missions, both Roman Catholic and Protestant, is a history of light and darkness: light derived from the spirit of dedication and sacrifice of many missionaries, perhaps the majority of them; darkness resulting from the spirit of conquest imbedded in Western culture.

In his classical work *The Other Spanish Christ: A Study in the Spiritual History of Spain and South America,* John A. Mackay shows that the Iberian conquest beginning in 1492 was in reality a religious epic inspired by the mystic motive of Roman Catholic King Ferdinand and Queen Isabel. With a real sense of mission, Spain approached the conquest of the New World for the purpose of converting it into a Roman Catholic continent. The cross and the sword worked in partnership and, in the name of evangelization, the sword took care of opening the way to the cross. For Mackay, this was the original mark of Spanish Christianity.

We must recognize, however, that the close association between mission and empire is also part of the history of Protestant missions. As David J. Bosch has affirmed in *Transforming Mission: Paradigm Shifts in Theology of Mission:* "Surveying the great variety of ways in which Western cultural norms were, implicitly or explicitly, imposed upon converts in other parts of the world, it is of some significance to note that both liberals and conservatives shared [and unfortunately many still share] the assumption that [Western] Christianity was [and still is] the only basis for a healthy civilization; this was a form of consensus so fundamental that it operated mainly on an unconscious, prepositional level."

What is new in what Willis Horst, Ute and Frank Paul offer in this book is nothing more than the rediscovery of *mission without conquest,* that is, a missionary alternative radically different from the mission shaped by the spirit of conquest described by Mackay and Bosch. It is an alternative forged in the heat of a long period of living with indigenous communities and of deep reflection on the meaning of contextualization of the gospel in a culture totally different from that of the missionaries.

From a biblical perspective, every disciple of Jesus Christ is called to participate in the mission of God in the world. One of the values of *Mission Without Conquest* is that it offers an excellent illustration of how to carry out this task. Of course, it is especially related to transcultural missionary work among indigenous communities that represent the most neglected sector of the population in Latin America in general and in Argentina in particular. At the same time, however, it shows what it means to practice the principles that must characterize every effort to communicate the gospel.

If this work inspires the readers to humbly share the good news of Jesus Christ in their own situation without a spirit of conquest, both the authors and the editors will be extremely pleased.

C. René Padilla
Buenos Aires, Argentina

Introduction
and Acknowledgments

Willis Horst

Through the centuries the church of Jesus Christ has sought to carry out its missionary task in ways that are effective and at the same time faithful to the manner in which Jesus himself lived and taught. Mission leaders have a growing awareness of the need to avoid practices that are paternalistic, dominating or conquering. In the face of the horrendous deeds done in the name of Christ during the conquest of America, mission among indigenous peoples requires heightened sensitivity.

Over 55 years ago the workers of the Mennonite Mission Team in the Argentine Chaco gave themselves to that search. Leaving behind all intention to conquer and rejecting the need to form a church of their own denomination, they forged an alternative style of mission. Their choice was to walk alongside of others who were also searching for Life, without claiming superiority. Rather, they chose to walk as Jesus walked, with an attitude of weakness and vulnerability, and thus to give priority to the personal and social wholeness of others.

Any action that diminishes the other is not worthy of being called "good news."

Mission Without Conquest is for all who are engaged in that search. Much creative work lies ahead as the church forges new paradigms in mission. We authors recognize our indebtedness to the legacy of the historic peace churches which provides us with a fundamental understanding of Jesus' message as the gospel of peace. We offer this book as a contribution to the growing interest in shaping mission around post-Constantinian nonviolent ethical practice. God has freed us from the weight of carrying out the mission as an obligation. God sends us out to share God's love with joy.

Mission Without Conquest begins in Chapter 1 with an incipient mission theology that legitimizes the universal human urge to find wholeness, fulfillment and meaning through spiritual quest. Chapter 2 tells of the walk of faith of the Toba Qom people in the Argentine Chaco following their conversion to the way of Jesus. Their story narrates the development of a thoroughly indigenous church as it was strengthened by the accompaniment of the mission team. This chapter also recounts the team's search to encourage the spiritual self-determination of indigenous communities which had received the gospel. By the mid 1990's, the "Mennonite mission team" was, in fact, deliberately interdenominational and international. The longest section of the book, Chapter 3, then documents how one family of the team put into practice the accompaniment model as an alternative missionary practice. This contribution is based on Frank Paul's travel diary of his extensive visits to indigenous congregations, which illustrate numerous aspects of interaction between guests and their hosts.

All but one of the contributions included in Part 2 were written by former members of the Mennonite Team, all of whom helped shape the alternative mission model. The inclusion of four articles by Albert and Lois Buckwalter is a special privilege. Albert and Lois were the artisans of the major shift in missionary strategy that foreshadowed much of the current emphasis in mission circles on the inculturation of the gospel and the accompaniment model. Finally, we are pleased to include the contribution of Juan Carlos Martínez, an indigenous voice with genuine perception of the urgent issue of land recovery as understood through the eyes of Mocoví spirituality.

The Appendices provide charts, essays and scholarly articles that give a significant bird's-eye view of Chaco indigenous culture and history, along with suggestions for visitors.

Ethnographically, the Toba belong to the Guaycuruan linguistic family. They have been known by the name Toba since the late 19th century, but in recent years it has become increasingly popular to refer to them as the Qom people, the term by which they designate themselves and which in their language means simply "the people." Therefore, throughout the book we opt for the composite term Toba Qom as a way of honoring their emerging identity without losing the historical designation found in the literature.

Given the continuing uncertainty regarding the most appropriate terminology, we use "indigenous people" as the currently preferred designation across much of Latin America for Native American, Indian, First Nations, or aborigine peoples of the Americas. In consonance, we most often use simply "non-indigenous" as the least racist term for all others, rather than "whites," "criollos," "anglos," "nationals" or other commonly used expressions which lend themselves to misunderstanding.

The authors wish to thank the many who helped make the English version possible. Most important of all, heartfelt thanks goes to Byrdalene Wyse Horst, who supported the overall process with her gifts of patience and watchful proofreader's eye. Numerous friends and supporters of the book provided translations and editing suggestions, especially Malcolm Sedaca, Ethel Yake Metzler, and Carmen Horst. Without the encouragement and guidance of C. René Padilla of Kairos Foundation, who served as the bridge with the publishers of the English edition, the book would not have seen the light of day.

Finally, we recognize the huge debt to the Chaco indigenous people who were our hosts throughout our ministries in their territory. Their example of faith in the midst of suffering provides continuing inspiration. The joyful worship and active social engagement of Toba Qom believers is ample reward for the missionary practice described here. The style of accompaniment as guest practiced by the Mennonite Team has, without doubt, helped empower the Toba Qom church leaders to continue their chosen path of spirituality towards maturity in Christ, not only in the church but in broader society. To be affirmed as persons created in God's image, of infinite worth, and with the capability to follow Jesus in their unique way is the most liberating and saving good news anyone can receive. Surely it is the opposite of being conquered.

Maps

Argentina and Location of Indigenous Churches

Map and location of Argentina
(not including areas of Antartica and Malvinas/Falkland Islands)

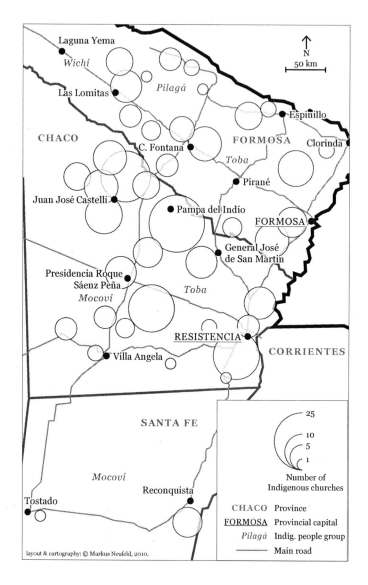

Location and number of indigenous churches in northern Argentina accompanied by Mennonite Team (year 2000)

Part 1

1

Religious Self-determination and the Autochthonous[1] Church

Toward a Theology of Self-determination[2] in the Growth of the Church

Willis Horst

Written in 1994 after twenty-some years of accompanying Chaco indigenous churches, Horst issued this clarion call for "religious self-determination" as a defining feature of the missionary impulse. Theologically grounded in God as the model, this view accents Bible translation into native languages and the Gospel itself, along with the missionary, as "guests" among those who receive them freely.

In this chapter I present a theological basis for missionary practice as it promotes the religious self-determination of the receiving culture.

All aspects of the cultural life-ways of a people are intimately interrelated. We cannot separate religious self-determination from other aspects of life,

---

1. Autochthonous. "Native to or formed in the place where found." Meaning N⁰2 in Webster's Concise College Dictionary, Random House, New York, 1999. Used here with the meaning of "a church formed and defined by those native to the place where it began or has grown."
2. Self-determination. I use this term to translate the Spanish concept of *autogestión*, since I haven't found an adequate alternative. *Autogestión* includes not only making one's own decisions about the direction one chooses to take but also being in charge of the process of moving forward toward that chosen goal.

such as the economic, or the socio-political. In fact, we can affirm that all other areas of life are influenced by the requirements of the religious system which gives meaning to the culture. In other words, the religious worldview[3] is what provides direction to all social aspects of a people.

Neither the Chaco first nations cultures nor those of the Middle East in Bible times separate that which has to do with religion from the rest of life. Western culture, however, through a long process of secularization and compartmentalization, has reduced the sacred to an increasingly limited area of life. Thus we live a false dualism which has led to a deepening crisis. Without religious guidance Western culture has lost its way.

Human capacity and the right to choose

Religious self-determination presupposes that every person and each people has the capacity as well as the right to negotiate and pursue[4] their own religious path. Humans are able by nature to choose among the various religious options which present themselves, and among the different components of whatever religious option they may find.[5]

Not all that happens or is present in any given culture or person is of God. Some elements are not life-giving. Undoubtedly, in any culture there are aspects, traits, or customs which do not reflect God's will. For example, we would not want to accept that a gene which predisposes any given person to suffer a negative health condition is bestowed on them by God, even though it were present in that person before birth.[6] In the same way, not everything expressed in any given culture is "of God." Neither did a pure culture ever exist in the pre-Columbian period of America nor at any time in human history.

---

3. By "religious worldview" I refer to whatever belief system defines ultimate values for a people, whether one of the recognized world religions, or any of their mutant versions, or secularism in its various forms.
4. I have opted to translate *gestionar* as "negotiate and pursue" in order to include the concept of being in charge of the whole process.
5. This is true also in societies in which communal identity takes precedence, although to a lesser degree, over the individual. Although the major religious choices in such a society may be made communally or by the person(s) in charge, each individual chooses the degree to which they adhere.
6. We cannot diverge here to discuss what some have called God's permissive will as over against God's absolute will. Obviously, the Creator allows negative aspects within the good creation which help move the evolutionary process in the direction of God's goals. This does not in itself oblige us to acknowledge that God desires the suffering or death which those negative aspects imply.

In addition, today the first nations peoples of the Argentine Chaco find themselves between two cultures – the ancient tribal and the more recent non-indigenous culture which surrounds and dominates them. An adequate respect for self-determination means that in relation to both the older as well as the newer culture, they themselves should have the power of decision as to which aspects they select to follow. The self-determination process includes the right to make decisions in dialogue with outsiders, but the responsibility for the choices made is their own. Self-determination implies that those best prepared to determine just which elements of a given culture are life-giving, or "of God," and which ones are not, are persons from that same culture who share its value system.

Historical memory of self-determination

If for some reason a people has lost its capacity for or its right to exercise self-determination, recovering it is a double effort of rediscovery and liberation from oppressive forces. This is where one who comes with the message of the gospel can make a legitimate contribution. Margot Bremer finds in her rereading of biblical history theological clues to help understand self-determination as the liberation God desires for humanity (Margot Bremer 1993). She suggests that the recuperation of self-determination is related to the memory of the past in which the people were in charge of their own life project. For Israel that memory includes the liberation from Egypt and their formation as a nation/people. But it also goes back to the pre-exodus times of the patriarchs and matriarchs. It includes the self-determination of Abram who in response to God's call took on an alternative life project, leaving Ur in search of "the promised land."

For the Toba Qom people the memory of the massive acceptance of the gospel in the 1940s, together with the subsequent formation of the self-managed indigenous church, has great significance and neither they nor we should forget it. The United Evangelical Church remembers that historical period as their "exodus" experience with the church's founder, Aurelio López, as their "Moses." However, it is also essential to recuperate the memory of the pre-conquest period of their history. During that time, as an ethnic group, they themselves practiced self-determination as they lived out their social project that resulted in life.

The Image of God

Religious self-determination was set in motion when God created the human being.

"From one person God made all nations who live on earth, and he decided when and where every nation would be. God has done all this, so that we will look for him and reach out and find him. He isn't far from any of us, and he gives us the power to live, to move, and to be who we are" (Acts 17:26-28a, CEV. See Acts 17:26-28 in its context 17:16-33. Also see Rom. 2:7, 14-16, context 2:1-16; 1 Pet. 1:10-11, context 1:8-16).

Each person and every culture has something of God within. God is present and active in all of Creation, but in the human in a unique way. We may identify this as the image of God. This presence can be discerned in several dimensions, one of which is what is often referred to as the life project. Part of the maturation of each individual is the development of a life goal – not only a professional vocation in the modern sense, but also the urge to realize a meaningful existence. Every culture as well has some concept of a better life, a dream towards which it seeks to move, an ideal place or state of being. That goal has many names and multiple definitions: utopia, shalom, land without evil, new heavens and new earth, the marriage supper of the Lamb, and others. As the Apostle Paul expresses in Acts 17:27, this dream functions "so that, even though dimly (imperfectly), they might find the Divine" (my translation).

The purpose of the gospel is to contribute to the life project present in every culture, to strengthen and enhance life wherever present. Jesus himself explained his purpose for coming and living out God's Way on earth in these words: "I came so that everyone would have life, and have it in its fullest" (John 10:10, CEV. See also Jesus' public declaration in the synagogue in Nazareth, Luke 4:16-21).

Christ in continuity with the one Creator God

Biblical faith understands the Creator of all as the one true God, the center which unites all things, that which holds the universe together (Col. 1:17). "For from God and through God and to God are all things. To God be the glory forever. Amen" (Rom. 11:36, RSV). Bible translator Edesio Sánchez Cetina[7] expressed this truth in the following words:

> "That [One] is the only and true unity to which are joined the various traditions, ethnicities, institutions, and theologies. No other unity fits within God than that of various diversities which respond to the multifaceted way in which God relates to his creatures." (Sánchez Cetina 1990:113)

Old Testament wisdom

Jewish wisdom came to recognize in Israel's tribal God the one, true Creator of all (e.g. see Isa. 40:28 and Deut. 6:4, RSV, "Hear O Israel: the Lord our God is one Lord; . . ."). The prophets followed after God searching and investigating salvation – liberation, healing and shalom for the people. There was apparently a thread of common understanding in Israel that the "anointed one" (messiah, christ), was somehow already present – though perhaps hidden and largely unrecognized – in Creation and in the history of God's people, Israel. That presence was understood as either the special strength (anointing in some cases) of God or as the wisdom of God which reaches across cultures and throughout time. (e.g. as wisdom in Prov. 8; Cyrus as God's messiah in Isa. 45:1ff).

Writers of the New Testament recognized this theological thread in certain contexts. The Spirit of Christ was already present in the prophets in their search (1 Pet. 1:11, see the context: vv. 10-12). Christ was the rock which the Israelites found in the desert following their liberation from Egypt (1 Cor. 10:4). Not only was God's Messiah already present within Israel, but was also actively involved in the history of those outside of Israel. Amos announced God's broader interest in an attempt to hold Israel accountable for its sins, saying, "Are you not like the Ethiopians to me, O people of Israel? says the Lord. Did I not bring Israel up from the land of Egypt, and the Philistines from Caphtor and the Arameans from Kir?" (Amos 9:7, RSV).

The same Spirit of God which had already been present in Israel worked in Peter's understanding to undo generations of blindness so that Peter could recognize again that "God shows no partiality, but in every nation anyone who fears him and does what is right is acceptable to him" (Acts 10:31-34, RSV). Paul, the Pharisee, had his eyes opened by that same Spirit to be able

---

7. All quotes from Sánchez Cetina are my translation.

to recognize that God will give eternal life "to those who by patiently doing good seek for glory and honor and immortality." God "will repay according to each one's deeds," there will be "glory and honor and peace for everyone who does good, the Jew first and also the Greek. For God shows no partiality" (see Rom. 2:6-11, RSV, including the whole context of chapter 2).

Christ in creation

Creator God, present in all of creation and also, in some way, in the history of each person and every culture, became present uniquely in Jesus the Christ. The creative light that shone at creation is the same light shining within the human heart making it possible to discern in Jesus the expected Christ. "For it is the God who said, 'Let light shine out of darkness,' who has shone in our hearts to give the light of the knowledge of the glory of God in the face of Jesus Christ" (2 Cor. 4:6, RSV). "In him all things in heaven and on earth were created" (Col. 1:15-19, RSV). Christ himself is the peace and harmony of the whole universe and in him everything finds its true unity (Col. 1:19-20, and Eph. 1:10). This Christ who transcends time and space is a cosmic reality.

Jesus, the Christ

Christian faith acknowledges that this cosmic Christ, present with God from the beginning of creation, took on flesh and blood (human life) in Jesus of Nazareth. Peter's confession "You are the Messiah" is key to the comprehension of the true identity of Jesus (Mt. 8:29). Jesus' followers confessed that for them Jesus was the expected Messiah. The first three chapters of Hebrews present Jesus as a historical event which awakens a new consciousness of God's project.

For the Jewish nation, Moses and the Torah personified its religious tradition. As the early Jewish believers came to recognize that Jesus was indeed the expected Messiah, they were enabled to transfer their ultimate loyalty from Moses and the Law to Jesus. It was Jesus the Christ, they declared, who "takes away the blindness" that kept the Jews from recognizing Jesus as the Messiah (2 Cor. 3:14-18, RSV). Jesus, the Expected One, who should have been the revelation of the true meaning of the Old Testament Scriptures, became instead a stumbling block for the Jews.

The early church understood the Jesus of history to be the very image of God. That is to say, it is in Jesus Christ that we see most clearly what the

Creator God is like, since in Jesus God became visible by entering human history (2 Cor. 4:4). According to the prologue of John's Gospel, the Word that was with God and indeed was God became flesh and tented among humans (John 1:1-14). Compare the report in John's Gospel (John 14:9) of Jesus' word to Phillip, "The one who has seen me has seen the Father." As Jesus announced in the synagogue at Nazareth, God's Spirit was at work in him to carry out the life project of the Jewish nation as the prophets had announced (Luke 4:16-21).

The church also confesses that at the end of history God will unite all things under Christ's authority (Eph. 1:10). In the new creation, there is no discrimination since "Christ is all and is in all" (Col. 3:11). Thus, Paul can write that when we have the mind of Christ we can know all things" (1 Cor. 2:16, RSV). For Paul, this mind of Christ which can "judge all things" seems to be a cosmic reality that he came to believe was present in Jesus of Nazareth.

Paul often makes reference in his letters to the Christ within. He seems to understand this as God's Spirit empowering the individual and the community in their life project. For example, in the letter to the Philippians we find this description of the life project which God was enabling in the church community at Philippi: "work out your own salvation with fear and trembling; for God is at work in you, both to will and to work for his good pleasure" (Phil. 2:12-13, RSV). Thus, Paul understood that the church, collectively, and perhaps each person individually, is both motivated and capable of pursuing their life project and that God is the enabling power.

In his letter to the Galatians (see Gal. 3:15-4:7), Paul compared the function of the Law of Moses to a slave tutor who led the Jews to maturity in Christ (3:24). Writing to the Colossians (Col. 2:8-23), Paul treated the Law as "human precepts and doctrines." "These are only a shadow of what is to come; but the substance belongs to Christ" (2:17, RSV). Thus Paul considered the previous spirituality as inferior to the reality of Christ.

The author of the Epistle to the Hebrews puts Christ forward as the continuation and culmination of Jewish religious history. Through the eyes of Jewish faith, with all of its culture, law and religiosity, Jesus is understood in superlative language taken from the Sacred Scriptures (the Old Testament, in Christian terminology). This can serve as a paradigm to help us see Christ in continuity with God in any culture, where the particular history and spirituality serves as that people's own "Old Testament."

Thus, the New Testament includes abundant evidence that from its earliest days the church considered that in Jesus the cosmic Christ was truly present and active.

Evangelization

The parable "The monkey and the fish" of Anthony de Mello (de Mello 1995:25) illustrates, in general terms, the history of the evangelization of the autochthonous peoples of the western hemisphere.

"What are you doing?" I asked a monkey when I saw him pull a fish out of the water and place it on the branch of a tree.

"I'm saving the fish from drowning," the monkey responded.

God is the model

In a theology for self-directed religious determination (*autogestión religiosa*) our model for evangelization is God's own self. God took the risk of trusting in humanity. God trusted humans to the extent of expecting that they would recognize God in a recently born infant and in a tortured man. God has entrusted the care and even the very destiny of Creation to humans made in God's own image!

We are managers of the mysteries of God – managers, nothing less! All we have has been given to us to administer for its true owner (1 Cor. 4:1-7). God offers the gospel to us, recommending it to us as to administrators of the creation. We, in turn, offer the gospel to the world as enrichment, an enhancement for the good of creation. Stanley Green, president of the Mennonite Mission Network of Mennonite Church USA, affirms that in the process of sharing the gospel with others we are also enriched.

The gospel is to be offered to others, not forced upon anyone. It is by invitation, not by obligation. We must reject all forms of violence in mission practice as being incompatible with the gospel itself. As Pablo Suess says, "The Gospel is always guest" (Suess 1995). The mutual respect implicit in an attitude of genuine intercultural dialogue is a growing imperative in a pluralistic world.

To each and everyone who accepts it, the gospel becomes a help in their religious self-determination. It becomes a valuable aid in the realization of their project of life, the desire for "shalom," the utopia for which all are searching. However, for that project to be truly life-giving, it must be submitted to the presence, the guidance and the correction of the God of Life. Otherwise, it may lose the way to life. In other words, God does not exist to serve humanity, rather humanity exists in order to serve its creator in the interest of Life.

Therefore we affirm with the whole church that Jesus is the way, the truth and the life (John 14:6); it is only when humanity chooses to submit to Jesus Christ and to his project that the salvation of the world is realized. It is in the way of peace, justice, love, forgiveness and reconciliation which Jesus offers that makes co-existence a viable option for the world's diverse cultures. Only the refusal to use violence against others – even enemies – will give birth to a common peoplehood living together in God's shalom. The goal of evangelization is conversion to the Jesus way of life rather than adhesion to any particular religion or Christian denomination.

Christ present in creation is the foundation

The basis of God's project of life for creation is the Christ already present in history, rather than the church. New Testament missionary Paul, speaking in a context of extreme denominationalism, said the only foundation has already been laid, which is Christ Jesus. No other foundation is possible (1 Cor. 3:10). That firm foundation was laid at creation, not when the church began.

The church is to be "reinvented"

In each culture the church is to be built on the true foundation – Christ. It should be configured according to local cultural perceptions rather than in ways brought by persons from foreign cultures. Brazilian theologian, Leonard Boff, in his book *From the Perspective of the Poor*, uses the expression: *reinvent* the church. Boff says that, "the church exists since the time of Jesus, but must always be reinvented; she is not a lifeless millennial old organization; but an organism which grows, is renewed and remade to the degree to which she penetrates history and responds to new challenges" (Boff 1986, my translation).

When a person knowingly accepts identification with Jesus:

- That person is now a Christian/believer/follower of Jesus/disciple;
- Their life enters a change process to become more like the "inculturated" Jesus (the Jesus seen from within their own worldview);

- Their goals and utopic dreams undergo a transformation as they come to understand God's project for Creation, according to the paradigm of Jesus.

Such persons, committed in some degree to the Way of Jesus the Christ, join with other believers to discern together and forge their own history; in this way the church is born anew. Boff, speaking of the grassroots Christian communities known in Latin America as *communidades eclesiales de base* (CEB) says:

> The CEBs, which include all the members of the church with their specific differences, make possible the recuperation and practice of that reality of the church as a communion of the faithful (*comunitas fidelium*). This is the oldest and theologically most accurate definition of the church. (Boff 1986)

Plurality

Religious self-determination presupposes religious pluralism. It is not a given that everyone – not even all persons within a given culture – will choose the same religious path. Let us, then, say goodbye to Christendom; that is, the "constantinization" of society. Let us also say goodbye to the dreams of proselytism, with its hopes to conquer an ever-growing percentage of the world for one's own church or religion. The Kingdom of God will be realized in the diversity of churches. Each people, culture and congregation has the possibility to understand and interpret the gospel message from within their own culture. This is both a privilege and a responsibility. "Where two or three are gathered together in my name, there I am in the midst of them," said Jesus, speaking of the local congregation and the process of community discernment (Mt. 18:18-20, RSV).

Each congregation, cell group or base community also will at times make mistakes in their discernment processes. That is why it is essential that each one be in dialogue with others within the universal church in an attitude of ongoing conversation. However, we must remember that those "two or three gathered together" have the right to make mistakes. The process itself is part of the learning. We should not make light of any sincere effort of religious self-determination, no matter how strange it may seem to us.

As a result of the process of religious self-determination within the wide variety of cultures, the diversity of churches, with their distinct spiritualities, complement each other, thus enriching the universal church. The more authentic the inculturation of the gospel in any given people, and the more liberty it enjoys in its reinvention of the church, the greater will be that local church's contribution to the worldwide church.

Bible translation

"It is characteristic of the colonizing mentality to not translate the Scriptures into the language of the receiving culture, but rather to translate the receiver into the culture and worldview of the colonizer" (Sánchez Cetina 1990:116). Religious self-determination vigorously promotes the translation of the Bible into the language of each people. The Bible came into being with a special purpose: that God's message reach all in the language and level of expression they can understand. Therefore, the work of translation is eminently a missional task. However, the translation must be done by native speakers, as Sánchez Cetina affirms:

> My experience as translator and coordinator of the translation of the Bible into maya, leads me to reaffirm the principle followed by the United Bible Societies: it should be native speakers who translate the Bible into their own language and not foreign linguistic experts. We who have been speaking an indigenous language since birth not only know the unique characteristics of that language, but also our own culture and worldview. Unless these elements are considered as a whole, the resulting translation will always have a strange flavor and will not readily be regarded as God's word for the people. (Sánchez Cetina 1990:96)

To place the Bible into the hands of the people in their own language encourages widespread reading and contextualized interpretation. Thus, the God of the Bible is incarnated in each culture.

Seeing translation as mission is a powerful affirmation that the receiving culture is the authentic destination of the divine saving promise and, as a result, enjoys a place of honor in the grace of God, at the same time it rejects every kind of cultural absolutism (Sánchez Cetina 1990:118).

To translate the Bible into the language of the people is to believe that through the Word the Spirit of God is the true teacher of those being evangelized. The Bible teacher or catechist from outside the culture is also a student of the same Holy Spirit.

Certainly, trained pastoral agents, although not from the local culture, can facilitate the translation process. Due to a more highly specialized preparation and broader experiences, they are equipped to serve as interpreter between cultures. Thereby, they can clarify the meaning of texts and contexts of the Bible. Nevertheless, they should limit their intervention in the hermeneutical process of the indigenous church to:

- Clarifying the text, and
- Evaluating interpretations of the text, without assuming they have the final word.

Specific applications should be left to the community itself, which is in the process of religious self-determination, working out their own salvation. There may be times to suggest alternative applications, but not to dictate rules about their appropriateness. Juan Luis Segundo says in *Hidden Motives of Latin American Pastoral Work*:

> When one goes to a different culture, what (s)he should do is tell the message of Jesus and his teachings, and let the people themselves generate their own traditions and customs, as the Word of God leads them. (Rooy 1993:53)

A widespread tendency among missionaries of any of the churches is to universalize their own interpretations of the Bible. However, as Sánchez Cetina writes, "Biblical diversity is a warning against all intentions to privatize God" (Sánchez Cetina 1990:115). This is true for our attitudes toward first nations believers as well as in regards to other churches.

The church should not give in to the temptation to control the message nor its testimony. Right from the moment in which the sovereign God desired that God's Word might reach everyone, that Word is subject to the dominion of the one who receives it, not of the one who sent it (Sánchez Cetina 1990:115).

Since as persons we are each formed within a particular religious tradition and a given culture, our egocentrism often urges us to want to correct that which is simply different. Following are some of the cultural features encountered in indigenous churches which those from outside often, in error, want to correct.

Cultural characteristic	Example
types of emotional expression	dance
ecclesiology	baptism
lack of formal leadership training	illiteracy
syncretism	use of the Bible as a power object

To entrust the Bible to the people in the language they understand best, shows that we believe in their capacity to continue managing their own spiritual path, as they have already been doing long before the missionary arrived. It also demonstrates that we believe in the power of the Holy Spirit to guide the process. The local people are capable of discerning for themselves the Word of God within the Scriptures, just as we consider ourselves to be likewise capable.

Any pedagogical intervention which respects the self-management rights of the local inculturated church allows the believers of each people, the church in every culture, the freedom to:

- Live their own spirituality,
- Interpret the Bible from within their own culture,
- Define their ethical practices in agreement with their own value system,
- Decide and manage their own church structures and liturgy,
- Elaborate their own theology,
- Spread the gospel in their own way.

Another quote from Sánchez Cetina is appropriate:

> As careful reading of the Bible will allow us to discover, it is not possible to make any rigid harmonization nor enclose the message in dogmatic systems without doing inappropriate violence to it. No theological construction or doctrine can capture completely the holy and infallible God. The Bible contains differing theologies which demonstrate the richness of human life under the one God. (Sánchez Cetina 1990:113-14)

By recognizing the above limitations, pastoral agents from outside open themselves to learn from the other and to continue growing towards the fullness of Christ, which is to continue their own conversion. As an additional blessing, we will be able to work in the same indigenous community ecumenically, without competition or proselytism, using the Bible to support the self-determination of the first nations church!

Goals and intentions

We want to be bearers of the gospel in healthy ways. What are the goals we aim for so that our missionary presence will promote religious self-determination?

- A spirituality which inspires and supports the *shalom* (well-being) of society. Salvation is to participate to a certain degree in the peace and well-being of the Kingdom of God. Salvation is multifaceted. It is always partial and incomplete in this life. To be Christian is to participate consciously in God's project, join with God in the carrying out of God's global purposes, and explicitly recognize that Jesus Christ is Lord.
- *Religious pluralism*, with mutual respect and interreligious cooperation on activities of common interest.
- *A church both authentically indigenous and Christian,* in dialogue with other communities of believers consciously committed to Jesus and to living out the Kingdom of God. Its spirituality will be informed by the cultural and spiritual values of its own worldview as well as by the word of God incarnated in Jesus and recorded in the Bible.
- A *dialogical relationship* with pastoral representatives of other churches, in the service of this specific church. We, as pastoral agents from outside the culture, are "accompaniers" in a fraternal relationship to the extent that we are freely invited. Freely, in the first nations context, means without pressures of proselytism, without power of decision in the indigenous church, and without transforming our relationship into one of resource gathering by indigenous believers.

Limitations

Finally, we recognize that self-determination will be partial and limited in scope. This will always be true because to a large degree our actions in life are responses to what happens to us, actions initiated and directed by others or by God. Our role as protagonists of history is always limited. However, the principle of self-determination does imply that we can choose our own response to what happens to us, within limits. This implies that there are real options, however small they may be, and that each and every human being is gifted with the capacity and the freedom to choose.

According to a United Nations report, "90 percent of the world population still lacks an effective management of those critical aspects which affect their lives," emphasizing that the largest groups of those excluded from decision-making "are made up of women and populations of First Nations minorities, even in the richest countries."[8]

A Toba Qom chief and pastor in the United Evangelical Church once hung a poster on the wall of his church house. Along with photos of first nations leaders, it featured the phrase, "Protagonists of history." For a long moment he pondered in silence the proposal of the organization that had distributed the posters. Then he observed, "Is it really true that we are protagonists of our history, or do they just tell us that and keep on managing us?"

---

8. Daily newspaper, *El Comercial* , Formosa, 14 de mayo de 1994, p. 9.

2

Toba Qom Spirituality

The Remarkable Faith Journey of an Indigenous People in the Argentine Chaco[1]

Willis Horst

In 2001, after thirty-some years of intense engagement with the Toba Qom, Horst prepared this outline of the emerging spirituality of the people he had come to know and love. Built around direct quotes from trusting Toba friends, this brief account depicts an experiential theology that is lively and uncoerced, authentic, inculturated, and still in process.

The Toba Qom people are one of several indigenous ethnic groups living today, as they have for centuries, in the low-land Chaco region of Argentina. With an estimated 80,000 members, they maintain a traditional relationship with their environment by hunting, gathering and fishing.

The Toba Qom present for us a remarkable example of a people whose unique spirituality has shaped their Christian experience. Their particular

---

1. The essay was first published under the title, "Spirituality of the Toba Qom Christians of the Argentine Chaco" in *Missiology*, Vol. XXIX, Number 2 (April 2001), pp. 165-184. In 2001 Mennonite Board of Missions, predecessor agency of Mennonite Mission Network, Elkhart, IN., shortened, adapted and reprinted it with the title, "Toba Spirituality: The Remarkable Faith Journey of an Indigenous People in the Argentina Chaco," as Number 19 of the *Mission Insight* series.

path toward Christ has resulted in a distinctively indigenous church, and a uniquely relevant theology worthy of being heard and respected.

Toba Qom spirituality, emerging in the church today, is not a formal, systematized, written theology, organized in terms of European traditions. Rather, it is a spirituality that sees Jesus through Toba Qom cultural glasses and that is lived out simply and practically in daily life.

The religious experience of the Toba Qom Christian movement teaches us that receiving Jesus Christ results in life and wholeness when Christ is authentically perceived and uncoercively interpreted from within one's own worldview.

Toba Qom traditional wisdom prepared the way for embracing the gospel

> *The one who does not share from the cooking pot*
> *will surely lose his or her way in the forest.*
>
> —Mocoví proverb

Every human culture accumulates a body of wisdom that defines that which is considered to be the proper, or correct, way to live. Each member of the culture acquires this wisdom as part of daily life. Wisdom reflects what is considered to be "just the way things are," dealing with appropriate human behavior and "correct" relationships of humans with regard to creation, to others, and to the transcendent.

This wisdom is contained in and transmitted by a people's myths, rituals, proverbs, dreams, celebrations, songs, religious liturgies, and popular adages repeated over and over again. In indigenous cultures, wisdom is also passed along through the stories told by elders or "wise ones."

Fundamental to the traditional Toba Qom worldview is the concept of the universe as a reality cared for by its "owners." All of creation, as well as each of its parts, "belongs" to its owner with whom it maintains a relationship. These owners are spiritual beings. They are not owners in the sense of having private property; rather, they are administrators in charge of some part of the totality which the Creator/Owner/Giver has made and constantly renews for the use of all. Thus, each area of "vital space" (forest, swamp, river, grassland, etc.) as well as each species of prey (or fruit or plant to be harvested for consumption) within that "space" has a spiritual caretaker. Consequently, life depends upon adequate relationships with these owners or caretakers. Life is understood as the struggle to maintain a state of tranquility, balance and harmony with all the created world and, especially with the owners or guardians. For example, before going out to hunt in an open grassland, the traditional Toba Qom hunter would pray, seeking the protection of the owner of that space as well as instructions as to where to go and how many specimens of the prey he is to be given. If he doesn't obey the instructions, especially by taking more than he is allotted, he risks harm through illness or death. The interpretation given is that the hunter, by his disobedience, disrupts the state of harmony. This is more than a simple violation of established taboos, since the real issue is the relationship with the owner(s) involved.

The experience of Benjamin, a 35-year-old hunter who lives in the outskirts of the city of Formosa, clearly illustrates this relationship. He is one of the few Toba Qom in the city who still hunt rhea on a regular basis. Fields are fenced and access to hunting areas is controlled by cattle ranchers. In such a restricted context, Benjamin explains his success by referring to a "voice" he often hears before and during a hunt, giving him instructions: "It's as though someone is going along with me, even though when I hear the voice and I turn around to look, I don't see anyone."

Toba Qom spirituality seeks for holistic health within this overall state of harmony. Health is understood to be a spiritual state, and healing a spiritual process. Illness is considered to be the result of actions that disrupt the desired state of harmony and tranquility, which is restored through spiritual "therapies."

In the context of the Toba Qom extended-family communities, there are spiritual specialists who either have greater innate sensitivity or are able to develop more sensitivity toward communication with the spiritual owners. These "power people" are traditionally the healers in Toba Qom society. They go through special "training" to prepare for using powers granted them by the spiritual owners for service to their community. They dedicate their very lives to maintaining and restoring the state of tranquility, balance and harmony with the surrounding world. However, these specialists may also choose to use the powers at their disposal for evil, inflicting harm on others. This occurs with greater frequency in the modern context than has been the case traditionally, and causes intense internal conflict in many Toba Qom communities.

Toba Qom traditional spirituality includes the following elements:

- **Integrality.** All of life and all of creation are spiritual. The spiritual cannot be compartmentalized or segmented from the rest of life. Every thing and every person stand in relationship with the "owners," the spiritual beings and powers. The Creator is Owner of all, the First and the Final Power, the Ultimate Giver.

- **Inclusiveness.** Truths that are complementary or even opposing are maintained together, included in the same overall unit. Truth is cumulative.

- **Person-in-peoplehood.** Individuals find their reason for being through integration into the ethnic group or clan.

- **"Roundness" of reality.** Cyclical repetition, the return, the circle, space and place, are some fundamental aspects of indigenous life.[2]

- **Holistic.** Maintaining balance and right relationship with the spiritual and physical surroundings is a basic definition or condition of life.

- **Concrete action as an expression of faith.** Dreams are to be fulfilled. One recognizes another person's faith by observing behavior.

- **Reciprocity.** The harmony and balance of all things is maintained through a system of reciprocity at all levels, governed by well-defined rules and relationships.

Much of the traditional Toba Qom wisdom described here – already present in pre-Christian culture – provided the Toba Qom people with a framework for comprehending and embracing the good news of Jesus in terms they could understand.

A powerful people movement among the Toba Qom is born

We heard that a powerful One (a god) had come down in the city of Resistencia, so we went – on horseback, mule, on foot, for days – sometimes suffering hunger or cold. We went because we wanted salvation.

—Felipe Cabrera, Toba Qom elder[3]

The evangelical movement among the indigenous peoples of the Argentine Chaco began more than 60 years ago. A few elderly Toba Qom who witnessed the beginning of this movement among their people are still living today.

---

2. Ideas gleaned from a personal conversation with Helena Oliver in 1997.
3. Felipe was a first-hand witness to the Argentine Chaco evangelical movement in the early 1940s.

Following their fierce defense of the land against invaders for 400 years, the Toba Qom had finally been defeated by military force in the late 1800s. Their native healers did not have sufficient power over the illnesses brought by the conquerors. A British missionary, who has lived in Formosa province since 1932, says that in the 20 years between 1937 and 1957, the indigenous population of the province was reduced from 25,000 to 6,000 because of illnesses brought by the "whites" – as the non-indigenous intruders are known. In those years, so many children died that the women's cries of lament could be heard incessantly day and night in the Indian settlements. Suffering and need were great. Traditional leaders had lost their authority. The streets of the city of Resistencia were said to be filled with "drunken Indians."

As early as 1934, the first non-Catholic mission, the British "Emmanuel Mission" was established in the Toba Qom territory of the Argentine Chaco. Within ten years, three additional foreign non-Catholic missions began work with the Toba Qom: Go Ye Mission, Mennonite Nam Cum Mission, and Grace and Glory Mission, all three North American. In addition, an increasing number of Toba Qom heard the evangelical message in denominational churches (especially Church of God and Baptist) in frontier towns. These efforts all helped set the stage for what followed.

In the decades of the 1940s and 1950s, a significant religious awakening took place among the Toba Qom. Through contact with pentecostal preachers, especially John Lagar of the Go Ye Mission, the Toba Qom began to believe in Jesus in large numbers. Through physical healings they understood Jesus as a great power. They understood that God loved, valued and accepted them as indigenous people, regardless of how they were rated alongside white society. They were enabled to leave the vices to which they had resorted in their state of cultural disintegration. Within a few years, hundreds of Toba Qom converted to Jesus and congregations of "believers" with local leadership sprang up in many of the communities throughout the Chaco.

This movement resulted in a revitalization of the Toba Qom people, which permitted them to continue existing within the world of *criollo* (non-indigenous) civilization that was encroaching upon them. Toba Qom social leaders were among the first to support the religious movement, since they recognized in it the possibility of surviving the profound crisis in which they found themselves and their people. As the movement spread, a novel evangelical religious expression took shape: the indigenous evangelical *culto*.

North American Mennonites began work in the Chaco in 1943, with what could be described as a classical mission compound. Following ten years of activities that showed little fruit for their labors, and faced with a deep sense of frustration, Mennonite missionaries were, by 1954, ready for change. Through the guidance of missionary anthropologists William and Marie Reyburn, Mennonite workers closed the mission and began a creative, courageous missionary strategy designed to strengthen the fledgling gospel movement among the Toba Qom.[4] They turned their backs on denominational proselytizing, and dedicated their efforts toward Bible translation and pastoral visitation. By encouraging religious *autogestión* (self-directed determination), in a few short years this ministry enabled leading Toba Qom believers to organize their own autonomous church.

"The church is like our Mother. We love our Mother."

That's why we celebrate the church's anniversary every year. The church is like our Mother. So we bring gifts for her, we celebrate, we praise, we eat. We love our Mother.

—Luis Mendoza, Toba Qom pastor[5]

In the late 1950s, Mennonite missionaries and some of the Toba Qom spiritual leaders agreed on the idea of organizing a totally indigenous church. Today, the Toba Qom attribute that idea to the Holy Spirit. This seems to have been confirmed by the unusual birth and growth of an authentically indigenous church that came to be called the *Iglesia Evangélica Unida* (IEU), the United Evangelical Church.

Because the Mennonites supported the Toba Qom in this important step by assisting with the legal process involved, they have had a special relationship with the IEU churches and its leaders that continues to the present. Mennonite missionaries together with Toba Qom leaders prepared the original handbook that provided guidelines for the church life and structure of the new organization. They deliberately left details vague and undefined in order to allow for maximum indigenous initiative in determining the future shape and theology of the movement.

It must be recognized that as the Toba Qom evangelical movement gathered strength and took on organizational shape, it achieved a legitimization not accorded to either their traditional spirituality nor to

---

4. See William Reyburn, *The Toba Indians of the Argentine Chaco* (Elkhart, IN: Mennonite Board of Missions and Charities, 1954).
5. Personal conversation with Luis Mendoza ca. 1992.

the Catholic faith. This came about through the legal documents (*fichero de culto*) granted by the national government in Buenos Aires, a required authorization for all religious organizations that did not form part of the established Catholic Church, the official religion of Argentina. Since these documents were not necessary for Catholic organizations, and because native spirituality did not qualify as an organized religion, evangelical churches were able to demonstrate written legitimization not available elsewhere. These legal documents became powerful tools in the hands of Toba Qom leaders as they sought recognition from local authorities. In addition, at this stage of history, leaders of the defeated indigenous peoples attributed great value and power to written documents of all types because the oral nature of their culture had been thoroughly disparaged as worthless by the dominating Spanish culture.[6]

Thus, an official government policy designed to curb the influences of non-official religions became, in effect, a great influence in just the opposite direction. At first, through affiliation with missions or denominational churches from outside, and later through their own autonomous indigenous church organization, the possession of important legal documentation strengthened the Toba Qom evangelical movement. Although this legitimization was not among the motives for accepting the gospel in the early stages of the movement, it became an important factor in giving impetus once the evangelical movement became organized.

Internationally recognized as one of the few examples in Latin America of a completely indigenous church, the IEU has come forth as a grassroots movement that developed its own leadership and organizational structure. Today, this church is a member of the Argentine Federation of Evangelical Churches (FAIE) and of the Latin American Council of Churches (CLAI).

The movement has been very missionary from its beginning, with congregations forming wherever Toba Qom settled to find work or traveled to sell their crafts. The majority of the congregations are in Formosa and Chaco provinces in northern Argentina, with the official headquarters in Presidencia Roque Sáenz Peña, Chaco province. Congregations exist, however, all the way from La Plata, nearly 800 miles to the south, to Salta in the northwest, to Paraguay near Asunción, as well as in Formosa, Chaco and Santa Fe provinces of Argentina.

---

6. See Pablo Wright's unpublished dissertation, "'Being-in-the-Dream.' Post-Colonial Explorations in Toba Ontology" (Philadelphia, PA: Temple University, 1997), pp. 480-482.

This growth is a result of the living testimony of faith of the indigenous people.

The coming of the gospel among the Toba Qom has broken down ethnic barriers and created a new family of faith

The United Evangelical Church is today a multi-ethnic church. Within a few years of its formation, congregations of other indigenous ethnic groups sought membership: first *Pilagá*, then *Mocoví*, followed by *Wichí* churches, some *Toba Qom* from Paraguay, a few *Quechua*-speaking congregations in the province of Santiago del Estero, plus fringe groups of non-indigenous *criollos, campesinos* (rural folk) and even gypsies.

The IEU is not the only Christian church among the several indigenous peoples of the Chaco, but it has gathered together the largest number of members. However, since 1990, the original organizational structure has divided, giving form to four or five new denominations in addition to the official IEU. While it is impossible to conduct an accurate census, at the time of writing this estimates calculate between 10,000-15,000 active members in well over 200 congregations which have resulted from the IEU movement.

Loyalty to the IEU as an indigenous entity has been expressed through the following theme song, which grew out of the early days of the movement and is still used today at anniversary gatherings:

> We are
> the United Church, the United Church,
> the people of God.

> We believe
> in the promise of the Holy Spirit,
> the Counselor.

Toba Qom Christians are finding their way between the spiritual legacy of their past and the radical newness of the gospel

To express their new faith, Toba Qom leaders chose some forms and expressions from Pentecostal churches and some from their traditional religion. On the surface, the IEU can easily be confused with pentecostalism. Since pentecostalism is the closest parallel expression of Christianity in the surrounding non-indigenous culture, many Toba Qom themselves accept this designation. However, there are enough distinctively indigenous characteristics of the IEU to clearly differentiate it from the non-indigenous pentecostal churches.

For example, due to cultural factors, the IEU has largely adopted child baptism in spite of being aware of the practice of Mennonite, evangelical and pentecostal churches of reserving baptism for adults, or at least limiting it to teenagers or older children.

Another difference may be seen in the IEU church services in the expressions of religious ecstasy. The Toba Qom personality is extremely sensitive to altered states of consciousness. Women are sometimes observed during a church service in a state of ecstasy brought on by heavy breathing with chanting (a technique of hyperventilation). Such ecstasy often involves oblivion to surroundings, and occasionally results in falling to the floor in a state of unconsciousness during which a dream or vision is received. Although the Toba Qom recognize this behavior as something from their previous religious expression, by using the Spanish term *gozo* (joy) to describe this behavior to non-indigenous Christians, it is accepted in the context of pentecostal Christianity as a form of possession by the Holy Spirit.

Because of the strangeness of some elements of IEU church services, many non-indigenous Christians consider the church to be little more than a pagan cult filled with superstitious practices carried out under the name of the gospel. Others, upon closer investigation, consider the IEU a syncretistic Christian church, because of what looks like a strange combination of Christian teachings together with ancestral Toba Qom beliefs and practices. There are even those who, through ignorance, consider the IEU as part of a fundamentalist conspiracy with North American roots, imposed and managed by outside interests for the purpose of dividing and conquering the people!

The IEU is, however, an authentic Christian movement of indigenous peoples living out its own spirituality. This indigenous spirituality is expressed in an authentic form of the gospel inculturated in a people with a worldview quite different from that of Western-oriented churches.

Orlando Sánchez, a former president of the IEU and one of the Toba Qom Bible translators, is a second-generation believer who has been preaching from the Bible for more than 30 years. He participated in a consultation in Ecuador in 1986 on the Latin American indigenous contribution to Christian theology. He has co-taught, in the bilingual teacher-training school in Sáenz Peña, a course on the history of Toba Qom culture and thought. Perhaps more

than any other Toba Qom, Orlando has reflected on the significance of the
gospel for his people and just how it is related to their previous spirituality. In
1984, Orlando expressed his own convictions regarding the relation between
Toba Qom spirituality and the IEU with these words:

> The IEU has its own authentic theology, which grows out of
> its own religious experience and from the Holy Scripture. The
> church is the center of life and interest in the community, given
> that the indigenous peoples have their own history, culture and
> language, which is thousands of years old. Their understanding
> of the universe and of nature as created, is their own. All the
> cosmos and its laws are expressed in their life and are the very
> reason for their existence.
>
> When the indigenous person heard the gospel, it was good
> news. It captivated his mind because many of the things that
> he already perceived by means of his own understandings and
> wisdom came into focus and became visible. Thus, the Christian
> faith and the Bible are expressed in a very strong way in the
> life of the indigenous peoples, and they define themselves as
> pentecostals. Ñim qad'ot (our creator) is one of the expressions
> used to refer to God. It is beyond doubt that indigenous people
> already had a notion of God in ancient times.
>
> Evangelization and the Bible did not destroy anything at all,
> such that for the indigenous the gospel has not been a process of
> brainwashing, but just the opposite. The spirit of the indigenous
> was freed through organizing their own church, where they
> themselves respond in their own way to the call of God. The
> indigenous person is an individual with culture. That culture is
> still intact.[7]

In this way, Orlando articulates both dimensions of Toba Qom
spirituality – continuity with the past *and* the radical newness of the gospel.
By keeping both of these dimensions together as parts of the same spiritual
reality, Orlando skillfully demonstrates the *inculturation* of the gospel, and
the radically indigenous nature of their own church.

---

7. From *Memorias del Gran Chaco*, Vol 2 (1998), p. 197. Translation my own.

Worship is at the heart of the Toba Qom religious experience

In the book of Revelation a vision of the end times shows a large number of people of God worshiping together. It says there will be many nations and languages. Since their activity is worship, it's obvious that what identifies them as distinct nations must be their style of worship. It pleases God for us to worship in our own way.
—Rafael Mansilla, Toba Qom church leader
and reservation administrator[8]

The primary function of the church service in Toba Qom spirituality is that of re-establishing the state of tranquility and harmony that is constantly being threatened by the interference of evil forces. Throughout any service the question is repeatedly articulated: "How many of you are contented?" or "Are you all contented, brothers and sisters?" The desired goal is that sense of well-being that results from right relationships with all the surroundings. Thus, reconciliation, healing and exorcism are important ministries in restoring damaged relationships. Prolonged stretches of singing, strong preaching and forceful prayer are spiritual forces useful in warding off evil.

Carrying out the church service in an adequate way becomes the most serious activity of the believers. They often refer to the culto, as well as to its different components, as "our work." In fact, one of the complaints of leaders of non-indigenous society is that the Toba Qom spend so much time and energy in church services, they are neglecting their other social responsibilities.

Regular church services are long, usually two to four hours, colorful, enthusiastic and bilingual. Frequently, multiple expressions occur simultaneously: dancing, audible prayer, preaching, ecstasy, children participating spontaneously, entering and leaving, moving about with relative freedom. Singing is predominant in the informal liturgy, as well as being a favorite youth activity and entertainment outside of services. Congregational singing expresses the collective lament of the people, and includes "praise songs," a unique musical form of repetitive medleys based on traditional chant.

Prayers are offered aloud, fervently and collectively. In rural churches the pattern still observed for congregational prayers includes closing windows and doors. Most services include an extended time for healing, often as part of the final prayer. The importance of following correct ritual observance for

---

8. Personal notes from a sermon given by Rafael Mansilla in 1994.

effectiveness is seen especially in the liturgy used for the celebration of The Lord's Supper. During this ritual, singing is a cappella and songs are limited to certain hymns translated from English hymnals of the period and introduced by missionaries during the earliest part of the movement.

Local pastors and other church leaders are usually men, although women are frequently called on to speak. Recently, women have organized themselves at local and churchwide levels, patterning activities after *criollo* evangelical churches in the area. Men evangelists have a popular role in current church life, and often organize extended evangelistic "campaigns" that are referred to as *movimientos* (movements). Evangelists are expected to be effective as spiritual healers, thus replacing traditional power-person healers within the church.

Large, seasonal, camp-meeting-style gatherings have a prominent part in Toba Qom church life. Birthdays, anniversaries and memorials are significant annual, festive events. These larger meetings provide opportunities to share with relatives from a distance, and for the interaction of youth. They are reminiscent of the traditional assemblies of several bands or groups for feasting during the annual season of abundance. The sense of well-being that results from these gatherings reveals their function as corporate healing services. Ambrosio Peña, an elderly *Wichí* man, expressed this sense of well-being when he said to me early one morning at an IEU gathering as we got up from our blankets under a tree at the edge of the clearing, "I'm contented, and I dance well."

Jesus Christ is, for Toba Qom believers, the completion and perfection of traditional spirituality

> So many of the teachings of the Bible are similar to the teachings of the older Tobas. When I remember the faith of the elders, I feel contented to be Toba. Rediscovering their theology is like a perfume for me. It's just like a huge tree over us, giving off a fragrance which we are breathing.
>
> —Joel Jara, Toba Qom pastor[9]

---

9. From unpublished notes presented at the second workshop on Indigenous Evangelical Spirituality, Formosa, Argentina, 1996.

The spiritual worldview of the Toba Qom is expressed in their wisdom. This wisdom prepared the Toba Qom to be able to perceive and receive Jesus. The book of Hebrews in the New Testament gives us a paradigm of how Jesus is understood in terms of the Jews' previous religious system. For the early Jewish Christians, Jesus was seen as the superlative high priest who had come to resolve what they understood to be the problem of humanity – separation from God due to sin. Similarly, the Toba Qom recognize in Jesus the final solution to their problem – disruption of the tranquility and harmony of creation due to the actions of evil powers.

Through the gospel, the Toba Qom found in Jesus One with power to restore wholeness. The Holy Spirit was understood as putting each believer in direct relationship to the Ultimate Owner of the whole of Creation. They recognized in Jesus the continuity and the perfecting of the spiritual presence that they already knew and experienced as an active force within their own culture, and with whom they were accustomed to relate. Thus, in a very few years the majority of the Toba Qom embraced faith in Jesus.

The following testimony from José Sánchez is an eloquent illustration of the relation of traditional Toba Qom wisdom and the gospel. José, an elderly Toba Qom clan leader, had trained as a power-person in his younger years. In middle age, he became a believer in Jesus. From that time on, he experienced "persecution" by other powers who wanted to discourage him from following Jesus. For José, the process of synthesizing traditional spirituality and present experiences of the power of Christ happens primarily in the context of the dream. In Toba Qom spirituality the dream is one of the primary spaces where communication with the transcendent powers occurs.

> Once while lying in the hospital deathly ill, as I was praying in the early dawn, I "saw" eight *pi'oxonaqpi* (power-persons) at my bedside. I said to them, "What are you doing here? Why have you come to me, seeing there is no other name given to humans for **healing**, except the name of Christ?" With that name, that word, they left.
>
> Later in a dream, I was about to be hanged from a tall tree by "the man of this world." At the last minute a "light" rescued me, taking me up through the air at such a great height that I was afraid of falling. Then the light spoke to me, "I am, I am the **light** of all humans who live on earth. So the one who follows me cannot be in darkness." So I said, "Aaaahh, so it was the same Jesus Christ, since that's what the Bible says. Now I understand."

I looked back over my shoulder then, and the same person was still coming after me. I said, "Now, what am I going to do?" The light said, "I'll take **care** of you. I put you into the very hand of God!"

Afterward, ferocious animals came after me repeatedly. Each time I said to them, "God is the owner of all you animals, because God is the one who made all the animals and humans – together. So you belong to God and must obey him." With that, they left me alone!

Finally, there appeared to me a headless woman sitting on my sickbed. Her voice came from her head that was hanging on the wall. She seemed to represent death. I said to her, "God is **fire**, God is fire. No one can touch where he is present." Then came smoke and when I looked, the woman and her head were burning. They both burned up. Thanks to God! So then I got well, and I told the people, "God is fire, and no one can come close to him."[10]

The previous paragraphs illustrate how traditional Toba Qom spirituality provides the categories for José's understanding of Christ. Each paragraph highlights at least one theme, which I summarize here in the order in which they occur:

- Jesus is the most **powerful** healer, restorer of wholeness ("the evil powers left").
- Jesus is the continuation of the **light** already present, light being a common theme in Toba Qom dreams and traditionally a positive and powerful symbol.
- An owner takes **care** of their "possession" if the relationship of reciprocity is maintained. This may be done by spiritual mediators. Animals as well as humans owe ultimate allegiance to their true Creator/Owner, and when confronted with that reality, they must submit.
- **Fire**, another traditional symbol of power, may be concentrated in the Ultimate Owner, who has authority over all his creation. The action of the Holy Spirit is also often referred to as "fire" in both Toba Qom spirituality and in non-indigenous theology.

---

10.   Personal conversation with José Sánchez in 1997.

The gospel came to the Toba Qom in pentecostal clothes. Such pentecostal forms as being filled with the Spirit, speaking in ecstasy, spiritual healing, praying fervently, repetitive singing, spirit possession, and exorcism were all forms that were easily understandable in terms of Toba Qom wisdom. Since there was broad coincidence between the two symbolic systems (traditional Toba Qom wisdom and pentecostal), the Toba Qom understood with little difficulty the significance of Jesus for their lives and that of their people.

In this way the wisdom of the Toba Qom culture prepared them to find in Jesus new dimensions of **power, love** and **life**:

- **Power** over the forces of death, harmful vices, illnesses, evil spirits; new power for survival. Spiritual strength has enabled them to forgive their neighbor and to refuse to seek vengeance for the death of a family member. Thus, the spiral of violence propagated by shamanic action is broken.

- **Love** in the renewal of relationships in the family, community and with other tribes. Understanding the love of Jesus has motivated more caring family relationships. This new love also enabled them to love themselves once again, after their devastating defeat at the hands of the conquerors.

- **Life** within the environment of the non-Indian world. The new symbolic system permitted them to reconstruct their world and find themselves whole again in that new world. Balance was again restored – if not wholly, at least in part – giving new life to Toba Qom existence. In addition, the new life that they were now experiencing in Christ, effectively energized some of the old cultural religious forms, such as prayer, dance and song, giving them significant functions within the new *culto*, the indigenous worship experience.

Self-respect, self-confidence and self-determination have come to characterize the Toba Qom Christian movement

The spirit of the indigenous people was freed through organizing their own church, where they themselves respond in their own way to the call of God. The indigenous person is an individual with culture. That culture is still intact.

—Orlando Sánchez, Toba Qom pastor

As a result of the military defeat by "Christian" conquerors, the Toba Qom found themselves in an advanced state of cultural disintegration at the historical moment in which they heard the message of Jesus. Not surprisingly, their initial reaction as early believers was to reject both the official religion of the conquering powers, as well as much of their own traditional religion, which they considered to have failed them.

With time, however, the Toba Qom developed an alternative religious experience that permitted them to maintain their differentiation from the dominate culture, while allowing them to achieve the respect of the non-indigenous Christians around them by also being considered believers in Jesus.

The result of this historical process over the past 50 years has been the strengthening of Toba Qom identity and the empowerment of the indigenous church. The Toba Qom experience the love and power of Jesus Christ in their lives. They are fully in charge of determining and carrying out their own faith and religious practice. Participating in the translation of the Bible into the Toba Qom language has contributed to the restoration of their sense of self-worth. This religious self-determination, together with other sociopolitical factors, has enabled them to recover their sense of confidence in being able to exercise choices that self-determination requires.

The healthy effects of the gospel on Toba Qom people and culture, strengthening self-identity in their struggle for survival, can be seen in the following dialogue, recounted by José Mendoza, a Toba Qom evangelist and youth worker, who lived in Lote 68, a settlement of more than 400 indigenous families near the city of Formosa:

> One time there was a man here in Formosa whom I'll always remember. He had money, a pickup, a large truck – he had everything. But he marginalized the paisanos, the indigenous people. Even though he gave them work, he looked for those who liked to drink and hired them. When they began working, he gave them a bit of wine, and by the time they realized it, they were too drunk to work, so he took them home and got them again the next day, but never paid anything more.
>
> One day I was waiting at the bus stop to come home, and that man came up to me and said,
>
> – "You've been here awhile?"
>
> – "Yes."

– "Which bus are you waiting for?"

– "The one that goes to Lote 68."

– "You live in Lote 68?"

– "Yes."

– "Are you Indian?"

– "Yes, why do you ask?"

– "Because I'm looking for peones ("workers") and I don't find any. I need six or eight, and I'll have them work for bread and wine."

– "And that's all you pay?" I asked him. "Only wine and bread to those poor men? And what will they put on if they don't even have a shirt and pants? You won't find that kind of worker anymore!"

– "Why?"

– "Because that kind of worker woke up and now lives in Christ, and Christ lives in him."

– "And just where did you learn that?"

– "From the Bible," I told him, "and from my pastor. My pastor lives in Lote 68. If you want to know about it, you're invited. The door is open. But those workers you hired for wine and bread, you won't find anymore. They're all believers now."

You know, when I told him that, it upset him.[11]

Finding a way to be both Toba Qom and Christian is the major challenge that lies ahead

Come stay with us, not for a short "cross-cultural experience" – make it a lifetime commitment; be good listeners; accompany us in recovering our cultural values, especially the language; teach the Bible in such a way as not to fracture the life-process of the indigenous people.

—Orlando Charole, Toba Qom political leader[12]

11. Personal conversation with José Mendoza in 1992.
12. Recounted by Luis Acosta in a 1998 conversation.

Younger Toba Qom leaders are increasingly demonstrating their clear sense of confidence that indigenous cultural identity holds the secret to the future. Milton Caballero, 50-year-old believer and community leader of a semi-urban Toba Qom settlement, expressed his hope in 1996 in these words: "We must try to make it on our own, and we must be strong in our own culture, because the civilized world has failed. We know where civilization is headed, and it is useless."[13]

IEU leaders are convinced that Jesus Christ is the hope for the future. Through their faith in Christ, they are transforming their own mythology. This can be seen in the way they tell the history of the IEU. They refer to the IEU as their mother, and the formation of their own church as their Exodus, with their church founder as something of a cultural Moses.

However, in the face of the globalization that the dominating Empire (world economy) is forcing upon all indigenous groups, the continuing survival of the Toba Qom requires a redefinition of their own identity as both Christian and Toba Qom. This includes defining and articulating their own theology.

In 1996, Hugo Díaz, a regional overseer of the IEU, expressed a growing confidence among Toba Qom church leaders in doing just that. Speaking at a study conference on indigenous theologies and discrimination, Hugo declared to non-indigenous church workers, "We no longer want you to come and teach us the Bible. We want you to come and read the Bible together with us."

In this new moment in history, the indigenous church is indeed actively involved in the process of redefining Toba Qom identity. Up until now, the methodology has not been that of developing a systematized written theology, but instead, a process that is coherent with their own spirituality. Identity is being worked out through the development of their own religious forms and rites. However, these clearly demonstrate the ambiguity in the struggle to define their identity. Will the Toba Qom continue to see themselves as evangelical, pentecostal believers who embrace more and more of the criollo culture, or will they define themselves more and more as Toba Qom believers? Or will, perhaps, both of these occur? The struggle is evident in the question raised by an elderly Toba Qom woman following a congregational decision-making discussion: "How can they show a video in the church service when we are searching for the power?"

---

13.   Personal conversation with Milton Caballero in 1996.

One of the areas that most clearly reveals the struggle for identity is the place given to the various power-persons in church life. What – some are asking – should be the role and space given to the shaman as healer in the indigenous church? What would be the Christology that theologically relates shamanism to the claims of Christ? Can the two coexist?

Today, this theme is being considered intensely at all levels of the church. However, rather than calling for official conferences at which written documents are drawn up to define doctrine, the struggle is reflected in the variety of forms and spaces given to shaman activity within the church service itself. Some congregations allow recognized shaman healers to participate in prayers for healing during the service's regular healing ritual. Others prohibit shaman participation during church services, but allow or even encourage shaman healing if carried out at the healer's home, which serves as a kind of professional doctor's office. Some churches allow power-persons to lead the praise marches and praise dances, while other churches prohibit their participation or limit them to non-leadership roles.

The theological work that lies ahead for the Toba Qom believers today has two facets: (1) the continued re-reading of the Bible in the light of their own traditional wisdom and of present-day reality, and (2) the reinterpretation of their own "Old Testament" myths, wisdom and sacred history in the light of Christ. This process has already been going on for 50 years, but today it is intensified because of the urgency for greater self-identity.

Toba Qom spirituality can contribute to the faith of Christians everywhere

> But the people of that time weren't like now. In that time they weren't united, each was only with their own culture, only with their own people; they didn't mix with others because they were somewhat like enemies. Now they are all mixed together – Toba, Pilagá, Mocoví, Wichí – by means of the gospel. Now they are all united because of the gospel, they trust each other. There wasn't trust before. Now because of the gospel, all accepted the same unity.
>
> —José Mendoza, Toba Qom evangelist[14]

---

14. Personal conversation with José Mendoza in 1992.

Indigenous wisdom, like all human wisdom, becomes hope only when it reflects divine truth. Or, stated from a Christian point of view, wisdom becomes hope only as it is submitted to and measured by Christ, who is the hope and finality of all creation. The wisdom of all cultures is perfected in the inclusive Christ, who respects and brings to completion what the Creator has already begun. There is new hope only in turning life toward the True Life – the New Humanity in Christ – in turning toward the new heaven and new earth where each unique spirituality is finally given its rightful place.

In the concluding paragraphs of this piece, I will attempt to interpret, from the perspective of the broader Christian faith, the deeper significance of the Toba Qom experience as it relates to Christ and to the worldwide church. This significance I understand in terms of *transformation and complementation*.

Transformation. The gospel affirms each person and the culture of each people as loved and valued by God. Jesus Christ comes to validate and complete whatever true Wisdom is already present in any given culture. However, since every culture is by its very nature a human product, no culture coincides perfectly with the kingdom of God in all its aspects.

There is, therefore, no such thing as a Christian culture, only cultures that include some of the recognized Christian values. Wherever the kingdom of God is preached, the tension with the evils of the system – that which the New Testament considers the "world" – will become apparent. This is true for Western, so-called "Christian" and post-modern cultures, as well as for indigenous pre- and post-conquest cultures. Christ will engage every culture in a transformation process that questions all those aspects within that culture that are not life-giving, while at the same time enhancing all life-giving values present there.

Toba Qom spiritual leaders are aware of this tension and search for the best way to guide the transformation process, as shown in these words of Rafael Mansilla, a Toba Qom church leader and reservation administrator:

> We don't want our culture to be destroyed, but neither do we want to revive all the beliefs and practices of our ancestors. What we want is the "purification" of our culture, a selective process that makes survival possible. In that process the Bible is our guide.[15]

---

15. From author's unpublished notes, 1996.

The transformation process does not erase the uniqueness of the culture. Rather, each culture is enhanced through its movement toward completion in Christ, who in this way becomes its hope.

Complementation. The Toba Qom image of Christ can help Western and other Christians complete their otherwise limited experiences of Christ. Although it is true that Christians still do not know what the complete image of Jesus Christ is going to be,[16] we do know that it will include Toba Qom spirituality. Had the Toba Qom never embraced faith in Jesus, or had their distinctive spirituality been erased in the process, their contribution to the complete image of Jesus Christ would still be lacking.

The wisdom of God, which has already been revealed in each culture, is completed in Christ only by recognizing Christ in the "other," in such a way that it is through "unity with diversity" that full salvation will come.

We see glimpses of this understanding of complementation in the New Testament. For example, the biblical author of the letter to the Hebrews recognized the incompleteness of the salvation of those who belonged to traditional Jewish spirituality, even though they were accepted by God because of their faith. Thus, all the ancestors included in the long list of "heroes of faith" in Hebrews 11 are considered to be within the Jewish religious tradition, in spite of their diverse characteristics (or perhaps because of them!) since they exercised faith. "Therefore, God is not ashamed to be called their God; indeed, he has prepared a city for them" (Heb. 11:16, NRSV). The author goes on, however, to say that "all these, though they were commended for their faith, did not receive what was promised, since God had provided something better so that they would not, apart from us, be made perfect" (Heb. 11:39-40 NRSV).

In a similar way, we also stand in complementation with other culturally conditioned perceptions of Christ. Only by coming together, while at the same time honoring our diversity, will we discover a more complete understanding of the salvation God offers. As we contemplate faces of Christ perceived through other cultural eyes, rather than considering them culturally limited, we might begin to understand them as culturally enriched.

With the Toba Qom and other indigenous spiritualities in mind, I offer this paraphrased inversion of the above truth expressed in Hebrews: "God had provided something even better so that we would not, *apart from them,*

---

16. See Anton Wessels, *Images of Jesus. How Jesus is Perceived and Portrayed in Non-European Cultures*, Grand Rapids, MI: Eerdmans, 1990, p. 174.

be made perfect." The true Wisdom of God in Christ is hope for the future as it embraces each cultural face of Christ without erasing the distinctiveness of any.

Grand Canyon Suite

I have been incredibly privileged
by the God of life—granted a vision
of the infinite, in the "Grand Canyon" experience
of beholding, from within, the sheer grandeur
of the Toba-Qom cultural formation,
built with layer upon layer of countless lives
shaped and molded by place and time
and by unseen powers
into an enduring spirituality
of awesome dimension.

Willis Horst, July 2001

3

Serving as Guest-Missionaries in the Argentine Chaco

Stories of Accompaniment

Ute and Frank Paul

This chapter is primarily comprised of a thematically grouped selection of Frank and Ute's personal diary notes written during visits to indigenous communities in the Argentine Chaco from 1995 to 2008. Describing specific activities, challenges, insights, and attitudes, the excerpts offer a detailed portrait of the practice of accompaniment. A brief historical summary and theological foundation sets the context.

Preparation for the Chaco

In 1990 theologian and pastor René Padilla invited us, Frank and Ute, to Argentina to work for a year under his mentorship. He and his wife, Catalina Feser, opened our eyes to the local Latin-American situation, especially regarding social conditions and the situation of the church. They gave us important insights and the opportunity to cooperate with them in a mission effort in an area of the poverty belt of Buenos Aires.

At that time we were a young married couple with two small children. We did not lack the courage to become actively engaged, but we definitively did not have the experience to live and work with people in such extreme circumstances. After our year of personal contacts and regular visits, the local youth group and a few adults with their children invited us to move into their neighborhood to encourage and strengthen their new church.

The following four years resulted in a kind of "school of life" for us. The people exercised amazing gifts as they organized their own church and initiated a vital community life. They showed impressive endurance amidst material poverty. Some of the broken marriages and families exemplified the strength of the gospel.

Although we were collaborating with them primarily as coworkers, it turned out to be unavoidable for us to bring perceptions and customs from our European background loaded with superiority. It was, therefore, not easy to be present with them solely as guests. However, the local leadership, self-confident enough to remind us of the role they wanted us to pursue, made clear that we were not the ones to make decisions for them. Rather, they invited us to support them in *their* effort to strengthen their church in accordance with their own ideas. We learned to accept this gracefully. They invited Frank to cooperate on the pastoral team, but not as pastor. He was expected to participate in a manner similar to that of the other two members of the team. Beyond this, they took for granted that he, like they, would earn a living outside the pastoral team role.

We were eager to join their team, but in retrospect realize how difficult it was for us not to feel superior to them due to our German cultural formation. The believers in the Faith and Life Church were gracious, kept their homes open, offered their friendship, and shared with us their faith and everyday life. Thus, we remember those first years in Argentina with profound gratitude. At that time we did not yet foresee what an excellent preparation these experiences would be for the challenges awaiting us in the Chaco.

In 1994, when our term of service in Buenos Aires ended, we, Frank and Ute, received an invitation to join the Mennonite Team in northern Argentina. Thus, from 1995 until 2008 we served with the Mennonite Team and lived in the Argentine Chaco. During those years of ministry with the indigenous people and their churches, our experience in Buenos Aires served us well. In the Chaco we needed always to keep in mind that the initiative should remain with the indigenous. We were there not to do things *for* them, but rather *with* them.

The Chaco and its people

The Gran Chaco is situated in the heart of the South American continent. It stretches over an area of nearly 97,000 square miles, about the size of the state of Oregon, and belongs politically to three countries: Argentina, Paraguay, and Bolivia. The Argentine part lies mainly in the northern provinces of Chaco, Formosa, Santa Fe and Santiago del Estero.

Originally the area was covered with swamps, palm savannas and semi-arid thorn forests. Today, large sections of the Chaco have been deforested and are now being used for agriculture, cattle and forestry. Where virgin forest still exists, it exhibits an enormously rich flora and fauna that withstands the aridity and poor soil. Precipitation diminishes gradually from the southeast to the northwest. During the cold season it sometimes does not rain for six to eight months creating critical shortage of drinking water. In this subtropical climate, large trees with deep roots thrive, for instance, the *quebracho*, the *algarrobo* (related to the carob), and a wide variety of thorny trees. Extended forests of palm trees grow in the eastern swampy regions. In spring, tree blossoms feed a large variety of bee species. Huge numbers of insects provide food resources for amphibians, birds and mammals such as anteaters and bats. Poisonous snakes and giant boas, caimans, piranhas, dangerous spiders and scorpions, peccary and even pumas are the characteristic wildlife of the interior of the Chaco. European immigrants considered it so harsh and inhospitable that they labeled it "the green hell."

Yet the Chaco had been home for indigenous populations for thousands of years. The thorny, almost impenetrable forest offered areas of protection, retreat and abundance for the aboriginal peoples. They had always been hunters and gatherers for whom subsistence determined lifestyle. The forest provided all they needed for life: meat, fish, honey, roots and fruits; shells for utensils, wood for fire and building material, plants for medicinal purposes, weapons, and fiber for clothing. They lived in small semi-nomadic family groups, moving frequently according to the availability of food. At certain times of the year they gathered with other groups to celebrate feasts.

An economy based on accumulation of goods for future need was unknown to them. They believed that the forest belongs to the benevolent Creator and to invisible intermediaries, whom they called "owners" and to whom they owed respect. A harmonious relationship with the spiritual owners of a certain geographical area, or of a species desired for food, was a prerequisite for the acquisition of resources. Anyone who wanted to hunt had to ask permission and obey the limits established by the spiritual owners.[1]

In the 18th century European invaders started building towns along the banks of the Paraná and Salado rivers. They sought to use the waterways that crossed the Chaco as means of access to the presumed riches – gold and silver – of the Andes. This encroachment left the indigenous inhabitants unable to roam freely throughout their traditional territory in search of food. Even more devastating were the military operations of the armies of the newly founded South American states, following independence from Spain. In their desire to free the land for colonization, they deliberately set out to wage war against the *indios* (the term by which the indigenous peoples were commonly known). In the late 1800s, just over 100 years ago, Argentine generals led annihilating campaigns against the few surviving indigenous populations. Even as recently as 1924 and 1947, in northern Argentina, national security forces carried out massacres on the reservations of *Napalpí* (Mocoví and Toba Qom) and *Rincón La Bomba* (Pilagá) with no subsequent judicial inquiry nor consequence for those responsible.

The Europeans came with a philosophy of the land profoundly different from that of the indigenous. Colonizers and military alike wanted to possess land as property and protect it against external claims. To this end, the Argentine land offices produced papers intended to document the rightful possession by the new "owners" with no consideration for the rights of the indigenous people who naturally had no such written documents. In the wake of the military conquest, European immigrants gradually invaded Toba Qom living space. When larger stretches of land were granted to a new "owner," the surviving indigenous families living within this territory were handed over as part of the package.

The Chaco indigenous tribal people did not surrender without fighting. They stood bravely against the foreign soldiers, but were finally overcome by the superior fire power of the invaders, by fraud and fictitious treaties, and by new diseases against which they had developed no immunity. The military conquest brought with it death, deportation, forced labor and compulsive Christianization. Today, only approximately 1 percent of the population of Argentina considers itself indigenous, while perhaps 3-5 percent of Formosa and Chaco provinces do so. However, it is recognized that more than half of

---

1. See also in this volume Albert Buckwalter's description, Chapter 7, "Important Considerations . . ." section: "Before the Colonization of the Chaco," pp. 177ff.

Argentina's 40 million people carry some degree of indigenous blood. The descendants of more than ten indigenous tribal groups live in the Argentine part of the Gran Chaco. The most numerous of these are the Toba Qom (about 80,000 individuals) and the Wichí (about 80,000). The Mennonite Team accompanies the Toba Qom, Mocoví and Pilagá peoples, who together make up the Guaycurú linguistic family. (See maps pp. 5-6).

The situation of these indigenous groups remains precarious. Among the poorest sectors in the country, they represent an unwanted minority in the provinces where they live. They commonly suffer discrimination by government administrative personnel and in public institutions of health, education and welfare. The recognition of indigenous rights at the national and international level is slow and tedious. In the Argentine Chaco, immigrants and their descendents hold a colonial mentality with respect to the indigenous population. Most Argentines expect them to adapt to the dominant Argentine way of life and abandon indigenous customs.

Many indigenous families depend on public subsidies or pensions, which too often are linked to political manipulation and obligations. Like other lower class Argentines, most indigenous people are not hired for permanent work and therefore have no fixed income. They accept work wherever possible: as handy men, day laborers for heavy, dirty, dusty jobs, harvest workers, ranch hands, and in the forests. Fortunately, traditional skills in basketry, weaving, pottery and other handicrafts allow them to generate additional income. Where possible, some men still prefer to hunt and fish for additional food.[2]

Although the general situation of the indigenous population of Argentina still appalls us, we have seen a steadily growing self-confidence in recent years. Many young indigenous leaders have accepted responsibility in their churches, as well as in their communities, determined to combat further discrimination and suppression of their people. An example is the 2005 peaceful protest held in the central park across from the government office building in Resistencia, the capital of Chaco Province. Hundreds of women, children and men rallied from the whole province. They camped out in the park under plastic sheets for four months, exposed to cold winter temperatures, in an attempt to draw public attention to the subnormal living conditions of the indigenous population. Although the results were not as

---

2. For more detailed comments about present day conditions, see the section, "Accompaniment ministries," pp. 118ff. See also Albert Buckwalter's comments in this volume, Chapter 7 "Important considerations . . ." section: "The Situation Today," pp. 179ff.

satisfying as hoped, this joint effort generated an amazing inner power which the government and the non-indigenous population could not ignore.

The Mennonite Team – an alternative missionary presence

From the beginning of the Mennonite presence in the Argentine Chaco, mission workers were sent by the North American mission agency of the Mennonite Church. Subsequent to the transition of the Mission to an accompaniment style in the mid-1950s, no attempt was made to include staff members from other countries or of denominations other than Mennonite. Requirements for all new workers included linguistic and anthropological training. However, by the early 1990s the team made a deliberate effort to seek persons other than North American Mennonites to join the team.

At the same time the team sought to broaden its involvement towards accompaniment in areas other than the explicitly spiritual, that is, church and Bible. The term "Mennonite Team" emerged in the mid 1990s to fill the need for a more adequate label in the interaction with other nongovernmental agencies involved with indigenous groups in the Chaco. By the late 1990s the Mennonite Team consisted of seven families from three countries and several evangelical denominations. They lived in four cities in the provinces of Chaco and Formosa. The name Mennonite Team has been continued for its historical legacy, although today less than half of its members belong to North American Mennonite churches.

According to their mission statement, the Mennonite Team members consider themselves ambassadors of Jesus Christ and guests of the people in the Chaco. They seek to call attention to God's presence and actions. Hence, a great deal of time and energy goes into accompanying and strengthening indigenous churches. Translation of the Bible and making its message available in the languages best understood receive high priority in order for the Toba Qom to apply the gospel in their own setting. In addition to the priority given to the churches, the team engages in accompaniment of the indigenous communities in the struggle for human rights, for wholesome living conditions, and for strengthening indigenous identity and culture.

The Mennonite Team seeks to accompany without creating dependencies or taking on any responsibilities rightly belonging to local leadership. Team members promote native leadership and the use of local resources. They seek to avoid paternalistic actions and undue interference in the indigenous communities. Therefore, they abstain from giving financial aid; avoid initiating, sponsoring or directing projects and do not accept leadership in local church groups. The team's activities of accompaniment are based on the conviction that all initiatives for action should rest primarily with the indigenous people themselves.

The Mennonite Team sees itself not only as a group of missionary workers in a foreign setting, but also as a spiritual community in itself. Members seek to function as a "church" by investing the time necessary to maintain a pastoral relationship with each other. The team functions as a community of followers of Jesus with a special mandate for ministry in the Argentine Chaco as fraternal companions of indigenous people.

Through the following activities the Mennonite Team carries out its alternative missionary presence:

- learn and use indigenous languages;
- participate in the translation of the Bible into indigenous languages;
- provide Bibles and other literature as requested;
- coordinate Bible Circles in collaboration with church leaders;
- publish the quarterly bulletin, *Qad'aqtaxanaxanec* ("Our Messenger"), edited by the team since 1955;
- visit indigenous communities and churches and participate in their services;
- receive indigenous guests in our homes;
- carry out pastoral visitation of indigenous persons in hospitals and prisons;
- document personal testimonies, life stories and oral histories;
- give advisory aid in pursuing indigenous rights, especially land rights;
- collaboratively assist with literacy efforts in indigenous languages;
- interact with other organizations in the larger Chaco region.

Today, after more than seventy years in the Chaco, the Mennonite presence, now known as the Mennonite Team (*Equipo Menonita*), continues its accompanying ministries. Much of the Bible has been translated into the three languages of the Qom people – Toba, Mocoví and Pilagá. Members of the Mennonite Team come from several countries and denominations. The experiences and insights of those first years still form the guidelines for all Team activities and are passed on to successive workers.

When we, Frank and Ute, became members of the team in 1995, we learned from the senior missionaries, some of whom had been living in the Chaco for decades. As we gained access to this enormous treasure, the opportunities to learn overwhelmed us. We want to share with others this treasure of mission as accompaniment rather than conquest. Therefore, we tell our story. We counsel those who go to other cultures to encourage the people to grow in their relationship to God within their own cultural forms of expression.

It would be difficult to grasp our style of accompaniment without a descriptive illustration. What follows is based mainly on Frank's personal, thematically structured notes written during his extensive travels in the interior of the Chaco from 1995 to 2008.

Later in this chapter we illustrate these activities with excerpts from Frank Paul's travel diary. However, in the following sections we include a description of missionary models, first from a contemporary colonial practice, then by a look at models taken from the Bible.

Mission in colonial style

Missionary conquest

Everyone entering into a foreign culture should aspire to be a learner; a guest, not a manager. As members of the Mennonite Team, our goal is to respect the local culture. With time, we become acquainted with indigenous people's wisdom, spirituality, customs, and special gifts, as well as their faults and failures. We share in the life of our hosts as invited guests, seeking to be aware of how our presence affects them in order to avoid being the cause of problems or internal conflict.

Unfortunately, Jesus' missionary mandate, the Great Commission, is often wrongly depicted as a spiritual conquest. Young Christians are sometimes urged to see themselves as "a new generation of conquerors." Christian missionary enthusiasm is often generated by referencing the military occupation the tribes of Israel carried out against the indigenous inhabitants of neighboring countries as described in the Old Testament. Unfortunately, that narrative is misinterpreted when used as motivation for spreading the gospel. An aggressive attitude is reflected in the many military terms used in sermons and songs such as "take possession of the land," "conquer the world for Jesus," "crusade for Christ," "win the battle," "soldiers of Jesus," among others. These phrases suggest a lack of sensitivity to the South American indigenous context. Upon hearing the word "conquest," Latin American indigenous peoples are reminded, first of all, of the violent military conquest in the name of Christ. In order to avoid false associations, military terms should be eliminated from missionary vocabulary.

Insensitive evangelization

Sometimes Christians who go to evangelize or to help indigenous communities lack the cultural understanding required for bringing healing and hope. In 2006 two of our Mennonite Team colleagues reported the following story which serves to illustrate:

> When we arrived at an indigenous community we had visited often over many years, local leaders told us the following news. A group of evangelical Christians had come there some months before from a distant city where they have a Bible institute. The visitors told of a vision they had received to "find and help" a certain indigenous tribe. Already on this first visit they offered financial aid to replace the small, old church building of wood and mud plaster with a new "respectable" building of bricks, a "worthy" house of God. Many years before, the members of the congregation had built the old church building with their own hands and means.
>
> The visitors apparently were not aware that there had been an independent indigenous church in the community for nearly half a century, nor that the New Testament had been available in the language for many years. They offered future Bible studies at the local church and also invited a young man recommended by the local pastor (his own son) to go to their Bible school in the city to receive an "adequate preparation" to be the future pastor of the group. Other members of the community told us that this young man was not a faithful member of the congregation and had even left his wife in order to go to the Bible school because he learned that married men were not accepted for training. An older pastor also travelled to the Bible school to study, but was refused acceptance with the argument that he had to care for his family. He returned home deeply disappointed.
>
> During two subsequent visits, professors from the city held Bible studies dictated in a language that required an interpreter

to translate into Spanish, with the promise of a written certificate for those who would finish the course. By their attitude these teachers were communicating, either consciously or without realizing it, that "a true church" should have the correct documents and that pastors should have a "proper" degree from a recognized institution.

The visitors furthermore urged the congregation to begin a Sunday school for the children (which a "proper" church ought to have). For this purpose they named a director and teacher (the daughter of the indigenous pastor), and offered her a salary to teach and to prepare the snack. She was instructed to keep attendance records with names and document numbers of the children who participated. These reports then had to be sent to the head of the church in the city. Some of the members of the congregation told us confidentially that the Sunday school did not always take place, but that nevertheless, the young woman faithfully completed the list monthly, creating suspicions that it was to keep her small financial stipend coming.

We were also told that another young man had started a correspondence course for pastors on the condition that he legalize his common law marriage. The church barbecued two cows for the wedding celebration. But when guests from a neighboring community arrived for the feast, they were refused entrance because they did not have official printed invitations. That was an incredible shock for the people. However, the young man told us with obvious lack of respect, "The elders and present pastors don't know anything. They don't have a title or certificate."

Despite all promises to the contrary ("we shall respect your culture and your traditions") the missionaries from the city interfered with the church services. With spiritual arrogance and ethnocentrism they openly criticized the existing forms of the congregation. On one occasion the church members had prepared everything for a baptismal service and cleared a spot in the nearby stream. Everyone gathered around for the service. When it began, the foreign visitor took leadership without prior consultation, filled a basin with water and sprinkled it on the candidates for baptism. The church members and the pastor were appalled because in their baptism ceremony the candidates are submerged completely. The congregation interpreted the foreign visitor's behavior as aversion to the "dirty" water, which, in their eyes, was a great humiliation.

The local congregation felt insecure in the presence of these outside visitors. During church services they did not feel free to express their happiness with the customary dancing. The pastor said to us: "If I cannot dance I feel spiritually dried up." Nevertheless, he accepted the presence of the visitors because he had been promised a new church building. To this end he even suffered voluntarily the humiliation in front of his own people when the foreigners said, "The pastor and the elder of your congregation do not have an official theological education, they cannot teach you anything."

The indigenous people have learned through past experience that outside financial aid to church groups is linked to constraints. Almost invariably the donors will demand conformity to their own culturally defined understandings of church life in order for the funds to continue. In this way the persons favored by the donation are under great pressure to meet the requirements. However, according to the wisdom of the hunter in indigenous culture, if the hunt is successful, the one who brings home the prey vindicates his position of prestige no matter what amount of humiliation or other demands he must suffer in order to achieve the end result. It is understood that he is only being astute as a hunter. The pastor told us decidedly, "We will wait until the church building is finished with their help. Then we will gather to decide what to do about the people from the city."

A wise, elderly leader of this same indigenous community has maintained a clear and deeply rooted faith in Jesus Christ. He confided to us, "Since I first learned about Jesus, 64 years ago, I hear God's voice every morning. When I get up I hear the voice. When the young man said to me, 'Old man, you don't know anything,' then I kept silent and listened. I said nothing. It may be that this young man knows something, but I know God."

Negative results

The foregoing example illustrates how a well-meaning Christian mission can cause internal conflicts within the indigenous communities. This type of mission cannot even be considered "gospel" since it interferes with local leadership, produces insecurity, causes division and belittles the people as ignorant, uneducated and even sinful. In the above mentioned case, the consequence of a well-intentioned "mission" was that most members of the community who did not receive financial remuneration left the church for fear that they would not be able to continue to worship as they chose. They later formed a separate congregation as an alternative.

Mission models from the New Testament

Jesus and the first missionaries exemplified a basic attitude and consequent action which can guide mission efforts today. Above all, missionaries should follow Jesus' example. Jesus said to his followers: "Peace be with you. As the Father has sent me, so I send you" (John 20:21).

Jesus

Life mission: to live with missional intent among the common people

John's Gospel states, "And the Word became flesh, and lived among us." (Literally, "the Word tented among the people," John 1:14). Jesus is described as the final and complete word from God, the one in whom God, the Father, was shown to humankind, yet who lived as a guest among his own people (see John 14:9b; Heb. 1:1-2). But, "He came to what was his own (home), and his own people did not accept him" (John 1:11).

The early communities of believers remembered and meditated on the self-emptying manner of Jesus. It is exemplified in one of the oldest Christian hymns, which Paul includes in his letter to the Philippians (2:5-11). We cite this hymn because we, along with generations of believers in Jesus throughout the centuries, understand that the self-emptying attitude of Jesus, who became a servant, stands as the measure by which all action in his name must be measured. Our missional message and goals, as well as the means by which we achieve them, must fall within the parameters of this model.

The Gospels repeatedly mention this attitude and behavior of Jesus, which even those who lived closest to him found difficult to accept and live out. Even after living with Jesus for many months, his apostles argued among themselves about which of them should be honored the most (Mark 10:35-45). Neither could they accept with the same approval as their teacher did, those who were considered sinners, unclean or inferior, such as women, children, the sick and disabled, and foreigners (Mark 10:13-15; John 9:2-5; Matthew 15:23; 26:6-8).

Jesus travelled around Palestine mingling with the people. During his journeys he stayed as a guest with those who received him (Matthew 8:14; 9:27-28; Mark 3:20; 7:24). He was known to take part in the customary religious and family festivities of his people. Thus, he aroused suspicion and indignation among the spiritual leaders of his time (Matthew 9:10-13; 11:20). Once, at a wedding celebration that had gone on for several days and had run out of wine, Jesus found a way to provide more (John 2:1-12).

Jesus ate at the same table with all who invited him. He was guest of ill-esteemed persons and listened to the troubles of his hosts. He allowed a woman of disrepute to touch him. He visited bedfast people and cared for them. Jesus did not consider illness a punishment from God. Even when he was teaching he was aware of the needs of his listeners (Mark 6:34-37).

Jesus taught in synagogues and the temple, but also often in the open air. However, only a few of his sermons have been recorded, although many of his conversations were. The times when he was alone are presented as interludes spent in prayer and renewal (Matthew 26:36-45; Mark 1:35). Mostly we find him speaking to one person, often surrounded by listeners. Jesus' conversations consisted not so much of spiritual instruction, but were more often related to concrete actions such as healings or about problems of life. Evidently, a considerable number of dialogues recorded in the Gospels were aroused by provocative questions raised by Jesus or by the people who approached him.

Jesus himself apparently felt like an ordinary man among others and he enjoyed being with common women and men. In his teaching, he used examples and comparisons taken from everyday life of the rural population. He was acquainted with utensils from hearth and home. He knew the struggle of daily work, the rhythm of seasons, seedtime and harvest, wind and weather. He understood the rules of economic life and was aware of the abuse of power by the wealthy and their allies.

Jesus wandered on foot over the country and was apparently not in a hurry. He took time for the needs of the people waiting for him along the road (Matthew 8:5, 28). Rather than spend the night in hotels or taverns, or eat in restaurants, he chose to stay in the houses of his friends (Luke 10:38-42;

John 11:1-5). He was not self-sufficient, but preferred to depend on the help of others for his personal needs (Luke 8:1-3). It is not surprising that Jesus instructed his apostles to go out in vulnerability and live as guests. "As you go, proclaim the good news . . . cure the sick . . . , give without payment . . . Take no gold . . . , no bag for your journey . . . Whatever town or village you enter, find out who in it is worthy, and stay there until you leave . . . It is enough for the disciple to be like the teacher" (Matthew 10:7-12, 24-25a).

Jesus was a Jew. Until the age of 30, he was taught and shaped by the culture and history of his people. Then he became an itinerant preacher and a rabbi. He selectively reinterpreted some of the spiritual and cultural teachings of his own people's sacred tradition. When he criticized practices of his time he intended to clarify God's original intentions: that love overrules law, that compassion is worth more than ritual sacrifice, that peace comes through justice and mercy, and that God's love reaches all people including enemies. (Matthew 5:17-48)

However, it is highly important for us to understand that Jesus' work of renewal (or purification) of the local culture and religion was carried out *as one who belonged to the local Jewish culture.* No one attempting to work and live in a foreign culture as a guest should assume that role. We can only exercise that right with integrity when we act from within our own culture. God works through local followers of Jesus to clarify his will in every culture and through them he effects the process of renovation.

Peter

Expanding mission: a paradigmatic change in self-understanding

All persons normally judge from the point of view of their own culture that which appears strange in those of other cultures. Each culture considers itself superior to all others. This behavior is called ethnocentrism. The early church began in the context of an ethnic people with an extremely ethnocentric orientation.

Following the outpouring of the Holy Spirit at Pentecost, the gospel of Jesus began to spread. The first to believe in Jesus as the Messiah were people with Jewish ancestors. It was their firm belief that a spiritual relation of non-Jews to the true God, Yahweh, was possible only on the condition that they convert to Judaism. This made spreading the gospel to the Gentiles in their neighborhood and surrounding countries almost impossible for Christian Jews.

One of the disciples who had a particularly difficult struggle in this respect was Peter. The story in Acts 10 shows that he was not aware of his ethnocentrism. It took a drastic divine intervention to convince Peter that God would accept people with non Jewish background just as well as people of Jewish descent. Only then was Peter ready to enter the house of a Roman officer who had urgently invited him – an action considered incompatible with Jewish laws. Peter had several heavenly visions which inspired him in such a way that later, in the house of the officer, he was able to state:

> You yourselves know that it is unlawful for a Jew to associate with or to visit a Gentile; but God has shown me that I should not call anyone profane or unclean. So when I was sent for, I came without objection. Now may I ask why you sent for me? (Acts 10:28-29)

In that same context Peter added:

> I truly understand that God shows no partiality, but in every nation anyone who fears him and does what is right is acceptable to him. (Acts 10:34-35)

Until then it was unthinkable for Peter that humans of any non-Judaic culture could have direct access to the gospel and the power of the Holy Spirit. However, following the visions in which the Spirit of God taught him, Peter began to realize that "everyone who believes in him receives forgiveness of sins through his name" (Acts 10: 43). Now he understood that a right relationship with God does not depend on fulfilling the Jewish laws. This was a new theology which was to be disputed intensely in the early Christian congregations and the cause of much conflict between Jewish and non-Jewish Christians.

Paul

Church growth in mission: the independence of young churches

Paul, a Jew, lived and worked in the Diaspora, in a multicultural context. He denounced the attitude of superiority of his own people. During the early years of the church Paul laid down the theological foundation for the understanding that God was already present in non-Jewish nations before they came into contact with the gospel. As a missionary he promoted the independence of the newly established, young churches in Europe.

In his well-known speech at Athens Paul said, "What therefore you worship as unknown; this I proclaim to you . . . he who is Lord of heaven and earth, . . . he himself gives to all mortals life and breath and all things . . . he made all nations to inhabit the whole earth . . . so that they would search for God and perhaps grope for him and find him" (Acts 17:23-27).

According to Paul's thought, God created each ethnic group and remains present with all peoples since their beginning whether or not they know God. God guides them, protects them and cares for their needs. God's wisdom resounds in their life experiences. Paul did not speak disparagingly of the religious ideas of others. He was convinced that each group of people has received from God their own land in order to develop their particular language and culture (cf. Gen. 10:5b; 20:31). Yahweh wanted and still wishes to be sought in order that all human beings can find God and walk in God's way. They will then discover that God's commandments generate and sustain life. Throughout history, the Creator becomes known in many ways. But finally, Jesus Christ uniquely reveals God so that all humankind might trust, obey and follow in Jesus' way (Heb. 1:1-2).

With this purpose in mind, Paul strategically chose several cities of the Roman Empire in which to preach – in synagogues, public places and private homes. Some persons began to recognize Jesus as God's special messenger, the Christ, and accepted his way. Paul gathered these new non-Jewish believers into house churches, instead of integrating them into the existing synagogues. He organized them, sometimes including Jewish believers, into groups that met in homes. If there was more than one in an urban area, they were considered to be part of the larger assembly, or church, which regularly held common services and feasts of the Lord's Supper. This gave them the occasion to remember the death and resurrection of Jesus, as well as to be part of one common body of Christ.

It was not Paul's intention to constitute a hierarchically structured religious institution which would then become the only door to heaven, but to inspire a way of life that reflected the practice of Jesus. Believers were expected to practice and extend the forgiveness and reconciliation which Jesus taught. They were to be open communities that transmit convincingly the love of God for all people.

From the very beginning, these Christian communities were heterogeneous social groups joined by their common commitment to Christ. Paul felt that every community of believers should be rooted in its respective cultural context, but continue to be inviting to strangers. These Christian groups organized their social life like that of an extended family. General care for the poor, the sick, the widows and orphans was part of congregational life. Thus, in the early church the practice of social justice developed in unmistakable contrast to the surrounding society. Christians seriously lived out their belief that God wanted fullness of life for every human being.

Paul expressed his conviction that Christian duties are not determined by one's race or social position (Rom. 12:6-8; 1 Cor. 12:4-11). Rather, the Holy Spirit offers talents and gifts to each one to be used for the good of the entire community. In using these talents and gifts, each member becomes dignified and important to the community.

Another Pauline teaching, that the body of Christ, the church, is one and universal holds great practical importance for missionary action. In his first letter to the Corinthians Paul describes all Christians in the world as one body, with Christ as the only head. When each congregation recognizes its worth to the others, no such thing as a self-sufficient church exists, nor one whose contribution does not enrich the rest.

Paul also wanted to avoid becoming a financial burden to the newly founded house churches. Although he knew that as a "missionary co-worker" he had the right to some financial remuneration, he earned his living as a tent maker (1 Cor. 9:11-15).

With the exception of Corinth, where he remained longer than a year, Paul stayed only a few weeks at places where new church groups came into existence. In each place he appointed those who should become responsible leaders of the group, and then moved on. He was led by the conviction that he was only a co-worker under God and he trusted that God was in charge of developing and caring for each new group he had begun. He expressed clearly his basic attitude towards the young congregations in one of his letters: "I do not mean to imply that we lord it over your faith; rather, we are workers with you for your joy, because you stand firm in the faith" (2 Cor. 1:24). However, he did maintain fraternal ties from a distance, through periodic pastoral letters and occasional visits when possible. If he was not able to go personally, he sent trustworthy co-workers.

We who minister as "fraternal co-workers" with the indigenous churches in the Chaco find much inspiration and guidance in the Apostle Paul. We are especially challenged by his encouragement of each local group to be in charge of their own church life. He taught the newly formed groups of believers to be independent in terms of their authority, but to develop caring relationship with other parts of the church as Christ's one body.

As a team we seek to follow the New Testament patterns we have discussed above through the following convictions:

- We do not take God to anyone. God has already been present in the wisdom and history of the indigenous people.
- We desire to discern where and how God is already at work, then join in to cooperate but without taking charge.
- We believe the indigenous churches are God's work, not ours. God guides and teaches them.
- We belong to the one universal body of Christ in the world. We have much to learn from the faith and practice of indigenous believers. It is not true that they need us more than we need them.
- We acknowledge our part of the international body of Christ, and, as members of the economically wealthier churches, we seek ways to share in solidarity and reciprocity. (2 Cor. 8:9) This practice of solidarity with the poor requires discretion and careful discernment.
- We recognize the Holy Spirit living in our indigenous sisters and brothers. We trust the Spirit to guide them and enable them to achieve an authentic expression of faith.
- We seek, as missionary guests, to avoid fostering dependencies or becoming a burden for the indigenous churches.

Guests in Toba Qom homes

In 1955, following the transition to an accompaniment style of presence, visiting and encouraging the scattered Toba Qom communities became the priority.

In Toba Qom culture the practice of visiting has a deep and long-lasting importance and provides one of the greatest joys in the life of the people. Particularly among big family clans constant coming and going means relatives visit unannounced. They follow their intuition, simply appearing at the homes of their relatives and staying as long as they like. Of course these guests are sheltered, fed and looked after as well as possible.

Hosts and guests alike frequently tell of being helped during unexpected visits. Rather than call attention to what could be viewed as a negative experience – a burden for their family – they are tuned in instead to the unexpected blessings in the ongoing circumstances of life. God consoles, and even sometimes admonishes them through visitors or hosts, which shows

God's concern and value of them as persons of worth. To be received and treated as guests by the indigenous people we considered a unique privilege.

"Wasting" time together

We members of the Mennonite Team are often asked what we actually *do*, when we say that we accompany and support the indigenous people. We respond jokingly that we sit around with them and drink *maté* (MAHteh) tea. It would not be an overstatement to say that these times of mutual encounter during our visits were our foremost contribution over the years. Drinking *maté* together provides the culturally acceptable way to build friendship and trust.

Of course, as newcomers to the team, we (Ute and Frank) first had to learn what our indigenous hosts expect from us – not so much talk, but silence and patient waiting. In Western culture it is customary to ask many questions to show interest. To do so during visits to indigenous homes or churches would be inappropriate. We are the guests; the indigenous families are our hosts. Bombarding them with questions can raise unnecessary mistrust, as they may wonder about their guests' motivation for soliciting information. To become respectful guests, we learned to remain quietly seated after the usual greeting ritual until our indigenous hosts start the conversation, which often takes quite awhile.

We gradually became aware of all that happened in the silence: our thoughts became quiet, our bodies rested, we noticed our surroundings. More and more we came to appreciate being allowed to recover after a long, exhausting journey without having to respond to constant questions. While we sat in a circle with other men, women quietly tended the fire, put the kettle on, and prepared the *maté* drink. When everything was ready the tea ritual began. The person responsible for serving the tea adds hot water to the cup of *maté* leaves and sucks the strong brew of green tea through a thin metal straw. Then the server pours more hot water on the tea and hands it in turn to each one seated in the circle, always in the same order. When any person says thank you, that one is skipped in subsequent rounds. This serving ritual continues, sometimes silently, and with great care. When the water cools, it is reheated.

The silence observed during *maté* drinking is not at all embarrassing, but was at first simply new for us. Time and again we invaded the silence with too many questions. Only when we kept quiet for some time did our hosts begin to speak of what really interested them. In such an atmosphere true encounter was then possible and we could also bring up our own concerns. Sharing the common *maté* cup and straw communicates more about acceptance than any words spoken.

In these encounters we learned to become vulnerable. Their great capacity for empathy spoke to our own sorrows and needs. When we were sick or depressed, they asked God to help us. They prayed for our children and parents. When our car stopped running, they made it their own concern. They rejoiced with us and wept with us, and we did likewise, in mutual care. They accompanied *us* as much as we accompanied *them*.

Here are journal entries made following visits to homes of indigenous friends.

> In the indigenous brother's patio we drank *maté*. The hours flew by in the light of the full moon as we sat with him, his wife and their three small daughters. . . . I didn't get tired at all listening to their life experiences and their stories. They expressed clearly their own theology and what they hoped their people would be able to achieve in the future. It was impossible for me to leave after one hour, as I had originally planned.
>
> *Piỹo' Lauac, Puerto Lavalle, 2005*

> As always, I was offered one of the few chairs. Several of the family stood at my side and asked me whether I had had a comfortable bus ride and whether it had been raining at home in Resistencia, too. Then they sat down not far from me and did not speak – for quite a long time. Meanwhile Doña Luisa prepared the *maté* tea. A few neighbors came by to greet me with a handshake and sat down in the silent circle. When this silent welcome ceremony had gone on for some time, they began to speak of topics that interested them.
>
> The night was spectacular because of the almost full moon above us. In front of us an open field extended to the distant forest. We enjoyed the light, steady breeze which kept away the mosquitoes. For hours the events of the last week were exchanged in this large family circle: An elderly man, sick with tuberculosis, had died; the local church had not been holding regular worship services for some time because of a conflict between the two male leaders; new families had been formed; the government

had ordered new houses built in other villages. Unfortunately the house of my Toba Qom family clan is without windows and doors because of misuse of public funds.

Pioq La'asat, Pampa Chica, 2005

The members of the local indigenous church told me during the evening service that other visitors did not stay long with them. They wanted me to know how delighted they were about my plans to stay with them for several days, accompany their pastor on his home visits in the mornings and to offer a Bible Circle in the afternoons. They decided spontaneously to hold worship services on the next three nights.

Laguna Pato, 1998

The wonderful dawn and the cloudless sky encouraged me. Even more so, the long time spent with Leopoldo López, who remembered the old days and his adventures with Aurelio and Albert. In worship one of the brothers said, "God does not send us letters, but sends us one of his children."

Lot 4, Pampa del Indio, 2001

Toba Qom teacher and friend Mario and I visited an indigenous church. He told me that he had promised a long time ago to visit their pastor. We were welcomed wholeheartedly. The pastor said with tears in his eyes: "Until now we have never been visited by a non-indigenous brother because we live so far away in the forest."

Colonia Aborigen, 2003

When I visited, the elderly pastor Ricardo González started talking with a lot of freedom. For me, it was another of those special experiences when a spontaneous visit seems to be prepared beforehand.

Ltañi Lai', San Martín, 2005

Experiences on the road

Visiting indigenous communities means traveling long distances. We Mennonite Team members intentionally live in different cities of this large region. Even so, some groups in the rural areas are over 220 miles from our homes, often in locations deep in the Chaco forest. Although the most important roads have been paved in recent years, many indigenous settlements can only be reached by roads which during the rainy season turn into mud and during the dry season into dust bowls. In addition, some of us also travel to indigenous neighborhoods in large urban centers that are up to 700 miles to the south.

During the first ten years Frank chose to use public transportation. When riding the bus, he was sometimes able to take along his bicycle. Often he had to walk and hitch-hike parts of the trip. The indigenous people rarely have vehicles of their own. When Frank arrived at their homes, exhausted and thirsty, they could readily understand the reason.

Later, Frank used a sturdy motorcycle for his long-distance trips, which made it much easier to transport the heavy box of literature. Note some of Frank's travel diary entries during those first years:

> I walked along the road with my backpack. Whenever a vehicle approached in the direction of Resistencia, I held up my thumb. Several times Toba Qom brothers on their way home with their bicycles recognized me and stopped to walk with me for a stretch.
>
> *Piguiñi Lai', Pampa del Indio, 2001*

> One of my Toba Qom friends advised me to take a shortcut to an unfamiliar bus stop. This is how he organized my departure: His son would carry the heavy box of Bible materials, he himself would shoulder my bicycle and I should follow with my backpack. All three of us walked barefoot, carrying our shoes, since they would have become stuck in the mud. When we finally reached the pavement my friend asked me whether I would like to clean my feet in the water of the roadside ditch. When I had finished he offered me a towel which he had obviously brought along for me to dry my feet.
>
> *Chimole, El Colorado 2001*

> The 9 o'clock bus to *Las Palmas* usually has room in the luggage compartment for bicycles. After arriving in Las Palmas, I rode the final kilometers to the community of *Laguna Pato* on small roads through fields of sugar cane and cattle pastures. When I arrived at my destination the pastor's wife asked whether I had had breakfast. Since I had not, she prepared breakfast immediately with everything she had: fried eggs and *maté*. Simply delicious!
>
> *Laguna Pato, 1998*

I had decided to visit a pastor on the other side of the colony. To do so, I had to go on foot first on a dusty path, and the last kilometers on a paved road. Just when I arrived at this road a young Toba Qom whom I knew stopped, invited me to sit on the back of his bicycle, and took me along. True "fraternal transportation!"

Tacai Lapa, Pampa del Indio, 1999

I had been invited several times to the birthday party of the Faith and Hope church in the indigenous neighborhood *La Isla*. I wanted to keep my promise and participate despite the fact that it had just rained and, because I was delayed by another visit, I would arrive in the dark. The mud made it difficult to walk the last two kilometers. My backpack and the Bible box became heavier and heavier. During the last stretch of the road the street lights went off and I was left in the dark. Fortunately I had a flashlight in my pocket.

The church building, to my surprise, was closed when I arrived and no one was around. After a moment I decided to try my luck at a neighboring indigenous church. I knew that it would be impossible for me to get home since by this time of the evening the last taxis and the bus to Resistencia had gone. After 15 minutes of walking I heard the songs of the believers of the Foursquare Church. They welcomed me warmly. On account of my wild appearance after my hike in the mud they called me *'cos qovi lqaic'* (i.e. the blond-headed wild boar).

Barrio La Isla, La Leonesa, 1999

Normally on Sunday mornings the road to Pampa del Indio is deserted. Walking along the road towards one of the churches, I was praying that somebody would come along and give me a ride so that I would arrive before the end of the service. Three minutes later a vehicle appeared and even stopped. It was actually a taxi, but when we arrived in the village the driver would not accept money from me.

Lote 16, Pampa Grande, 2000

I stood at the side of the dirt road that goes to the roundabout at *Villa Rio Bermejito*, 40 kilometers away. A heavily packed pickup stopped. They were musicians on their way to a weekend dance event. They made enough space for me to sit in the truck bed between their big loudspeakers. My 'taxi' was not very fast, but I was happy. The pick-up made so much dust on the road that I could breathe only by filtering the air with my handkerchief.

Piguiñi Lai', Pampa del Indio, 2001

On my way home I joined a group on a truck that a local politician had provided. Fifty people had to find space on the open truck bed. The clouds of dust were so thick we couldn't see anything and had trouble breathing. Mothers with babies covered them with towels. When we arrived we looked like mummies.

'Ele' Lpata'c, El Espinillo, 2003

Always welcome

Indigenous families in northern Argentina make room for unexpected visitors. When Toba Qom speak in their language of their home they say *yi qarma* (our place). This refers not only to the house itself, but to the living space around the house, which often serves as sleeping shelter for everyone, and usually includes several generations.

In rural areas their small houses tend to be some distance apart, so that neighbors are barely visible. The surrounding forest provides building material: wooden poles, grasses, and mud. The land around the house is kept cleared as a precaution against snakes and other dangerous animals. Some raise a few domestic animals such as goats, chickens or pigs. The most serious problem in these areas is the lack of safe drinking water. In urban areas most of the newly arrived Chaco indigenous families live together in slums or in government housing projects. Family groups are large and space is crowded.

A different cultural lens might see it as a burden to receive guests, given the scarcity of food. But Toba Qom cultural habits take such hosting in stride: knowing how to share is their highest cultural value. Reciprocity as a way of life means that the one who gives today will receive when he or she is the one in need. So they make room at the table, give up their beds, share what they have, or borrow from others to provide for visitors.

We were included in this chain of giving and receiving. Like their own relatives, we arrived with the clothes we had on our backs and generally with no gifts. By depending on them, we entered into the reality of their daily lives. In times of harvest there was always plenty, and in times of scarcity there was always *maté* to share. It seemed to us that people perceived our willingness to eat whatever they had as a significant gesture of solidarity and acceptance.

It was also good for us as visitors to learn to get along with less than our usual plenty.

Staying in Toba Qom homes we were able to share in daily life and become closely acquainted with the living conditions, difficulties, wisdom, and joys of their families. We received their generosity and their hospitality. Often they allowed us to become their friends. These are some of the life experiences we value most highly.

> My Toba Qom family asked me to make them a new barbecue grill. The one I had built for them two years before from a bicycle wheel rim had rusted and completely fallen apart. Only the wire was reusable. As a thank you they gave me a sack full of manioc roots.
>
> *Pioq La'asat, Pampa Chica, 1998*

> In the morning, on my departure, my hosts of the local church lamented that they'd had nothing to share with me but a piece of candy. They prayed for my journey and for a bite to eat somewhere else. Their prayer – and mine! – were unexpectedly answered at my next stop. Without knowing about my growling stomach, brother Horacio invited me to join him at his table for stew.
>
> *Tacai Lapa, Pampa del Indio, 1998*

> As soon as my tent had dried in the sun I got ready to go home. As always, I was given presents to take home. This time it was a big pumpkin and manioc roots.
>
> *Pioq La'asat, Pampa Chica, 1999*

They already knew

In the earliest years, because there were few phones, we often arrived at people's homes unannounced. Many times we noted with amazement how our indigenous friends seemed to know ahead of time about our coming visit. Their keen intuition and expertise in detailed observation of their natural surroundings allows them to perceive other modes of communication. This is still true even after the advent of mobile phones. They readily understand a hint from their own thoughts, the cry of a bird, a dream.

> At noon I visited one of the pastors in *Maipú* colony. He told me right away that he had not gone to the woods to collect firewood

with the others because he had sensed that someone was coming to visit him.

La Leonesa, 1998

As I prayed in the morning I thought of visiting the indigenous colony at Costa Iné which was 20 kilometers away. I invited our 11-year-old son Johannes to accompany me. We rode by bus and walked the last seven kilometers. As we walked through the fields and woods there was so much to see that Johannes never asked me when we would arrive. The last kilometer a passing vehicle picked us up.

When we arrived in the colony the old pastor welcomed us. He offered us two chairs and sat with us. After a short while Johannes disappeared and joined the other children of the neighborhood in visiting the newborn pigs, playing with other animals, playing hide-and-seek and watching television.

When I was alone with the pastor, he told me that he had been expecting our visit because in the early morning a certain bird (*vi'iyin*) had announced two visitors with two trills. I was thoroughly astonished because I had invited Johannes to the journey only at noon.

In further conversations Hilario taught me the messages of other birds. Some of them indicate danger, others announce joyful events. How interesting! That reminded me of an unusual definition of culture which I found affirmed here: "Culture consists of customs which human beings shape as a response to the voices they hear around them" (Patricio Doyle learned it from the Wichí people).

Costa Iné, 1998

Sharing the household and the soup pot

By 10 o'clock the heat was unbearable. Through the half shade I got a good sunburn without realizing it in time. The tent, an oven! Outside, *viudita* flies pestered me. I almost returned home early!

Pioq La'asat, Pampa Chica, 1999.

The whole extended family was in the courtyard of the house enjoying the conversation. The children came and went, playing with the domestic animals and with me. I think they trust me. They'd show up beside my chair for a friendly touch on the head or back. As always, the little daughter of the youngest son sat on my lap and now and then whispered something in my ear.

Pioq La'asat, Pampa Chica, 2002

I first visited a couple who are both almost 80 years old. They were surrounded by grandchildren. The couple told me that one of their daughters had died not long ago and they had taken all the orphaned children into their home.

Pioq La'asat, Pampa Chica, 2003

My Toba Qom friend Mario's house, located on the outskirts of a small town, was like a hostel. His sister-in-law was visiting with several of her children; a friend had arrived that afternoon; their own eight children had a number of friends over. Mario and his family had even set up a tent on the grass behind the house! Apparently Mario and Inés, his wife, receive visitors every day from the neighboring indigenous colony asking for counsel and all kinds of help. I was deeply impressed by the way Inés and the family stayed calm and friendly through it all.

Quitilipi, 2003

Once when I stayed in the countryside in a pastor's house where there wasn't much, I was struck when he said: "We are blessed because we have enough to eat every day." Later, when we were getting ready for the service, I was astonished when he offered me his deodorant!

Tacai Lapa, Pampa del Indio, 1998

I was moved by this family's situation. A one-room house, beds made of bundles of grass. I didn't see a table or chairs. But they invited me quite unselfconsciously to share their soup pot!

Laguna Pato, 1998

The past few days with my Toba Qom family were quite depressing because there was simply nothing in the fields. Absolutely nothing! The only food was some packages from Catholic Charities and the contents of the plastic bag I had brought along as usual for sharing (for the "big kitchen"). The few hives we found in the woods had no more honey. There wasn't even fishing line for fishing in the river. When I left they suggested I wait to come back until there was 'something to chew on', but not, they said, because I had not brought enough food, but because "we feel ashamed" (about the situation).

Pioq La'asat, Pampa Chica, 1997

When I arrived at Lot 16, intending to participate in the anniversary, I found only the bones of yesterday's barbecue. They had advanced the celebration one day because of provincial elections. Thank God they prepared tea and invited me to some homemade bread. I was really hungry.

Piguiñi Lai', Pampa del Indio, 2001

When I asked for water to wash my face, Pedro and Aurelio immediately understood my unspoken message: They took me to a neighbor's house with an enclosed place where I could pour a whole bucket of water over myself.

Mala' Lapel – San Carlos, 2001

The evening service lasted until 1:30 a.m. After a brief discussion, the elders asked a younger man to take me along to his house, where I was to stay with him, his wife, and their three children, who were sleeping. Without asking questions, they made fry bread, even though it was late. I did not look at my watch, but I am sure that several hours passed while the three of us sat and talked in the courtyard in the light of the full moon.

Pioq La'asat, Pampa Chica, 2003

On my way I met a Toba Qom man. When he found out where I was headed, he asked me to visit him in his home for awhile. His wife welcomed me when we arrived. She introduced me to each of their three children. They served me fried eggs with onions and fry bread. Three hours flew by. It seemed to me that this unplanned visit had been arranged by God, so, although I don't always do this, I offered to pray with them before I left.

Piguiñi Lai', Pampa del Indio, 2001

Accompanied by my daughters

The family welcomed us with great joy when they realized that this time, Loti, our eight-year-old daughter, had come with me.

Before that day, they had only seen her in a picture. We put up the tent before it started to rain again. Then they invited us to come inside their house. Loti very soon made friends with the other children. She was able to communicate in Spanish with those who attend school. Every now and then she would come to ask me about a Toba Qom word. On our way there we had already practiced a few. In the afternoon, Loti had her wish of riding a horse come true. One of their grandchildren, a ten-year-old, took his sister and Loti on a long ride. We could hear them laughing in the distance. I was moved by the attention we got: Loti and I ate with the adults at the table. When they realized that Loti loved watermelon, they served her several portions. Whenever my daughter wanted to ask me a question, she would do so in a low voice in German. That initiated a conversation among those present about a shared reality: raising our children in a Spanish-speaking context while trying to keep our mother tongue. Loti amazed me. She had no problems relating to the other kids, or with having to eat a different kind of food, or with the need to go to the forest for lack of a bathroom. She stayed long periods of time by my side, asking many questions or laying her head on my lap. Having Loti beside me made me feel so happy to be a father.

Pioq La'asat, Pampa Chica, 2003

For that whole previous day, our daughter Ana had been packing her backpack for her first trip to the countryside with her dad. On the bus trip she sat on the very first seat, observed everything and made a lot of comments. The children in the family gave us a beautiful welcome when they saw us coming. They yelled, "The German man came with his daughter!" We sat and had *maté* tea together. All the children came to see Ana. It took half an hour to break the ice. Then a twelve-year-old girl, also called Ana, managed to take my daughter over to see the animals. Shortly after that, she was riding horse with a group of kids. From then on, my Anita had a great time. The girls showed her how to take a bath in a designated place in the thick forest. Every now and then, Ana would come to ask me something or to hug me. At night, she fell asleep by my side in the small tent without any problem. Being a father is marvelous!

Pioq La'asat, Pampa Chica, 2000

Suffering, pain and hard work

People were celebrating these days because the men from the reservation and the nearby areas had been able to join an employment welfare program: they will be paid two hundred pesos a month for six hours of work per day. With their labor, the county wants to build a new access road from the highway to the reservation.

Pioq La'asat, Pampa Chica, 1997

Due to a lack of money, they were only able to get a cow's head without the tongue for one peso. We used every bit of meat and brain and ate it with onions and garlic.

Pioq La'asat, Pampa Chica, 1997

My host could not hide his frustration. The local government had not plowed a single Toba Qom farm during pre-election days. The exception had been the non-indigenous people's farms. He also regretted that the indigenous community's candidate had not won the county election. The Toba Qom people were hoping that for the first time in their history this candidate would call an indigenous council which would represent them alongside the county council. But a man favored by political cronyism won the election.

Colonia Maipú, 1999

The subject dominating the community these days was hunger. The entire town had its school dining room services cancelled the day after the provincial elections. People are searching for food. I was told about possible protests and lootings if things continue this way. The people from the settlement I have been visiting told me that they are okay because they still have some manioc and the first pumpkins to make a stew each day. They can also barter for flour and oil. The father of a family used that opportunity to tell his children who were present that it is better to work hard, plant and hoe the garden, and not beg or sell oneself to politicians.

Pioq La'asat, Pampa Chica, 1999

The local pastor's wife received us in her yard. As we talked, I learned that there were no worship services in any of the three churches due to water shortage. The only deep well could just barely serve the animals, and the county was not bringing water to the community cistern.

Chimole, El Colorado, 1999

I was present during the visit of politicians from one of the political parties, who came to check the electoral roll in order to determine who could vote in the primaries as "independents." It was incredible how they talked to the people, always addressing elders informally, making promises to bring them all kinds of things. Before they left, they handed out a few things. Heriberto refused to accept clothes as gifts, only food for sharing. Afterward he said, "There are some who go aimlessly, lost like an airplane without a pilot. That is why they accept whatever gift is offered."

Pioq La'asat, Pampa Chica, 1999

I was told that the "sweet-fifteen" birthday celebration had been called off because one of the girl's brothers had been seriously bitten by piranhas. Early on the following day, I walked to the road with my young daughter, Ana, who was with me those days. We went to the hospital to visit the injured boy. A doctor met us at the door. After telling him who I was, he asked, "So you guys help civilize them?" I almost fell over backwards! We found Florencio accompanied by his sister and with an IV. He had eight stitches near his navel.

Pioq La'asat, Pampa Chica, 2000

My host family's oldest son asked me to help him gather some firewood and pick up dry branches in a non-indigenous neighbor's lot. Suddenly, while we were collecting, an enraged man appeared and pointed his gun at me. I gazed at him open-mouthed in fright. He was the owner of that small farm, a man known as a mean, evil person who owned large extensions of land in the area.

It was like an ugly movie: the guy with his gun, a bandaged bruised eye, badmouthing indigenous people, using a quite rude language to express his anger to us, the alleged thieves of fallen branches. Eventually he calmed down, thank God. He put his gun away and let us leave, although we could not take with us the dry branches we had collected.

When we got back home, I was surprised by the way the Toba Qom family reacted to what had happened. Apparently they were not that shocked over the incident. They already knew that neighbor. He is the same man who encloses them in their lot with a barbed wire fence, leaving them without an exit to the road, something which, according to the law, he must allow. I kept wondering whether collecting dry branches was really stealing or rather, providing for one's basic needs.

Pioq La'asat, Pampa Chica, 2000

The eight little pigs were sold a short time ago, traded for corrugated sheets of roofing, a horse, clothes and chicks. They did not have enough barter goods to get vaccines for their horses. It is a very painful situation: in the past few months, five horses died for not being vaccinated.

Pioq La'asat, Pampa Chica, 2000

After the worship service, one brother took me to his place. In his wood house his daughters let me use one of their two bedrooms. In the church service, the father of this family had shared his pain: "I realized that there is almost no communication in our family because they are always watching television." He regretted that he was the only one who attended the service, the rest of his family stayed home to watch the famous show "Big Brother."

La Leonesa, 2001

A couple hosted me in their home with special affection. They told me about the community. "They took down the wooden sign at the entrance to the community which said, '*Lma' na Qompi – Bienvenidos*' (the Toba Qom people's place–Welcome) because they no longer want to be Qom."

That Sunday I noticed how in a four-generation family – from grandmother to great-granddaughter – indigenous features gradually disappear due to the mixing of races, along with their customs and their own language. Would this be the result of the official policy called "assimilation"?

Basaíl, 2001

When I arrived, people were weeding and plowing the small farm. The corn and the melons were almost ripe already. The pumpkins had sprouted again, after an unexpected late frost in the area.

Piguiñi Lai', Pampa del Indio, 2001

I was told that they were hoping they would receive financial assistance in order to repair their farming tools. There really were lots of weeds and only a small section of their farm had been prepared for sowing manioc and sweet potatoes. It is obvious that their subsistence level does not allow them to buy tools. Besides that, someone stole one of their three horses.

Piguiñi Lai', Pampa del Indio, 2003

We took the horses to the pond again. We built a fence for the nineteen chicks. They taught me how to hoe their farm. The new manioc is coming up. I am starting to understand a little about the problems in the community: someone hurt his neighbor's horse on purpose; another person stole barbed wire during the night. I was present when a group of men got drunk with 96 percent pure alcohol mixed with a little water.

Pioq La'asat, Pampa Chica, 1999

The next morning a few of us went early to harvest cotton at the farm of a man named García. It was the season's first harvest. The earth was still wet from last week's rain. Who can imagine the armies of mosquitoes attacking us? Thank goodness my long-sleeved shirt covered part of my neck and ears. The low quality of the cotton made it impossible for us to harvest anything but the whole cotton boll. Still, the final output of our hard labor was very low. Then I heard they paid just five cents per pound. By noon no one wanted to continue.

Pioq La'asat, Pampa Chica, 1998

In the morning we took out the manioc stalks from the hole, where they had put them a few months ago, and cut them in pieces. The father of the family marked the rows through the field with four horses. Although the heat almost killed us, several of us continued with the task. One would make small holes with the hoe and the other would throw a piece of manioc in there and cover it with his bare feet. We were able to complete fourteen rows of about one hundred feet each. When we stopped working at eleven, I was totally exhausted.

Pioq La'asat, Pampa Chica, 1998

This time I learned how to use cow's feet in a stew: you cut them in half between the two hoofs and boil them for several hours. The cartilage gets very soft. Then you eat everything with bread.

Pioq La'asat, Pampa Chica, 1999

Unusual nights

One of the privileges of visiting indigenous communities is being able to stay overnight. Even when there is no more room, they make room for visitors, in the house or in a nearby community building. We sense their trust and generosity as they allow us to enter into their private family space, especially when we are welcomed in their own homes.

During the years of his intensive Toba Qom language learning process, Frank used to stay several days a week in a rural community. He had a special arrangement with his host family: they took care of his small tent between his visits.

> For that night, the pastor's wife had placed a mattress in the only room they had, next to their children and grandchildren. The parents themselves slept outside. I will never forget when they invited me to come inside after the evening church service. With a flashlight, they lighted the place they had prepared for me, and I saw that the floor was already covered with sleeping children. After thanking the parents and God, I lay down.
>
> *Tacai Lapa, Pampa del Indio, 1998*

> I survived cold nights thanks to my poncho and the sleeping bag I had brought. In the morning, when the sun was rising, I joined the family, who was sitting around the fire drinking hot *maté* tea. As I got involved in the family conversation, I felt the whole experience was worthwhile.
>
> *Pioq La'asat, Pampa Chica, 2000*

> For that night I was offered one of their two beds. On the following morning the parents told me that their young son was surprised that I had decided to stay with them. In the church service I had also heard, "Our brother Frank came to visit us

again. But today, for the first time, he is staying overnight." The four days I lived with that family were very special: we ate what they had; they took me on their bicycle to the church building more than a mile away. They allowed me to enter in their lives.

Colonia Maipú, 1998

The birthday worship service ended after midnight and everyone got a slice of cake. Soon everybody returned to their homes and left me alone in the empty church building. I was hungry, but all the stores had already closed. I did not even have mosquito repellent. As I thought and prayed about what I could do, a neighbor came who was not from church. He was looking through the church building's open window. What a surprise when I came back from the restroom and found him with a mattress he had brought me from his house! That was divine providence!

Ltañi Lai', San Martín, 2001

I decided to fix my little tent. The previous week a few young goats had jumped on it. It took me several hours to sew the big hole they had made. But the following morning, when I was not paying attention, the goats came back!

Pioq La'asat, Pampa Chica, 2001

I finally know how it feels to sleep on wooden bed slats. It was even harder to deal with the wind and the cold because the entrance to the house was covered with only a curtain. I should have brought at least some warm clothes instead of traveling light. Apparently I was not the only one feeling cold: when I got up to get warm by the fire, two women were there breastfeeding their babies.

Lote 4, Pampa Chica, 2000

The family told me that someone had burned down their house and they had lost everything. They were slowly gathering the basics again. Still, they made room for me on a mattress. The boy who slept next to me that night was quiet, but I was surprised when another boy woke up in the middle of the night, probably looking for his usual bed. In the darkness he touched my face, my beard, my nose . . . to find out who had taken his place.

Laguna Lobo, 2001

I was given a bed made of sticks and a mattress made with piled-up clothes. It was quite comfortable, except for a stinking odor nearby which I could not locate.

Piguiñi Lai', Pampa del Indio, 2001

As soon as I came back to the camp, a few drops of rain fell and then a heavy rain. Since I was not able to sleep in my tent, I had to make do with the floor in the house. If there are no mosquitoes, you can be fine anywhere. But with those aggressive beasts around, not really!

Pioq La'asat, Pampa Chica, 2003

When the church services ended, everybody went home. The doorkeeper asked me, "*¿Hua'ague ca 'ad'ochaxa'?*" (Where are you sleeping tonight?), as if I already had a place to stay overnight. I realized that they are used to seeing non-indigenous visitors go to town to sleep. He had mercy on me and took me to his house. He shared some bread and homemade *dulce de leche* (a traditional caramel spread) with me. After eating – simultaneously fighting thousands of hungry mosquitoes that also wanted to eat – he prepared a bed for me in his bedroom with the windows shut because of the mosquitoes. But it was so hot inside it felt like a sauna. I tried in vain to sleep. My host noticed this and took a bed outside for me. Together we hung up the mosquito net I had brought along in my baggage and I was finally able to get some rest.

Ltañi Lai', San Martín, 2003

Many of us were sleeping on the floor of the church building. At 4:30, my neighbor woke up to heat water. I think I was the last person to get up, about 6:00, to complete the circle of men who were already sitting around the bonfire. We drank *maté* tea while they chatted about old times, about mutual acquaintances, about alligators and tortoises' egg-laying habits, and about Bible texts. It was amazing! We watched the sunrise and kept on chatting.

'Ele' Lpata'c, El Espinillo, 2003

The language student

One of the Mennonite team's areas of accompaniment concerns "valuing the indigenous languages and trying to learn them." Each one of us has used different approaches to language learning.

After trying a few different methods, Frank had the opportunity to live every week with a Toba Qom family in a rural area. They invited him to stay with them and he was able to interact freely with the whole family clan, which included several generations. They shared their work, weather conditions, the abundance in harvest times, as well as shortage, joys and jokes, conversations, and their pot of food, to which Frank contributed some basic ingredients.

While they shared their life with us, Frank, and then also Ute, gradually learned the language as something related to everyday situations. Sometimes with a machete or a hoe in one hand and a notebook in the other hand, learning was a slow and often discouraging process, although still fascinating. The world of a language with completely different roots from those of Spanish or any other European language seemed like an impenetrable forest that would only open itself up with great effort, until it began to show its beauty and depth.

The grandfather and patriarch of the Toba Qom family, but also the many children, became the *gringos'* teachers, who came frequently, set up their tent and twisted their tongues trying to pronounce some words. We joked for years about some funny expressions.

It was a long road to earn their trust: some members of the family waited months before they accepted a guest and talked with that person. There was great mistrust of a non-indigenous person's intentions. "What does he really want?" "Is she trustworthy?"

But years of visits allowed us to develop close bonds. The family got to know Frank, his preferences, thoughts, strength, skills and weaknesses. In turn, he saw children being born and raised within the family clan. On some occasions, Frank traveled to that home with our daughters.

> The manual water pump is working less and less. There is dust settling around the borehole. The water comes out so slowly that people prefer to get it from the well, although that water is really murky. I offered to stay by the water pump until the bucket filled up again, so that my family and I could drink clean water. I use that time to chat with kids and adults who also come to get

water. When nobody comes, I have time to memorize new Toba Qom words.

Pioq La'asat, Pampa Chica, 1997

Little by little, our mutual trust is growing like a plant. They started to make jokes with me.

Pioq La'asat, Pampa Chica, 1997

I was trying to open a plastic bag that was closed with several knots. I struggled unsuccessfully for a long time. One of the children brought me a knife, but I told him, "*Ñaq huo'o da iualaxavic*" (I still have patience). Amazed, he replied, "*Nachi mashi 'am qom le'ec*" (So you are already a Toba Qom man). Then I recalled what they had once commented, "*Na doqshi le'ec saxaỹit ỹalaxadaic*" (Non-indigenous people are always in a hurry).

Pioq La'asat, Pampa Chica, 1998

It was a beautiful experience this week when the elder agreed to read Moses' stories together. He enjoyed reading aloud in his own language. I was very happy too because I was able to understand more than in everyday conversations. It was easier to follow the text if I listened to an authentic voice.

Pioq La'asat, Pampa Chica, 1997

I was not able to travel this week because of the rain, so I reviewed my language notes from the country. I am starting to recognize words that were unknown to me a few weeks ago. Now I need to memorize them.

At home, 1998

They spoke a lot to me in their own language, and I tried to answer some things. The fact that they are now willing to speak to me in Toba Qom is really a step forward.

Costa Iné, 1998

I was very happy this week as I came back home, since I had been able to use what I learned. I am also getting to know the network of family relationships.

Pioq La'asat, Pampa Chica, 1998

I deeply enjoyed my time among them, especially at night and early in the morning, when I was alone among all the people. In terms of language, it was quite intensive because I was allowed to just listen to their informal conversation and their group interaction without switching to Spanish for me.

Yaicangui, Resistencia, 1998

While drinking *maté* tea, they talked about the sow and whether or not she was pregnant. The children mentioned that her udder looked swollen and that could be a sign of her pregnancy. The Toba Qom word for udder and teats was new for me, so I repeated it and jotted it down in my notebook. One of the children explained to me that they use the same word for women. Apparently his mother did not like that, because she told him not to teach me those terms.

Pioq La'asat, Pampa Chica, 1999

I really enjoyed that they have talked to me in their own language. I feel like I can have a slow conversation without constantly resorting to Spanish. That's better than nothing!

Margarita Belén, 1999

It was a splendid morning in the country, with quietness everywhere and a special dawn. The elder spent several hours reviewing and adding to my notes. As years go by, I see that he is leaving the heavy work at their small farm for his children. Now he has more time to share his thoughts with me and he does so with confidence.

Pioq La'asat, Pampa Chica, 2001

I came back from this trip with a sense of gratitude, especially for the profound conversations I had, even though it is still hard for me to catch everything they say when they speak fast, thinking I understand it all.

La Leonesa, 2001

Customs and culture

In every culture, one's own language is much more than a means of communication. With one's mother tongue, one can express how the world is perceived and understood. Our Toba Qom language learning has been closely linked to acquiring a broader perspective of indigenous life.

Becoming familiar with life in the indigenous communities was like a journey of exploration to an unknown world. The peoples of the Chaco have lived in this region of forests, rivers and swamps for thousands of years. With awe and respect, we walked the paths of others, realizing our limitations. Our own knowledge and customs were of little use. We had to rely on their wisdom to survive in their context. We did not know the medicinal plants or the water sources, nor could we read nature's signs and take the necessary precautions. Except during the brief times when we bathed among the trees, we were not allowed to go into the forest on our own due to the many dangerous insects, poisonous plants and snakes, even pumas we could have met up with and not known how to react.

The experience of our limitations in that setting helped us appreciate even more our hosts' vast knowledge and abilities. We learned to open ourselves to accept their customs and culture, and gradually distance ourselves from Western culture, the cradle of thought and action we carried inside. Their values challenge ours, their silence challenges our noise, their restrained and patient words challenge our verbosity, and their respect challenges our tendency to make judgments.

> I went with the men to collect honey. In order to get it, we felled a tall tree. But we found out that the larvae had already grown inside the honeycomb. Back home we started to suck out everything we could. When you bite the larvae, they release a white liquid. I tried not to look at what I was eating: the beeswax, some honey and the larvae. All together, it had a sweet and interesting taste. In the afternoon we took down an old house in order to save the ridgepole and the wooden post and then use them for another construction. It was hard to take them out, since they were buried deeply.
>
> *Pioq La'asat, Pampa Chica, 1998*

> They showed me how they get the honey out of the honeycomb: they wrap the honeycomb completely with a piece of cloth and squeeze it until the sweet liquid comes out. The beeswax is used for sucking or chewing. Once spit out, dogs, cats and hens eat that.
>
> *Pioq La'asat, Pampa Chica, 1999*

> In a conversation we ended up talking about the birds that tell them of visitors coming to a place. They said that the birds were their ancestors' "telephone." Somebody recalled a meeting with the renowned man, Pedro Martínez. This general chief had

heard a bird whistling. So he sent his "officers" to the town of Presidencia Roca because there would be a visit there. And so it was: they found a government official of President Juan Perón.

Somebody in the family mentioned they needed to go and get repellent because there were so many mosquitoes. I thought, "How are they going to get repellent if they have no money?" Later I had to laugh at myself and my ignorance because we went to get dried cow dung. That was the mosquito repellent. They burn it and the smoke wards off insects very effectively.

Pioq La'asat, Pampa Chica, 1998

The pastor told me he and his family had come back for good from the countryside where they had moved several months ago. There they had been ripped off by the chief. They were not the first people to suffer that misfortune. The pastor did not want to fight with the chief, nor report the case. Instead he chose to leave the area, spending their last savings on transportation. He said there was a lot of work in that area, as well as opportunities to hunt wild animals in the thick forest, and that the children felt very comfortable in the country. He left behind his garden, his house, some chicks, trees he had planted; and all because he did not want to fight.

Qochiiñi' Lai', Presidencia Roca, 1999

During the last few days they had started looking for *cotapic lmala'* (young red quebracho) sticks to continue building their big family house that had been stopped for months due to the priority of work on the farm.

Pioq La'asat, Pampa Chica, 1999

A nice wind began to blow at night which drove the mosquitoes away. The elderly man started to talk about what his grandparents had told him regarding their customs for finding a partner: "Young people did not chat as much as they now do. Rather, one day they would dance and drink in the forest. When the men were so drunk that they fell asleep, the women and the girls followed them. Using a rope, each woman tied up their previously chosen man and took him to a small thorn house in the thick forest, where they had placed some 'mattresses'. That is how couples were formed."

Pioq Laasat, Pampa Chica, 1999

They took me out to look for the special grass they mix with mud to build houses. We had to walk a long way to find it. I learned how to cut it.

Pioq Laasat, Pampa Chica, 2000

After the morning tasks – getting water, feeding the animals – the young people invited me to "go fishing." We took machetes and bamboo spears with iron tips. Next to a shallow murky ditch, they taught me how to get the *poxosoxoi* (catfish). We soon caught several big fish. Back home we grilled the *tallin* (wolf-fish) in pieces. With the catfish they made a tasty soup. A feast on a weekday! The stews of the previous days had almost no meat.

Pioq Laasat, Pampa Chica, 2000

As we talked with the Toba Qom man in the sun in front of his house, he kept working on his clay pots. He started telling me about some of the teachings he still remembers from the elders:

- In the past, men were strong because they respected women's menstrual periods. Women kept by themselves during that time.
- In the past, parents used to have their children get up before sunrise because dawn was sacred. Now young people wake up late.
- In the past, we were taught that when sharing our meal we could not argue; rather, we had to eat quietly and silently. Now they come to the table and start yelling and arguing. That is why food does not sit well with them. Or they go with their plates and watch TV. They do not pay attention to what they eat.
- In the past, they purified water by putting white ashes in the pot they used to carry the water. That was what they did if the water was cloudy. The dirt settled with the ash.

Fontana, 2003

As his final words in the church service, the leader reasoned, "Tomorrow is Monday, the day of the hands, since God gave us five fingers to get something (a job)."

Laguna Lobo, 2003

The members of the local church told me their version of Bernabé's death: he had dreamed that in order to be healed he had to go to the town of La Leonesa. He went there with bad health and stayed for a good long while, in January or February, in order to recover. While there, he said to us that he had been "told" to move to La Leonesa. The people from La Leonesa had offered to build him a house. But for some reason he returned to his house in the indigenous community, where he soon got worse . . . until he died.

Colonia Maipú, 2003

At the gathering three musicians sang traditional Qom songs with old melodies. They played the guitar, the *bombo* (a traditional Argentine drum) and the *nvique* (a one-string violin). Many people gathered around them and started dancing. Everyone enjoyed the humorous lyrics which were repeated many times.

Mala' Lapel, Colonia San Carlos, 2005

The pastor told me the story of a skin disease which, according to doctors, was long-lasting and incurable. He said that with the Lord's guidance he had been able to discover that a person known to him had hurt him causing that illness. The man confessed this to him, but he died soon after that. He had received a notice in a dream that if he did not stop hurting others, God would cut his life short, and he did not pay any attention to that word.

Ltañi Lai', San Martín, 2005

An elder told me that a non-indigenous pastor wanted him to study at a theological seminary in Montevideo. But his mother-in-law cried a lot, because she thought that her daughter would never come back or that she might be stolen if she went so far away. So he respected her fears and did not attend the seminary.

Rosario, 2006

Guests in the indigenous churches

Promotion of the indigenous church

The indigenous churches in northern Argentina are among the few spaces left in the life of the local indigenous communities where members and leaders are free to make their own decisions. Outside their church life, the indigenous people are normally relegated to an inferior position of receiving orders, advice, instructions, or acts of charity. They are frequently considered ignorant; or worse yet, treated as "uncivilized" in offices, schools, hospitals, political settings or on the street. However, in their churches they become respected adults, capable teachers, leaders and servants of the community, thoughtful pastors who are aware of the needs of the congregation. They are fully capable of managing church life.

Their self-management includes liturgical autonomy, choosing of leaders and pastors, and planning evangelization efforts. It also means the self-financing of church buildings, events, leadership and other needs with their own or collected resources. Indigenous congregations regularly celebrate church anniversaries; organize church conventions, evangelistic and worship conferences; coordinate gatherings of singers or pastors – often with big crowds – all with no need of external intervention. Were they to receive a salary from a non-indigenous denomination, the indigenous pastors would become employees of a foreign institution.

In order to respect their autonomy and advocate for their leadership, as fraternal workers we hold no formal positions in indigenous churches and officiate no church sacraments. Neither do we play a role in their internal decisions. Doing so would perpetuate a colonizing and alienating model which creates obstacles, or even makes the inculturation of the gospel impossible. The trust established over the years of walking alongside as fraternal workers allows the indigenous church leaders the freedom to express their faith in their own liturgical forms, even in our presence. They know we are not visiting in order to question or evaluate.

As guests, we have witnessed the strength, perseverance, faith and wisdom that God pours out on our indigenous brothers and sisters. Their deep thinking and contextualization amazes us. We often witness their wisdom in solving problems in their own cultural manner. Their words of advice, testimonies and thanksgiving encourage us. We are convinced that Jesus' good news illuminates and transforms from the very core of every culture, without violating or destroying it.

Frank reports:

At the commemoration of the founding of the local church building there was a lot of time for sermons. The sermons of J. (Josh. 1:7) and A. challenged youth to be brave and determined, following the example of deceased ancestors.

La Leonesa, Chaco 1998

Toba Qom pastor Alfredo Arce and I attended an evening service. We were surprised to see that most of the children participated, dancing in their colorful outfits (worn over everyday clothes). Also, a girls' choir and then a boys' choir sang. Amazed, we asked who their teacher was. They answered that the children had learned by listening, because they were always near the pulpit, listening to the adult singers and music groups.

Chimole, El Colorado, Formosa 1999

The church building is a simple wooden structure. We could feel the strength of the songs, and the passion of the believers to live out their testimony in their neighborhood. Some non-indigenous neighbors that attended the service had come to faith in Jesus through the indigenous witness.

La Plata, Buenos Aires, 2000

Born of a division, there have been two churches here for years. It was nice to hear that the two pastors had agreed to celebrate the Lord's Supper in a single united service, alternating the place monthly. Pastor Rafael Mansilla noted that this year had been designated as the "Year of Reconciliation."

Mala' Lapel, San Carlos, Formosa, 2000

The musician that played the *nvique* (one-string violin), a traditional Toba Qom musical instrument used in seasonal tribal celebrations, said: "I would like to reclaim the *nvique* for church use." He commented that once a pastor had told him this instrument was demonic. The musician raised his *nvique*, asking, "Where is the devil in this instrument?"

Mala' Lapel, San Carlos, 2003

I was told that one local congregation is getting smaller because the second pastor and his relatives rejoined a church they had left 20 years ago. Someone else told me that another church decided to change its name and join a different "domination" (term the indigenous use to refer to "denomination," a confusion of the two terms in Spanish, which is not their native language).

La Leonesa, Chaco 2000

Right before the third prayer a young woman was led to the pulpit, so they could pray for her headaches. Within moments a spirit possessed her. The young woman started to roll around on the floor completely out of control. The dancers surrounded her and prayed for her. The leader of the service asked the congregation to sing. Since the dancers couldn't calm the young woman down, they stepped back to leave space for the pastors and her mother. Meanwhile the leader and the evangelist told the congregation not to be afraid. They warned the people that the gospel was not to be taken lightly, and that it was important to follow Jesus wholeheartedly in order to be protected from evil spirits. After persistent prayers the young woman calmed down.

La Leonesa, Chaco 2000

As the afternoon cooled, I arrived at the local IEU. Every night of the week they held worship services with a Toba Qom evangelist from a nearby province preaching. He had brought amplifying equipment and his entire family as singers. So many people gathered that the meetings were held outside. Nearly 100 dancers from neighboring churches occupied a large open space in the church yard. Most of the visitors had to stand because few chairs were available.

Ltañi Lai', San Martin, Chaco 2001

I witnessed a service in which a group of children, ages six and older, participated in the Lord's Supper for the first time.

Yaicangui, Resistencia, Chaco 2001

The pastor proudly explained to me how they had replaced the church roof: they did not want to get anything through political means, but rather by their own effort. They decided that when each member collected the Head of Household unemployment payment, they would contribute 30 pesos for the renovation, the cost of one piece of roofing. In just a few months they restored the roof. Last month they decided that each member would donate 5 pesos to cement the dirt floor of the church.

Piyo' Lauac, Fortín Lavalle, 2002

The evening service was held in a building with no roof. However, that turned into an advantage because later when the electrical current decreased so much that the bulbs were barely glowing, we enjoyed the light of a full moon. It was cold, but no one wanted to leave. Many were invited to speak in the service.

Piguiñi Lai', Pampa del Indio, 2002

The pastor's wife is now in charge of the church because her husband voluntarily stepped aside and passed on the leadership to his wife. During the service he confirmed his decision by sitting back near the door among the rest of the men.

Piguiñi Lai', Pampa del Indio, 2003

For the first time, I saw that a brother who, along with two elders, was leading the Lord's Supper, solemnly washed his hands before distributing the bread and the wine.

Choxodai Nauec, Campo Medina, 2003

The pastor explained to me that among the Toba Qom the native healers used to surround the sick person and sing and dance. They don't want to lose this tradition now in his church, but rather give it a new spiritual meaning. Therefore, once a year they organize a procession through their neighborhood where at each street crossing they stop to dance in a circle and pray. With this ritual they intend to help the neighborhood heal from violence, drugs, depression and other social diseases.

Yaicangui, Resistencia, 2003

I arrived at the annual conference of a large indigenous church. A forest surrounds the church building and the trees provide good shade. Many people had come from Pampa del Indio, La Leonesa, J. J. Castelli, San Martín and Bartolomé de las Casas and gathered around the fires. Music groups played all night long. People were happy. I thought how beautiful this was and imagined the Israelite camps must have been like this: tribes and families around their fires. Each group ate the food they had brought. Members of the local church had butchered some of their own cattle so they could distribute meat to everyone. Every group prepared their own space to sleep under the stars. When I came to understand what was unfolding, I approached the group of people that I knew. They welcomed me with open arms and shared their food with me.

'Ele' Lpata'c, El Espinillo, 2003

The women were in charge of the service. An elderly woman started the meeting, then turned it over to a younger woman who asked the congregation to pardon her lack of experience since she had never led before. They want the youth to learn to lead worship services. The young woman, with a list of names of the visitors, called some of them one by one to participate.

During a lively song the young woman began to dance in ecstasy. She didn't fall down, but she did collide with other dancers. Another woman took her arm to steady her, but was careful not to obstruct her expressions of joy. When the musicians finished playing, the young leader broke into tears. Everyone waited patiently for her to regain composure. After a while she found words to express what had happened. She said that she had always loved to observe the dancers, but had never felt that same joy. After her explanation she continued leading the service.

A sense of astonishment lingered with me long after the church service, as I considered the enormous respect my brothers and sisters have for each person and their feelings, also the patience with which they guide their youth toward maturity.

La Leonesa, 2003

July 8 is an important date for the believers of Maipú Colony. On this date many years ago their spiritual leader, Mateo Quintana, received the Holy Spirit. They celebrate July 8 with a special devotion akin to a local Pentecost. They all dress in festive attire, especially the women, who wear blue skirts and white blouses. The church was nearly full and everyone sang with enthusiasm; many danced in a circle, some alone. I felt very grateful for the relationship of trust we had established over the years, happy to witness their expressions of faith and memory.

Colonia Maipú, 2003

At the end of the anniversary celebration of the local church, the congregation went outside and circled the church, walking and singing. The leader at the head of the procession carried an Argentine flag. Stopping at each corner, they read Bible passages and everyone prayed aloud simultaneously.

Misión Laishi, 2006

Sharing trips and visits with Toba Qom pastors

From the beginning of the United Evangelical Church, the indigenous congregations in the Argentine Chaco have had their own leaders, missionaries and evangelists, men and women of faith who heard God's call to take the gospel to other places. Sometimes they share the gospel with their own people, other times with people in neighboring towns, and even among those that in the past were enemies.

The missionary spirit is still strong among the Toba Qom believers. When they hear God's voice, they do not hesitate to travel, even pack their belongings and move to another place with their entire family. The Toba Qom remember their native missionaries with appreciation and great respect. They especially recall their perseverance under adverse conditions during their travels. These outstanding leaders endured heat, cold, hunger, thirst and persecution. The following is an example from some decades ago.

Pastor Abel Palomino said that when he was 18 years old, he travelled to Paraguay, along with Miguel Velázquez, Chávez Pereira and Orlando Sánchez, to make the first contact with the Mak'a tribe. Because the Mak'a had the reputation of being aggressive, the Toba Qom were fearful. Abel Palomino remembered how the police and others along the way advised them not to enter Mak'a territory. The Toba Qom, however, continued until they came upon a Mak'a group in the outskirts of Asunción. Suddenly they found themselves surrounded by people armed with bows, arrows and rifles. After a frightening moment, the Mak'a leader not only welcomed them. He invited them to stay for over a week. He even ordered the young Mak'a hunters to hunt armadillo, when he heard that this was a favorite meal of the Toba Qom. They held services together and the Toba Qom preached.

By the grace of God, several Mak'a were deeply moved by
the visitors' words and experiences. Today the Mak'a have a large
congregation, with the inscription of Psalm 96 on one wall which
reminds people of Orlando Sanchez's sermon.

La Leonesa, 1999

Frank had the opportunity to accompany Toba Qom pastors on their
journeys to visit indigenous churches. Those were special times of fellowship
and learning.

For a few days I (Frank) visited Toba Qom pastor Alfredo Arce.
He had received the calling from God in a dream to go and
strengthen the churches among the Mocoví tribe. He moved
with his whole family, consisting of eight persons, to Santa Fe
province. There he collaborated with several fledgling Mocoví
churches. Beside their new home his family began a small
vegetable garden. They visited neighbors and members of the
congregation, prayed for the sick, and did everything they could
to encourage others. Together they have started to construct a
church building in Los Palmares, a kilometer away, where Pastor
Alfredo and his family stay on weekends with a Mocoví family.
On Wednesdays Pastor Alfredo bikes 10 kilometers to another
Mocoví community to encourage the people there.

Berna, 1998

This trip with a Toba Qom pastor was of great value because I
could observe his style of ministry and learn from his experience.
One day, following afternoon naps, he did not speak a word for
quite some time. It was hard to be silent, but I didn't want to ask
him what was going on. I just stayed by his side. The next day he
broke his silence and over dinner he told me about the death of
his two children, and how he dealt with his grief as a father and
as a pastor.

La Leonesa, 1999

I accompanied an elderly Toba Qom to a community that neither
of us knew. I learned so much from the way he related to and
communicated with the people. He always waited for people to

offer us something to drink or eat. Only once did he ask for a glass of water. We slept on the porch at one of the homes.

Chimole, El Colorado, 1999

With a Toba Qom pastor I took a bus to visit some people in Lote 39 of the reservation. We attended the evening service and he was asked to deliver the final sermon. In his enthusiasm he preached for over an hour. Undoubtedly he is an excellent Bible teacher. Not only did he know how to incorporate in his sermons what previous speakers had said, he also knew how to interpret the Bible like a Qom, using illustrations from his personal life and context.

Colonia Aborigen, 2000

Ute reports:

Once we received a telephone message that a Toba Qom newborn baby had died in the hospital. We knew the baby's parents. I decided to visit the mother to share her grief, help with administrative details and wait with her. She was alone because her husband was working away for a few days and still hadn't arrived.

In the meantime a Toba Qom pastor arrived at our home to visit Frank. When he heard that I had gone to the hospital, he decided to go too, even though he did not know the family. He found us in the hospital courtyard and sat with us without saying a word. I thought he would console the grieving mother and me, and then leave. But, to my surprise, he stayed several hours as we waited for the baby's body. After a while he began to talk about his own pain when two of his children died, and how God showed him in his dreams a path of consolation.

When the young Toba Qom father arrived several hours later, the four of us walked over to the morgue. We entered that cold, inhospitable chamber and spoke to a nurse who was insensitive to the parents' grief. With no gesture of sympathy, she brought the tiny naked body in a cardboard box, handed it over to the shocked parents and, pointing to the small coffin, she said to put the body into it quickly. However, the parents were overwhelmed with pain when they saw their dead child. The pastor took the baby's body into his arms and laid it lovingly in the small coffin. He prayed with a loud voice as is customary of Toba Qom believers and filled the cold place with warmth, hope and love.

After the pastor nailed the cover onto the coffin, he carried it with the parents in a solemn procession to the ambulance that would take the family back home to their reservation where they would have the burial. We said goodbye with few words. I went back home amazed with what I had just experienced: I had gone there to accompany a woman in her grief, but I was also accompanied.

Ute, Yaicangui, Resistencia, 2001

Frank reports:

Abel Gómez, the Toba Qom pastor with whom I traveled, was received by the Mocoví people as a spiritual father and missionary. In an open, fraternal dialogue the local church leaders consulted with him about difficult topics in the life of their church. Pastor Abel shared freely about his many experiences. He had baptized sixty people and established a new church in his area.

As Abel's traveling companion, I was especially inspired by what the young local Mocoví pastor confided to me later: "Pastor Abel respects me, as I also respect him." He was referring to the Toba Qom missionary's respectful attitude of not intruding in the internal affairs of the new Mocoví church, and Pastor Abel took great care that the members not look down on their inexperienced pastor.

Los Laureles, 2005

At a friend's house I mentioned my desire to visit Lote Cuatro about 10 kilometers away. He got up without a word and soon returned with a borrowed bicycle. A half hour later another man asked to join us. The three of us biked across several fields and through woods until we arrived at the Lote Cuatro community. There they introduced me, their German brother, to some of their neighbors.

Tacai Lapa, Pampa Del Indio, 1998

Visits in worship services

One of our ministries as a Mennonite team is visiting indigenous churches.[3] With over 250 congregations, we cannot go to each place very often; perhaps every three or six months. Even if only once a year, our previous visit is still remembered. Quite often we hear them say at the welcoming in their worship service, "This is the fraternal worker who always visits us."

We are not members of any local congregation, nor do we accept positions within the churches. We do not participate in any decision making or express unsolicited opinions, so as not to affect the autonomous life of the congregations. We are convinced that we should neither usurp leading roles that belong to indigenous people, nor interfere in their native expressions. For that reason, even when we are sometimes invited, we do not lead their worship services, nor accept being in charge of the Lord's Supper, baptism or other ceremonies.

Worship services are central to indigenous church life and embody Chaco indigenous cultural characteristics. The communitarian and inclusive nature is reflected in the large number of people invited to participate throughout the meeting. When we visit we are also invited to share with the congregation. Worship leaders are responsible for selecting those invited to speak, in most cases, without prior notice. Contributions may be life experiences, faith testimonies, joys or troubles, biblical reflections, songs, readings or greetings, depending on the desire of the person invited to share.

The indigenous concept of time is seen in the great freedom given to the length of these contributions. Often the worship leader apologizes for not being able to allow everyone to participate due to time restrictions, even after many hours have passed. Besides, since most speaking is spontaneous, those coming to the front normally make reference to or incorporate what previous speakers shared. Thus, the message of the worship service is woven around one or several interconnected themes.

The egalitarian nature of indigenous culture is also expressed in the worship services. Even though sometimes a recognized preacher or evangelist is designated to bring "the final message," no one person stands out, due to the many speakers called on.

There are nearly always visitors at indigenous gatherings. Many come to see their relatives, to help with a special event, such as a birthday or anniversary celebration, an evangelistic rally, or to hear certain invited

---

3. See map p. 6 for location of churches in the provinces of Chaco and Formosa.

leaders or co-workers. Some travel many miles – by foot, bicycle, horse and cart, truck or bus – driven by the desire to see a particular person again or by a notice received in a dream showing them a specific place.

> It was my third visit to that place and I was surprised that the brothers and sisters said, "This is our brother Frank who always visits us."
>
> *Puerto Tirol, 1998*

> When I was invited to share a reflection in the church service, I decided to read a long passage from Genesis 3 in Toba. Later, the local pastor stressed that the Garden of Eden symbolized the church. It had to be cared for because it is under Satan's deception. I felt that without prior coordination between us, we had worked well as a team: I read the passage from the Bible in Toba and he interpreted it from his culture and local situation.
>
> *Pioq La'asat, Pampa Chica, 1998*

> A Toba preacher instilled fear in those who were at the worship service through his contribution, due to the supposedly imminent persecution of believers. He based his message on what he had heard about the meaning of the "Y2K" effect. When I was called to say something, I decided to read Jeremiah 29:11-14 as a message of encouragement and confidence about the future.
>
> I was glad when later that same preacher thanked me for my message and praised me for having improved my Toba language skills.
>
> *Yaicangui, Resistencia, 1999*

> We were eight people sharing a beautiful and emotional worship service without musicians. Everyone participated with expressions of gratitude.
>
> *Margarita Belén, 2000*

> A lot of people had come for the anniversary. Since the church building is only twenty feet by twenty feet, chairs were taken outside for the four-hour worship service. Almost all of the brothers and sisters from the local board of directors were invited to talk. They also collected presents for the church and prayed for the new members and eight young brothers and sisters that

had just renewed their commitment to the church. What great team work!

La Leonesa, 2001

"The meeting place is a low and humble church building, with a kerosene lamp. But I like it and there's joy," a Toba brother who was visiting from Resistencia told me. I had only been there once, but apparently everybody remembered me and welcomed me with open arms. I was called right after the songs. Many elders were present, glad to see the *qomagui* (foreigner who is like a Toba). One brother told the congregation that he had dreamt about me that morning anticipating my visit. As a way to end the long worship service, the local pastor mentioned how the different expressions of gratitude intertwined.

Colonia Maipú, 2001

At night, I took part in the worship service. An elderly woman came to the pulpit. She could barely walk with the aid of her walking stick. She spoke to the congregation, and even though we could not understand her words, she was apparently filled with joy.

Fontana, 2000

In one part of the church service, a public exchange of presents was proposed as a way of saying that God's blessing is for sharing. Since it was Mothers' Day, some had decided beforehand to bring gifts; others responded spontaneously to the invitation. Impressive! I got a present, too: one brother gave me a cassette tape from his music band.

Ltañi Lai', San Martín, 2000

The evening worship service started outside in the big yard. During the first two hours, the leaders were in charge of the "march," the "dance," the "wheel" and the "round" – the four "jobs," as they are known.

Many were invited to share something, each one after several rounds of dancing. Everything was peaceful, harmonious, nobody dominated the ceremony. The cold under the starry sky was really intense, but nobody seemed to notice. We spent the last three hours of the worship service inside the church building, with music played by the groups that were present and words from visitors. One of the preachers gave a contextualized message on Jotham's fable (Judges 9), which deals with the behavior of a false leader, characterized by being empty inside, by being a liar and by lacking a true calling.

Tacai Lana'q, Colonia 10 de Mayo, 2002

When I was called on, I commented on the value of each person's own name. I read the Bible story of Daniel and his friends, whose names were changed by force. I compared it with the history of indigenous people in Argentina that were stripped of their own names when they received national identification cards. Then I read and commented on current laws that allow registering children with indigenous names, even if these do not appear on the Division of Vital Records' lists. It generated a lot of interest.

Piguiñi Lai', Pam pa del Indio, 2003

After the worship service, some lay down around the bonfires, others on the floor of the church building. I was among them, too. My neighbor stood up at 4:30 to heat water. Soon, about ten men had gathered by the bonfire, drinking *maté* tea and chatting about old times, about mutual acquaintances, about alligators and tortoises' egg-laying habits, and about Bible texts. It was amazing! I was the last person to get up at around 6:30 to complete the circle. We watched the sunrise and kept on chatting.

'Ele' Lpata'c, El Espinillo, 2003

The worship service took place in the big churchyard with just one light. Many people danced in "wheels" and "rounds" during the first hour and a half of dancing. Others prayed intensely for an elderly woman who was seated in the center of the dancers' circle. What had bothered me somewhat as a disturbance of the church service was obviously accepted by those present as a community prayer and healing ceremony.

Villa Río Bermejito, 2003

I heard something that is said quite often at churches about fraternal workers' visits: "We prayed that God may send us a servant and one is here today. That is why we are glad about your visit, for you have come to encourage us and to bring us a good word." In one part of the church worship, the members of a local music group were called to the front. Many of those present talked to them and prayed for one of them. It was a community warning about certain perils and behaviors, and as such, a public way of supporting these young men.

Piguiñi Lai', Pampa del Indio, 2003

The worship service was a true anniversary party. Almost all of the local churches were represented, and they had called off their own worship services. The heat inside the church building was almost unbearable, but people still sang fervently without looking at their watches. All musicians and singers were invited to participate. A big gift collection was taken up for the church – "our mother." The gift had obviously been prepared in advance and wrapped up with a special wrapping paper. People prayed while touching the walls of the church building. Someone read a broad historical account of the founding generation and present congregation. Of course everybody shared a stew at 10:30am. They also announced that, after years without baptisms, the following morning they would baptize and receive thirty-six people into the church.

La Leonesa, 2005

What a beautiful worship service! The elderly pastor, Ricardo González, always welcomes me like a father; he, along with others, make me feel at home at their church gathering. He is used to giving plenty of participation to those brothers and sisters present. He also usually reads and interprets many Bible passages throughout the worship service. He uses the Toba language Bible extensively.

Ltañi Lai', San Martín, 2005

Communicating in the local language

The indigenous people of the Chaco are a minority; they do not reach 10 percent of the population in the northeastern Argentine provinces. They are extremely marginalized. Through the original Argentine Constitution, the state defined the relationship with indigenous people as one of "conversion to the Catholic faith, civilization and assimilation," and they were denied, among others, the right to express themselves in their native languages.

Although since the reformation of the Constitution in 1994 the state acknowledges the preexistence of indigenous people and their cultures and guarantees bilingual intercultural education, history has left them with truly profound psychological scars in terms of their ability to value their language. Feelings of shame, fear and even rejection are common and greatly hinder the transmission of their indigenous language to their children and grandchildren, especially among urban and semiurban populations.

Throughout our visits we have heard countless times the following expressions or interpretations:

"We don't teach our language to our children because we don't want them to suffer as we have for not speaking Spanish."

"When my grandparents talk together in our language, they do it quietly in a corner."

"Nowadays children resist learning our language."

"I don't want them to speak in our language because then they do badly at school."

"When the children are older, I'll teach them to speak our language."

"I was hit at school every time I spoke my language."

"Our language is of no use for our youth when they need a job."

Along with other endangered languages, those of the Chaco have lost their status and functionality as the Spanish-speaking, non-indigenous society overran important communication areas, such as schools, hospitals, public administration and paid jobs.

Besides this, with the advance of rural electrification, mass media is playing a significant alienating role within the intimate space of indigenous families. Especially through television, the values, customs and decadent messages of western society are transmitted in Spanish many hours of each day.

The invasion of the Spanish language is also strongly felt in indigenous churches, even though this is an autochthonous space. In worship services, the people sing their own songs, but often they also sing hymns learned from non-indigenous churches. They are used to reading the Bible in Spanish. Few of them are able or try to read in public from the Bible portions translated into their own language. Following the reading in Spanish, the explanation can then be bilingual, in Toba and Spanish, depending on the region and personal history of the one speaking.

But we are also witnesses to the deep restoring and healing power experienced by our indigenous brothers and sisters when they feel God's love. We see them raise their heads with strength and pride, recover their sense of dignity for their culture and language, and pass it on to their children and grandchildren. They themselves attribute that new feeling to the Creator's acceptance, who loved them as a people with its own language and culture.

With this background, we as a Mennonite Team consider it very important to:

- visit those homes and churches that try to convey the value each indigenous person and people has before God;
- make the effort to learn an indigenous language and to communicate with indigenous persons in that language;
- promote the translation and distribution of the Bible, as well as reading and recording it in their languages;
- collaborate with the recovery and extension of those areas lost to indigenous languages: by informing of the right to register and use indigenous names, by pleading for the designation of interpreters at hospitals and in the courts of justice, by accompanying bilingual intercultural teachers, and by networking with other support groups;
- write about the importance and intergenerational transmission of the language in the bulletin *Qad'aqtaxanaxanec*, published by our team;
- collaborate with the publication of writings by indigenous authors, preferably in their own language, such as biographies, historical writings, memories and oral histories;
- promote literacy in indigenous languages;
- discuss the use of indigenous languages in personal conversations.

A fraternal worker who learns an indigenous language shows the greatest sign of contextualization, even when this may be a slow process.

> I was welcomed with great joy. The brothers and sisters who were invited to participate in the worship service after me, echoed the few words I had spoken in Toba, really very few! This encouraged them not to be ashamed of speaking their own language and teaching it to their children, many of whom do not speak Toba any more.
>
> *Makallé, 1998*

At the Bible circle I used the biblical text in Toba *(qom l'aqtac)* all the time and did reading exercises with those present. This had a strong and visible effect: in the following talks and gatherings, the participants made a lot of comments about their learning experience. They expressed great satisfaction for "reading in our own language."

Colonia Maipú, 1998

Those who were at the Bible circle expressed themselves freely in their own language, except when I would ask them to explain to me in Spanish what they had said. Even more difficult was when my questions in Spanish had to be translated into Toba for all those present. I realized that there was a huge difference between talking about biblical issues in Spanish and talking about them in Toba. It seemed that my questions in Spanish made it difficult to understand things. Still, I was surprised by some examples of theological interpretation: they translated the "Lord's Supper" as the "healing meal."

La Leonesa, 1999

There was a church service at night. I could barely understand anything that the elderly women said when they spoke. But I am glad they spoke because I feel that they are slowly beginning to trust me. One brother read and interpreted Hebrews 10:36, using the Toba version for that passage. It was the first time he did this. The preacher for that night also read about the woman at Simon's house (Luke 7:36-50), verse by verse, using the Toba text. Then he told the whole story in both languages in his own words.

Piguiñi Lai', Pampa del Indio, 1999

As in other indigenous neighborhoods where non-indigenous people live nearby, I saw that many Tobas are embarrassed to speak in their own language, even in their family setting with their children. I hope I have encouraged them a little by telling them about our situation as a German family living in Argentina. We only speak German among ourselves.

La Plata, 2000

When I was called on in the worship service, I tried to use Toba for the first part of my expression of thanks, but several Tobas almost died laughing listening to me. Then the preacher used

Proverbs 1:8, 4:1 and 6:20 as a biblical basis to talk about the pastor's role as a spiritual father for young people and about the value of learning to listen to what a father in the faith can teach. He used my effort to learn Toba as an example of the value of their language. He publicly acknowledged the mistake he had made by not teaching the Toba language to his own children, now already adults.

Colonia Aborigen, 2000

When I was called on, I read from the leaflet with biblical texts in Toba *"Da huo'o da ỹi'iỹaxa"* (When I am afraid) for the first time. I handed out a copy to everyone there. I was surprised by their interest in it and the encouragement they felt for learning about reading in Toba Qom, something unknown for many. Some even decided to read along with me from that leaflet in a low voice.

La Leonesa, 2001

It was a long church service with many visitors. Ten of them were invited to participate. They had come from Campo Alemani y La Pampita. There were many "joyful ones," as dancers and singers are called. Great was their surprise when they saw the "bearded man," myself, *mayi detaqa naua qad'aqtaqa* ("one who speaks our own language"). Then they talked about how important it is not to stop using their mother tongue.

Tacai Lana'q, Colonia Diez de Mayo, 2001

I was asked to read the Bible in Toba in public. After I thanked them, an elderly woman came to me. She embraced me and prayed aloud for me in her language, expressing to God that she wanted to pray for me, as a mother pleads for her child.

Villa Río Bermejito, 2003

The elderly Salustiano López gave me these words, "Non-indigenous teachers and missionaries have to first learn and become familiar with the indigenous culture. God does not like it if we only want to 'reap.' Even if someone speaks our language imperfectly or just a little, it still is a powerful sign for us that he or she want to become well acquainted with us."

Rosario, 2006

I had decided to read the complete story of Elijah on Mount Carmel with the prophets of Baal in Toba. I was amazed that people followed the long text – which I commented on here and there – with their voices, shouting "Amen!" and with other expressions of affirmation.

La Leonesa, 2002

Testimonies of faith

The purpose of the following examples is to show the power of the gospel inculturated among the Toba Qom people. These are personal testimonies that emerged in conversations that show autochthonous views about God's work among them and how it influences their ideas, their feelings and the way they interpret their experiences.

Here is a testimony of healing from a Toba believer: "When I was sick, the doctors didn't know what to do with me at the hospital. But one night I heard a voice telling me, 'Leave the hospital and ask your mom to pray for you. You will be healed.' I had to sign a paper in order to leave the hospital and I was healed."

Costa Iné, 1998

I went to visit a Toba pastor. At noon he shared with me that which he had: *torta frita* (a fried bread) and *maté* tea. He told me about his life: He had abandoned the way of the gospel for some time. He ended up in jail and was sentenced to several years in prison. There he reconciled to God and began to talk about God's love to other prisoners, some of whom were feared for their violence. He told me about the change in some of them who now serve God and their neighbors. His wife put up with the long waiting all those years and today they continue to be together, united.

Qochiiñi' Lai', Presidencia Roca 1999

A young man told me that he used to get together with his friends and get drunk. While intoxicated they would throw rubble at the roof of church buildings in their neighborhood to mock evangelicals. Then he was arrested, but while being held in jail he changed: "He entered into the gospel," as the Toba express it. Once he was free again, he began to help at a church in his community as a preacher and evangelist, and speaks to young people who are lost just as he used to be.

Fontana, 2000

A visiting pastor introduced me to his wife. The tone in his voice expressed such happiness and pride that it left me wondering. She was a woman who would easily go unnoticed. Later, during the church service, I finally understood; he introduced her to everybody and gave thanks to God for her, his partner in life's struggle. He said that at times when he had felt weak, his wife prayed for him. Thus he was strengthened and stood up again. One could see the unity between the spouses, as well as in their shared ministry in the worship service.

I could see how in that church's anniversary all those who came were included, even a drunk man, to whom they served lunch with respect just like everybody else, and also a non-indigenous man who spoke nonstop taking over the conversation.

Margarita Belén, 2000

One brother felt free to talk for more than an hour about his adventures as an evangelist and about how God "tested" his faith when he had no money for his trips, although he did have a clear calling to go to a certain place. "I don't ask churches to give me anything for my trips, I just pray and the Lord always helps me."

Fontana, 2003

An elderly man told us that many years ago, when he was seriously ill and had lost a lot of weight, another believer visited him after receiving a "message" and prayed for him. He felt a "fire" inside of him. He sweated so much that twice he had to change his clothes. Later, after another message, the visitor gave him a vegetable and milk diet. Fifteen days later, the recovered man received the baptism of the Holy Spirit while alone in the countryside. He did not eat for two weeks until Aurelio López, a Toba Qom missionary, arrived. Although Aurelio did not know him, he prayed for the man when he got to the door of his home.

Colonia Aborigen, 2005

One evangelist told me that last year he was in intensive care for nine days, unconscious, with an artificial respirator. He had had dreams and messages from God before and after awaking which helped him understand that God knew about his secret drinking habit when no one else was aware of it, and was giving him one last opportunity to change.

La Leonesa, 2005

A pastor shared that he does not want to be authoritarian on ethical issues, not even with examples from the Bible, because he believes it is better to let the Holy Spirit and God's Word convince us of our mistakes at the appropriate time. For instance, he told me about a stubborn brother who with this approach is "taming" himself. He also told me about another person who received the Holy Spirit, whose experience was so powerful that people thought he was insane. He said he had seen Jesus' image walking in the church building. After a while Jesus came close to him and "got inside" of him. So he started to shout "Hallelujah!" praising God loudly with his arms up for several hours. He felt so happy that he did not eat for twelve days.

Ltañi Lai', San Martín, 2005

The elderly Toba Qom Salustiano López shared the following experiences: "I never say anything to someone who does something wrong. I even hug him as if I loved him more than I love others, so that he sees his mistake. Some day he'll remember I hugged him. Paul says something similar when he talks about the ugliest part of the body, which gets more attention. The ugliest part is our feet, because they are always dirty.

"Our first trip with my wife, Florencia, was from Pampa to Quitilipi. We had to go through a thick forest called Cancha Larga. It was drizzling. We spent that night in the forest, up in a tree, tied up. A puma came near and started to walk around the tree. I said to Florencia, 'God sent us this puma to look after us, so that no one comes close,' because we were near the path.

"The next morning we found a house in the middle of the forest, and the man who lived there welcomed us and invited us to stay so we could eat and rest. He asked the reason for our trip. We explained and then preached from the Bible. He asked, 'Is it a religion?'

I replied, "No, it is salvation. You have to surrender to it.' However, we 'lost' him that day, because we had been taught that a person can only yield to God at a church with the presence of a pastor. How wrong we were for not praying with him right there and laying hands on him! In the afternoon the man gave us a big piece of beef jerky and cheese. Then we left.

"Florencia had dreamt that in the afternoon we would find a red truck. That's why we didn't stay at the man's house, even though he invited us. We kept on walking and saw some tracks first and then a truck. It was red! The driver gave us a ride. He told us that he was a friend of Chief Ramón Gómez, from Legua 17, who is Florencia's father! He lodged us in his home that night. Next day, he had two of his sons help us cross the gully on horseback in order to get to Quitilipi."

Rosario, 2006

Bible interpretation through indigenous eyes

Each person understands what happens to them or what they are reading on the basis of previous experiences. That explains why no two individuals can interpret the same event in exactly the same way, especially if they belong to different cultures and speak dissimilar languages.

This also applies to how we understand God's work in all of creation. Although it is the same God at work, we understand according to our past experience, our language and our culture.

No people can grasp completely who God is, all that God does in and with God's creation, nor the full meaning of Jesus' life and death. We need each other to help us recognize how partial is our point of view and to broaden our own understanding. Thus, we believe that as fraternal workers we cannot assume the authority to teach indigenous people how they should understand God's work, or how to apply the Bible's message in their lives.

Our challenge is to be among them, share with them and, above all, listen to the way they express in their own words and in their own manner what they experience in life and how they interpret the Bible. Those spaces for expressing themselves emerge in a natural manner during our visits.

In the Bible circle about the Beatitudes, we discussed what would be the most appropriate Toba Qom word to define "peacemakers." They chose the word *laxadaicpi*, (the obedient ones), who would set themselves apart from those who *qaica ca qaipi'iỹa'a* (don't trust anybody) or the *loquiaxaicpi* (quarrelsome).

Colonia Maipú, 1998

A Toba Qom pastor preached that prayer can touch a person's heart better than words, but that at the same time, that person is responsible for opening the heart from the inside. Another believer symbolized a man or woman whose life is covered by sin by placing a hymnal on the floor and covering it with a piece of cloth. He said that a person in that situation doesn't get moving when someone calls them because they can't hear anything. Only when the Holy Spirit calls them can they move and go where God wants.

Isla de La Leonesa, 1998

One brother said, "We must not *conquer* souls, but bring spiritual food to them; then they will come to church of their own choice, seeking more from God."

Qochiiñi' Lai', Presidencia Roca, 1999

The young local preacher talked about Jesus as "the light" according to Matthew 5:14-16. He contextualized "the mountain" mentioned in the text as *aviaq* (forest), where one can get lost or stumble without light.

Pioq La'asat, Pampa Chica, 1999

In a gathering of Toba Qom pastors, they chose specific terms in their language to describe the different church ministries:
- conduct the worship service, "to take care of one's work"
- blessing of the children, "to commit children to Christ"
- the Lord's Supper, "the healing meal"
- baptism, "to be washed"
- consecration of utensils for use at the church, such as plates, brooms, instruments, etc. "to set apart for God's work in the house of prayer"
- prayer for healing, "to pray over those not well, the sick"
- intercessory prayer for unbelievers, "to pray for those who do not yet come into our house of prayer"
- consecration of new church worker, "to set apart one of our brothers or sisters because of their future work for the church"

- anniversary of the church building, "birthday of the place for singing"
- reconciliation with the church of one who had left, "to return and come inside again to surrender before God."

Palauo, El Colchón, 1999

I heard a biblical interpretation by Silvano Sánchez: "God loves us. We see this in Genesis, where it says that God made us in his own image. God didn't want to be alone. That's why God had a special kind of love for clay. God shaped with his hands and kissed it. Brothers and sisters, God kissed it! God kissed us with his mouth. And God shared life with us. And said to us, 'Arise and walk!'

Laguna Pato, 1999

In a Bible circle we talked about what would be appropriate for the Toba Qom people to do on a Sunday, a day of rest. They distinguished "not appropriate physical work" from "appropriate spiritual work":
- "we give our attention to the day of rest"
- "to relax peacefully at home"
- "to refuse to work for money"
- "to make an effort to do something even if it is difficult"
- "it depends on each person, it refers to the situation of families with very young children"
- "to gather firewood and prepare a bit of food"
- "to praise God at home and at church."

Mala' Lapel, San Carlos, 2000

The pastor preached about the Lord's Supper based on 1 Corinthians 11:23:
- We must not close the Lord's table, but leave it open for everybody. Otherwise people would have to go elsewhere to seek a solution for their problems (such as health issues).
- The cup changes evil thoughts (Heb. 9:14).
- He shared another idea: "Just as people know that you are Toba Qom when they see your face, so they should be able to identify you as a believer."

Machagai, 2000

The Toba Qom pastor Alfredo Arce preached about Joseph's example and strength. He talked about the "gift of lying," which Potiphar's wife had, and about Joseph's decision not to let her seduce him.

He compared this with the poor advice given by an elderly woman from church to her granddaughter, who had an argument with her young husband. The grandmother told her, "Let him find another one! He is not the only man around."

He recalled as good advice that when he was fourteen years old, his mother said to him, "When you like a girl, you should have a serious thought. Once you make up your mind and choose her, 'auchoxoden acamayi (be understanding of her; literally 'care for her,' 'forgive her')." To extend this lesson to the youth, he turned to Ecclesiastes 11:9, 10, explaining that "the vanity of youth" mentioned in the text means an immature way of thinking that is not yet solid.

Colonia Aborigen, 2000

The Toba Qom pastor preached on Romans 2:6-11: "We are no longer afraid of God's judgment. Just like when the police come to our house, we don't get scared because we didn't do anything wrong."

He also talked about the authority of God's ministers in their field of work, which is the church. "Other authorities, such as a policeman or a judge, have to respect us, just as we respect them in their roles." As his contribution for the worship service, he said, "You really need to know God's voice." To illustrate this, he told two personal stories where he had heard God talking to him: Once God told him he had to "love everybody equally." Another time, when he was discouraged, he heard the words of 1 Corinthians 15:58, "Your labor in the Lord is not in vain."

Colonia Aborigen, 2000

I wrote down some phrases from the sermon preached by an elderly Toba Qom man:
- "The Holy Spirit has to merge with our spirits, so that he can talk to us, explain things and control us" (Jas. 3:3).

- "The Holy Spirit won't leave you in peace with something he doesn't like. If you messed up, he will bother you in the night. You can't preach while still being tied to the earth" (Mt. 18:18).
- "When the word of God comes in, it's bitter and makes sin ache. But when it comes out and heals, it's sweet."
- "One doesn't receive the Holy Spirit all at one time, only step by step, so that we are not overcome."
- "The Holy Spirit makes us like children. He makes no one big" (Mark 10:14, 15).

Piguiñi Lai', Pampa del Indio, 2001

At night I took part in the worship service of a church called "Heavenly Vision." The large church building provided the dancers with plenty of space. The praise dance occupied two thirds of the time of the entire worship service. Many participants were wearing their special dance clothes, and many children and teenagers participated in the dances, called the "movement," the "round," the "wheel." The pastor read the text from Ephesians 6:13-15, interpreting the dancers' clothing as a spiritual armor.

Rosario, 2003

The preacher for that night compared the insects flying around the gas lantern in the church with the evil that surrounds us: "Bad things are like those bugs, they can hurt you. But if the Holy Spirit lives in you, it's like the heat from this lamp that burns the insects." Another young brother compared a tame ox with a tame donkey: "Although both are tame and good for work, the donkey will always keep its bad habits. For example, it kicks when you least expect it. So, do you have the spirit of the donkey?"

Piguiñi Lai', Pampa del Indio, 2003

During the evening worship service, a local preacher shared his pain for not being raised by his own parents. He encouraged those present to value their parents and their advice while they are alive. Then he called two elderly people to the front, whom he considered his spiritual parents, and he cried out of joy for and with them. The rest of the believers were moved to hug their own parents, too.

La Leonesa, 2003

The final speaker at the church service was the pastor himself, whose eyes filled with tears as he shared that he couldn't read or write, but he had received the word that to God he is worth more than gold, that he is like a jewel, and that he has no reason to think he is worthless as a Toba Qom. Then, in tears, he sang for ten minutes, repeating the words of the chorus: "How wonderful it is, when God loves me." He also said that he has learned not to look down on anybody, as he once did when he sent a nun out of his house. He publicly acknowledged that he should have welcomed her for what she is worth as a person in God's sight.

Rosario, 2003

The morning church service is always a treasure. I can always learn new things about the history of this community with their charismatic prophet, Mateo Quintana: "He wasn't guided by papers, but by revelations." One brother talked about the danger of dealing with the Bible: "The Bible is life, but if you play with it, it can kill you. It's just like water, which is also life, but can kill you if you can't swim."

Colonia Maipú, 2000

Conflict situations

Sometimes we have spontaneous conversations where we hear about internal problems within communities or churches: conflicts among leaders, divisions, fraud, mistakes. Since we know that our suggestions or solutions could easily be inadequate, we try to limit our role to that of active listener. By not taking sides in a conflict, we are able to talk with either group or person involved. We are careful not to talk negatively about an absent third party.

Sometimes we simply read a portion of the teachings of Jesus, such as: "So when you are offering your gift at the altar, if you remember that your brother or sister has something against you, leave your gift there before the altar, and go; first be reconciled to your brother or sister, and then come and offer your gift" (Mt. 5:23-24). However, we try not to use the Bible as an undercover way of imposing our own idea. We trust that God will guide them in the way of peace.

In order to foster "the dialogue between the Word of God and life" we have organized conflict resolution gatherings. We tried to use these encounters as a space where those present would not necessarily treat a specific conflict, but rather recall testimonies from their culture and history that account for peaceful solutions in tense or dangerous situations. We had truly profound and intimate discussions, where people would recall life stories from their most cherished leaders. These stories were also connected then with the message of the Bible.

Our hope is that these spaces for dialogue and for getting to know one another will nurture and illuminate current practices of conflict resolution.

> The pastor shared with me his decision to leave the association of churches they had been part of for a long time. He talked about his disappointment that there was fraud among denominational leaders during the church's national elections. Neither had they fulfilled their promise to come and visit his community and church. (2001)

> The couple talked with me for several hours. It's clear that the role of a third party is a valid one. (2001)

> Even though we didn't know each other personally, we had an intense conversation about the challenges, joys and frustrations of his work, as well as about church and faith-related issues. Some children from the neighborhood were around and brought us fried bread, but that didn't prevent him from expressing how he felt. (2001)

> I talked with the pastor and his wife in the yard for nearly two hours. He commented on his church's current problems and how some people link them with the complicated illness of one member and the family problems of another member. For internal conflicts, he tries to keep contact with both of the groups involved. He is happy about a recent public reconciliation, although he feels that the roots of that conflict were not dealt with. (2002)

> As I was talking with three pastors, I heard their concern about current church practices. The big regional gatherings, now organized for music and praise, are not being used for teaching – which, according to them, is not the same as preaching – something that the Toba Qom former missionary Aurelio López used to do.

One of them told us how one time that missionary [Aurelio López], prior to a convention, spent the night in prayer. "Every time I woke up, I found him praying." In his wisdom, the elderly missionary knew that they would have to deal with tough issues. So for the first morning of the conference, he prepared a biblical teaching for the pastors. That led those present to ask forgiveness of one another for their bad thoughts. (2005)

Accompaniment ministries

Communitarian Bible reading: the Bible Circle

What we of the Mennonite Team now call the "Bible Circle" is our attempt to respond to the Toba Qom believers' request, one of whom once put it this way, "We no longer want people to come and teach us the Bible. We want them to come and read the Bible together with us."

The Bible Circle is based on a key symbol of indigenous spirituality: the circle. To be "in the circle" means to be "at home" where one can talk about the things of God and about life in a natural way. Focusing attention on the circle rather than on the Bible itself as the means of God's communication is also a way of distracting from a natural tendency of the Toba Qom to see the Bible as a "power object" in itself.

The purpose of a Bible Circle is to meet God in community around the Bible, to experience an encounter with Jesus. It does not aim at increasing or verifying biblical knowledge as such, nor does it claim to be a masterly Bible study, where one person knows more than the rest and transfers knowledge. Rather than convince everyone to think the same way about a biblical text, the purpose is to hear each other and learn from each other. By learning to accept each other in diversity, participants discover how to work together for the common good. This leads to a mutual commitment to serve both God and the community.[4]

> The local leader conducted the Circle in a clear, organized fashion. He always began by asking a brother or sister to offer a short Bible meditation. He was conscious of the time frame, the need for spontaneous prayer, the conclusion, and coordinated with the person in charge of the evening worship service. He

---

4. See Chapter 10, "The Bible Circle" by Horst and Paul, pp. 203ff.

consistently helped me write down what participants had said in Qom and translated my questions for them. It was obvious that he was very interested in fostering and strengthening the use of their language. At the end of the meeting, he asked each participant to comment briefly on the weekend's activity, and then they saw me off with a long prayer.

Lote 68, Formosa, 2000

Since many had work commitments, we decided to have the Bible Circle two hours before the evening worship service. As people arrived, we did some reading exercises. It turned out to be quite difficult because apparently many had never read in their own language. In the conversation someone said that Jesus is God's voice, the clearest and most important person among all divine revelations.

La Plata, 2001

For the first Bible Circle there were about eighteen participants from six churches. Among them were also four people from a non-indigenous neighboring church that conducts a Sunday school class which a group of Toba Qom children attend. So the whole activity was truly communitarian and intercultural.

At the beginning of our gathering, I took a long time to explain what I think is the fundamental difference between a Bible Circle and a Bible study. The former intends to emphasize the importance of each person's contribution and the freedom to speak in any language. The latter depends on a teacher who leads a biblical lesson with or without people's participation. Later, I heard several affirmative comments saying that the Lord himself, represented by the Bible at the center of the circle, was the teacher who was teaching us.

I chose Matthew 6:5-8 for the first conversation, which was about prayer. Each one received the text in an understandable Spanish version and in *Qom La'aqtac*, one text on each side of a single sheet. After a warm welcome by the local pastors and my general introduction about the idea of the Bible Circle, we read the Spanish text several times, one verse each, and compared it with the texts each of us had in our own Bible. We wrote down difficult words on a big piece of paper on the floor. Then we did the same exercise with the Toba Qom text.

It took us quite a long time because some had never read in Toba Qom. But those present enjoyed their attempts. It was a good start, but we needed to practice more in order to grasp the idea of the text being read. Still, we had a number of examples that showed how the Toba Qom text clarified what they thought the Spanish text did not make clear. For instance, the word "synagogue" is translated as "the meeting place of the Jews."

After the reading, we only had time to talk about church customs which agree or disagree with Jesus' teachings on prayer. It was striking that Jesus said God knows beforehand what we will ask.

La Leonesa, 2003

The last text we explored in both languages was Romans 8:14, 15, 26, 27. Everyone commented on the Pauline text that says that the Holy Spirit makes us pray. Several participants felt moved by the simple biblical text, which emphasizes the Holy Spirit moving among us and generating prayer inside of us. An elderly woman, who was very shy when she first started talking, seemed to come to life as she felt others listened to her and respected her.

La Leonesa, 2003

Bible translation

Beginning in the 1950s, Bible translation became a central part of the ministries of the Mennonite mission. In a shared effort, Mennonite missionaries, Albert and Lois Buckwalter, several Toba Qom translators and the United Bible Societies completed and published the first translation of the New Testament in 1981. Then they translated selections (40%) of the Old Testament.

A new and complete translation of the Old Testament into Toba Qom began in 2000, following a request from indigenous churches in the Chaco region. The current translation process uses a new method: those in charge of translating the text into the indigenous language are no longer non-indigenous specialized linguists and theologians, but rather, a translation team formed of Toba Qom people themselves. The four leaders from different Toba Qom denominations – three men and one woman – were chosen for their Bible comprehension and their knowledge of both their mother tongue and the Spanish language, as well as for their good reputation.

At first we suggested that each translator work individually on an assigned book of the Bible and then their colleagues would review the draft document. Eventually they adopted a more adequate work approach, which apparently fits their cultural style: the entire team reads, discusses, considers, and translates the text while one of them writes down the agreed translation. The goal is not to produce a literal translation of a particular Spanish version into Toba Qom, but to read several versions, understand the key idea and express it appropriately in their own words.

Other indigenous and fraternal brothers and sisters assist the Toba Qom translation team as a way of providing advice, coordination, technical support (with the use of computers) and help with administrative duties between the translation team and the Argentine Bible Society.

Also helping are a number of readers that represent different Toba Qom dialects. They receive drafts of the translated biblical texts and read them very carefully to spot words they do not know, words they do not understand and words that could turn out to be confusing in their region. Then they provide alternative words. The readers' observations are then reviewed by the translation team.

> We started working together on the book of Jonah. We made up four mixed groups considering the different represented dialects. Each group read one chapter in order to identify words or phrases that weren't fully understandable. Then each group handed in their suggestions to the whole team, where each proposal was discussed. Some were accepted or modified by general consent; others were rejected after being discussed. There was a very interesting dialogue when they talked about the expression of mourning by the people in Nineveh, since they recalled they own similar old customs.
>
> They reached a unanimous consensus in every case, so the translation team always received one suggested alternative from them. No one got angry, and no one ever imposed his/her suggestions. Almost every individual involved took part in the discussion. People were so excited about the whole task that the group suggested that they stay together for a while after dinner. So we finished our task for that day at about 10:30 pm!
>
> *Readers Workshop, Resistencia, 2005*

Audio Scriptures

In collaboration with the Argentine Bible Society, our colleagues are working on the production of recorded biblical texts read and sung in Toba Qom, Mocoví and Pilagá. These recordings are a response to a basic need of indigenous peoples who continue to be oral cultures and prefer to hear rather than read the text.

This represents another kind of Bible translation: the preparation of the texts for audio scriptures. It involves adapting the text for listening to a spoken story in dialogue. The process includes choosing and preparing readers for each character, then the recording. Musicians record background music. The copies are produced in a variety of formats: cassette, audio and mp3 compact discs, and Megavoice mp3 players[5] for the physically challenged and the elderly.

> As soon as I got to the bonfire, the family asked me if I brought "gospel cassettes." The only thing I had was the text from 1 Timothy 1-6 read in Toba Qom. Everybody sat down and listened to the cassette recording. No one was allowed to interrupt. The songs in Toba Qom at the end of each chapter helped them concentrate during the break. When the tape reached the end, they played the same recording again. When the text gave practical advice, people made brief comments. Then the neighbors borrowed the cassette until the following day. How simple, relevant and interesting it was for them to listen to an ordinary reading of a short book of the New Testament! What a pity we have not been able to make more recordings yet!
>
> *Pioq Láasat, Pampa Chica, 1999*

Publications

Through our visits we intend to strengthen the initiatives of indigenous brothers and sisters. We want their voices to be heard. The bulletin *Qad'aqtaxanaxanec* (Our Messenger) has been published for fifty years with that goal. Originally begun as a pastoral letter to maintain contact with church groups between visits by missionaries, today five thousand copies of this brief quarterly publication reach virtually all the indigenous churches in the region.

---

5. These solar powered, solid state players are available through Megavoice, Jacksonville, FL, 32218, USA.

It includes testimonies of life and faith, meditations, a short Bible story, pictures and dates about important events in the life of the congregations, such as anniversaries, birthdays, praise events and evangelistic rallies. We also publish articles of general interest to the communities: laws, information about other indigenous peoples, land, and bilingual intercultural education. We give preference to bilingual articles to accommodate the growing number of indigenous voices.

We encourage the people to write their contributions, or, with their consent, we record their words and then transcribe them. When a written contribution exceeds the space provided in the bulletin, we publish it as a separate piece of literature.[6]

Other recent literature

In response to requests from indigenous church leaders the Mennonite Team has published a wide variety of materials related to the needs of the indigenous churches.[7]

Toba Qom pastor, Cornelio Castro, and Mennonite fraternal worker, José Oyanguren *Netoqqui*, together have prepared several new publications: a bilingual literacy book, Old Testament introductory courses, and a complete Toba Qom primer.

Mennonite Team member Willis Horst prepared a Toba Qom-Spanish bilingual Handbook for Ministers. It represents the fruit of countless conversations and meetings with pastors of the different indigenous denominations about the tasks and work carried out in their congregations. The manual of 322 pages reflects Toba Qom, Mocoví and Pilagá theology and includes a number of cultural notes which recognize the uniqueness of indigenous spirituality.

In addition, Frank and Ute Paul published illustrated stories of Bible characters and leaflets with thematic biblical texts all translated in the indigenous languages.

> I went to La Leonesa to cover all the local pastors' homes and hand out the latest issue of *Qad'aqtaxanaxanec*, (*The Messenger)* as several months had passed since my last visit there.
>
> *La Leonesa, 2000*

---

6. See list of materials by indigenous authors in Bibliography, Part I, p. 247.
7. See a partial listing in Bibliography Part II, p. 248.

Pastor Ocampo showed me that, due to my mistake, the date for the local church anniversary had been published with an error. Then he told me more of the story of Toba Qom missionary Florencio Núñez, about whom he had read in the previous *Qad'aqtaxanaxanec*.

Lote 16, Pampa Grande, 2000

Pastor Antonio León told me he would like to write about the history of the beginnings of Toba Qom churches for *Qad'aqtaxanaxanec*. He said he saves a lot of old pictures which he would lend me for this issue.

Piguiñi Lai', Pampa del Indio, 2000

I took the new Toba Qom leaflet containing Bible passages about trusting God when we are afraid. The congregation received it with great enthusiasm. I think that seeing printed material in their language encourages them and makes them want to read it.

La Leonesa, 2001

Pastor Audón León handed me the writing he told me about, a testimony of his father's travels and ministry.

Piguiñi Lai', Pampa del Indio, 2001

Toba Qom elementary school teacher, Mario Fernández, showed me an essay he had written about the Napa'lpí massacre. Besides historical data, it includes interviews with survivors which he gathered with his colleague, Juan Chico, and his own spiritual interpretation of the event: the blood cries out to God from the ground, according to Genesis 4:10.

Colonia Aborigen, 2005

Literature sales

One of the important ministries of our team has been the provision of Bibles. Of course, God does not speak only through the Bible; rather, God also speaks to indigenous people in culturally appropriate ways: through dreams, visions, thoughts and corporate worship, as well as through creation herself. However, knowing that we are not exclusively in charge of teaching the truth, we promote the Bible as a tool God uses to communicate the Word to humans. Therefore we trust the Bible and consider that those who use it to learn to walk in Jesus' way will discern for themselves what they need to know to grow spiritually.

When we visit communities, we promote the use of simplified versions of the Bible that people with little reading practice and limited Spanish skills can understand. We also encourage the use of the New Testament and Scripture portions translated into the three indigenous languages of our area. We sell these Scriptures at a symbolic price, less than Bibles in Spanish. The Argentine Bible Society provides us with Bibles and biblical materials at a generous discount, to make them more accessible.

Except for the quarterly bulletin, we do not hand out materials for free, in order not to promote dependency. Sometimes we exchange Bibles for indigenous handcrafts. We often see the positive effect of the effort to buy a Bible or other material, because then the item is more highly valued.

On our visits we also carry a collection of other materials such as the Toba, Mocoví, and Pilagá dictionaries, and the Toba translation of the book by Antoine de Saint-Exupéry, *The Little Prince (So Shiỹaxauolec Nta'a)*. In addition, we take along *Memorias del Gran Chaco* (Memories of the Great Chaco). This two-volume work, prepared by members of the Interdenominational Conference of Missionaries of the Argentine Chaco, presents the unofficial history of the European invasion of the Argentine Chaco during the past five centuries. It is history from the little-known perspective of the defeated, told through testimonies gathered from the indigenous people themselves.

> Pastor Mario Núñez and I traveled to several churches in the area by bicycle. I took along my box of biblical materials. Although people did not seem to have cash, they ended up finding some money for Bibles, hymnals, and illustrated Bible stories. On our way, we stumbled upon an elderly brother and his wife who were taking firewood home. When Mario told them about what was in the box, the man said he had lent out one of his copies of the hymnal a long time ago and later gave another one away as a present. I was surprised to see him take out of his pocket a fifty peso bill (which at that time was equivalent to fifty U.S. dollars), and stock up on everything he wanted.
>
> *Laguna Pato, 1998*

I was there for a Bible Circle. Those who little by little came to the church building wanted to see my box full of Bibles and other materials. Soon it was almost empty. Lunch. Nap. Visits. Then people had to go to town to receive their pay. So there was no meeting.

Colonia Aborigen, 2000

I visited some Mocoví communities and everywhere I went, people bought Bibles, although none in the Mocoví language. "It's not the kind of Mocoví we speak," they explained. Is it true that there is so much difference between the Mocoví dialects that people in that area speak and the one spoken in Southeastern Chaco? Or perhaps no one I met could read in their own language.

Northern Santa Fe province, 1999

Those present were very interested in my box of literature for sale, but no one had any money. On the last day of the gathering I offered to barter literature for handcrafts. My box was emptied in one hour, and I ended up with a pile of baskets. Everyone was very happy.

Yaicangui, Resistencia, 1999

Several people bought materials. Some who only had Bibles they had borrowed from other people asked me to come back the following month when they will have received their pay.

Yaicangui, Resistencia, 1999

Many looked at the Bibles, but nobody has been able to buy any in the last few months. I could only sell booklets that cost five or ten cents.

Ltañi Lai', San Martín, 2000

They had asked me to bring a lot of literature for them to buy. I sold almost everything.

La Plata, 2001

The church service with the Lord's Supper finished at midnight. I was so sleepy I almost fell off the bench. After that, many wanted to see what I had in my box. They bought practically everything!

Piguiñi Lai', Pampa del Indio, 2001

We spent many hours chatting under the shade of a tree. Every now and then, someone would come to greet us and look at the box of biblical materials.

Basaíl, 2002

Land and territory

Land is one of the vital spaces without which indigenous peoples of the Chaco region cannot survive and maintain their culture. Although it is impossible for them to revert to their ancestral way of life, having their own land to settle on makes it possible to connect with the natural environment and experience many of the dynamics and conditions which gave birth to and nurtured these cultures. Land security also allows for the constant reformulation of cultural aspects, including language, which are no longer feasible within the confines and pressures of urban life.

After a grueling struggle carried out by the leaders of virtually all the indigenous peoples of Argentina, the last constitutional reform, held in 1994, acknowledged the right of these communities to receive the ownership of those lands which are "suitable and sufficient" for their holistic development. Unfortunately, despite this all-important legal achievement, this declaration of rights does not easily become a reality. Powerful economic interests, bureaucratic ineffectiveness, corrupt interests and the profound prejudices of many provincial officials, have turned this struggle into a long and painful, often unrewarding experience.

For this reason, in the mid-1990s several fraternal workers of the Mennonite Team began to accompany some the indigenous peoples' claims for land in Chaco Province. Their technical expertise in land surveying and organizational development, and close relationship with many indigenous communities guided their efforts. They have also joined with other nongovernmental organizations, Catholic and Protestant, in partnering with indigenous leaders and representatives to advocate for land acquisition.

A coordinating board, composed of indigenous leaders, provincial government officials and representatives from the different partnering institutions became the main agency of action. As a result, a 370,650 acre reservation bordered by rivers was turned over to Toba Qom communities of the Chaco Province. Another large tract of approximately 791,000 acres of public lands in the Chaco Impenetrable region was also designated for a future reservation. However, over time it became obvious that the government authorities were refusing to allow this process to move forward. The task became tough and tiring, and, in some cases, even became necessary to take legal actions against the provincial government to demand an answer to the indigenous' requests.

The case of El Tabacal, near the town on La Tigra, Chaco Province – quite small in terms of acres, but fundamental for the empowerment process that community experienced – was emblematic. Their struggle lasted for more than a decade, and throughout all those years the Mocoví community claimed ownership of over 114 acres of fiscal land enclosed by a wire fence adjoining their humble little homes. Although this legal claim was clearly just, according to constitutional rights, the officials of the Colonization Institute, the government entity in charge of granting land titles for public lands, systematically ignored it for years. Colonization employees favored the request of a non-resident farmer, who also claimed ownership of that same propriety, a decision that violated current legal norms.

Finally, the Mocoví land organization decided, with the accompaniment of the Mennonite Team and others, to initiate a legal injunction against the Colonization Institute. They eventually obtained a legal sentence in 2006 that favored the El Tabacal Mocoví community. This was a breakthrough decision for the Chaco Province.

But perhaps most significant throughout this long process was that the team's nonintrusive way of accompaniment yielded its fruit, by respecting the rhythm and decision-making processes of the leader and members of the community. El Tabacal community itself played the leading role for the victory in a remarkable community process of growth and self-worth. This cannot take place when an outside benefactor – a person or an institution not belonging to the indigenous group – underestimates the indigenous people's own capacities and takes ownership of the struggle.

> On the road to Yataí we found several groups of men working on a future wire fence. The thirteen extended families of the community had received 4,450 acres, the largest portion in the redistribution of the former Las Palmas sugar mill plantation. I was able to talk for a while with the president of the association, Hirónimo Álvarez. He and the others expressed their joy, their hope and plans for the future.
>
> *Yataí, 1998*

There are fifteen families living in Costa Iné. With the help of a Catholic Charity sister who had recently passed away, they received three parcels of land and the houses where they are now living. They are cultivating a small community farm and currently looking for more land because they are surrounded by ranchers and farmers on whose lands they work as temporary farm workers.

Costa Iné, 1998

I really liked how this group of people has a strong communitarian history with former chief Mateo Quintana that binds them together. These people had suffered for many years while living at Las Coloradas under very difficult conditions, because they were never allowed to collect firewood from the private woods nearby. Mateo Quintana made it possible for about eighty families to receive 3,200 acres in the Maipú colony. He had a vision that God would do this, and that they would have a school as well as a concrete church building which then actually happened.

Colonia Maipú, 1999

We took a bus to Reconquista and from there another one to the community El Palmar, a little more than a mile south of Berna, on Highway 11. El Palmar is a 25-acre Mocoví settlement they recently received when they could no longer live near their boss from long ago. They told us that the soil was not good – it was white, due to the crystallized salt that had accumulated on the surface – so nobody wanted to buy it. Today they see God's help as the soil becomes fertile again, without any human intervention. Grass started to grow back and they are sowing vegetables on their small farm.

Now there are about ten concrete houses and a community hall which every morning functions also as a school building for the adults. Each house has its own solar screen. A sign at the entrance proclaims that this is the first indigenous community in the province of Santa Fe with sun-powered energy. Since all the children had to walk or go on bicycle to the town school, over time the families with children slowly moved to the Mocoví neighborhood in town to be nearer the school.

Reconquista, 1999

We talked about Alfredo's job as president of the neighborhood committee and about the surveying of the Cacique Pelayo neighborhood and its one hundred and eighty-six houses, most of them almost finished. Alfredo explained what he had come to understand: "Our biblical wisdom is apparently of no use if we have the same miserable neighborhood for decades with no improvement." That is why he made a deal with Pascual Ávalos. He left the pastoral role in Pascual's hands and started working in the neighborhood. "But I never stopped singing or attending the worship service."

Several neighbors publicly approached the then candidate for governor, Ángel Rozas, during his pre-election visit to the neighborhood. Since then, things started to work better. They struggled to be recognized. The previous neighborhood committee had political connections but did not accomplish anything. They did not want to pass the records on to the new committee. The group of neighbors got in touch with the Provincial Housing Institute and found out that the money for the land measurement projects had already been deposited in a bank account some years before.

Now they are applying for more land in order to buy enough for the approximately fifty young families, which were left with no place to live in Cacique Pelayo. They are forming a new committee with legal status in order not to be dependent on the Fontana municipality.

Fontana, 1999

I got off the bus in Presidencia Roca and headed to Ambrosio Francia's house. It has been a long time since my last visit. He lived in Pindó for awhile. Francia has a daily radio program at the local station and he gets along with the mayor, although he tries to stay away from party politics. Seventeen families in the next block received houses. He is very thankful for the way God is blessing him for the good of his people.

Qochiiñi' Lai', Presidencia Roca, 1999

There is some frustration because, apart from the 370,650 acres received, land recovery in general has made little progress. Officials showed up and did virtually nothing. Apparently the government sees itself as crowned with enough laurels. The challenge for next year is to agree on a document which includes everything still to be done concerning land problems. It would be presented and discussed in a hearing with the new minister.

CeCaPI, Pampa del Indio, 1999

In the afternoon we were able to walk about eighteen blocks to the neighborhood called La Quinta, where three days ago ten Qom families from different towns in the Chaco Province had occupied a block of land ceded to them by the city. Each family, with Faustino as their chief, was building their own humble little house. Apparently more people who want to move to this new Qom neighborhood are already on the waiting list.

La Plata, 2000

Human rights

The Argentine government ratified those international treaties which acknowledge human rights and the applicability of crimes against humanity – such as military campaigns and massacres of indigenous people – and define indigenous people's rights as collective and cultural rights.

Besides this, the 1994 Constitutional reform acknowledges a multicultural and multilingual society, the pre-existence of the indigenous peoples, the state's duty to ensure them lands on which to live, according to their cultural standards, and also guarantees their bilingual intercultural education. Nevertheless, indigenous communities are far from seeing the actual implementation of these, their now legal rights.

For the most part, the national and provincial representatives show no real interest or effort in enforcing these current laws. Often there are only promises and gifts, such as token bags of food or brick houses. That represents a patronage approach to politics, in which politicians try to "buy" voters for the coming elections through welfarism.

Unfortunately, far too few communities possess communitarian land titles that guarantee their right to stay in their traditional environment. Where those land titles actually exist, the basic services for all citizens are very often not present. The greater the distance from the province's capital city and from the eyes of mass media, the worse the situation becomes.

Health care is inadequate, in part due to a lack of indigenous public health agents who understand illness and treatment according to indigenous culture.

Common formal education still serves mainly to "civilize" indigenous children, to assimilate them into the surrounding society and to make the indigenous people feel like foreigners, ignorant and despised in their own land. Many schools with even a majority of indigenous children are led by teachers who do not speak the indigenous language. No multilevel education programs of study exist that are truly intercultural and bilingual, nor are there adequate scholarships available, which are fundamental for advanced education. Few indigenous individuals have a university degree.

Indigenous communities often lack knowledge about their legal situation and their own rights. For instance, when they want to register a newborn at the Civil Registry with an indigenous name, they are often refused, even though an existing law endorses this possibility. Also, quite often indigenous leaders are deceived or paid off for a low price. With some truth, we hear people say, "In the past, they killed us with weapons, now they do that through laws."

As fraternal workers, we try to cooperate with those indigenous organizations that seek ways to demand the state to comply with human rights requirements. Our desire is to maintain our role of accompaniment as we cooperate with individuals and organizations that strive to strengthen indigenous people and their leaders' self-management.

> The Chaco Province Finance Minister wanted to meet with us at noon. We were more than twenty people, mostly representatives from the three indigenous groups in the province plus some delegates from partnering organizations. Suddenly we were informed that only the representatives of the National Catholic Indigenous Ministries Team would be admitted. Mabel Quinteros, general secretary of the Team, explained that we had come as a group to talk with this government official.
>
> Finally the Minister agreed to our request and we all entered his office. He allowed each one to speak before he showed openness to dialogue. Orlando Sánchez, a Toba Qom professor, introduced each one of us and explained the reason for the requested interview. He read the list of demands prepared at a previous meeting. The requirements included the implementation of intercultural bilingual education throughout the province, and the participation of indigenous parents in that process. Several mentioned concrete problems in certain rural schools, where supervisors are hindering legitimate demands and the implementation of changes towards an education that is appropriate for indigenous people.
>
> The Minister himself is a professor and knows what actually happens at these schools. But unfortunately, he seems to ignore the real challenges posed by an intercultural bilingual education. He fails to recognize the need for genuine participation of

indigenous teachers and especially of indigenous parents in the educational process. Mabel's recording of the session may help the official not to forget his promises.

Yaicangui, Resistencia, 1999

Colombo, a congressman from the *Justicialista* political party, participated in the meeting called by the Indigenous Committee for the Defense of the Right to Intercultural Bilingual Education (IBE). He had suggested presenting a bill to develop an IBE program with teacher training and certification, and to create an Office for the IBE in the Ministry of Education.

The challenge was to know how to take advantage of this lawyer's disposition and good intentions without letting him take ownership of the Indigenous Committee's grassroots initiative, or use this cause as a political tool. That afternoon, they split into work groups and then each drew up a summary. Their goal is to present their own bill proposal at a special meeting with the Education Committee of the Provincial Chamber of Deputies, to be convened by congressman Colombo.

Piguiñi Lai', Pampa del Indio, 2000

I traveled with a lawyer friend to Pampa del Indio. In the community called *Taigoyi'* the officials from the regional land committee waited for us. They were interested in receiving counsel about the ongoing local police brutality and impunity. They claimed they are victims of an alliance among current politicians, the justice of the peace (formerly a teacher), and the chief-of-police.

We met at the community hall with thirty indigenous people. Many shared in their own language their unpleasant experiences with the police and asked advice for varied specific legal problems. The lawyer was sympathetic with the victims and offered to come back to support the initiative that emerged during their conversation: to invite two delegates from each one of the sixteen regions in Pampa del Indio, in order to create a Toba Qom human rights committee which would represent the community when needed.

Piguiñi Lai', Pampa del Indio, 2003

Here I heard the indigenous name of one of the pastor's young daughters. Her name is Soxodai (the kind one). I was interested in learning more about this subject, since there are very few indigenous children with Toba Qom names. The pastor explained that once he asked a teacher what the name Yamila, her daughter's name, means. He was told about that name's Arabic origin, so he began to think that it would be much more appropriate to choose a name from their own language for his future daughter.

Santa Rita, Pampa del Indio, 2002

It was the day that ended more than a year of boycott against the local school. The conflict had originated due to problems with the public school, established in the community nearly forty years previously.

[Historical note. In the 1960s the education department of Formosa Province, in the absence of a school on the reservation, named a self-taught Toba Qom man of the San Carlos community, Carlos Mansilla, as teacher of the children. Carlos held classes in the local church building and taught in the Toba Qom language. Thus, a whole generation of children grew up literate in their own language. When an official school was established by the province in the 1970s, non-indigenous teachers were brought in. From then on, instruction was in Spanish, with no more literacy in Toba Qom.]

Now, for some time most Toba Qom students had finished their primary education without being able to read or write at all. Also, parents were fed up with the mistreatment their children suffered at the hands of some of the teachers. They held the principal responsible for her mismanagement of the school cafeteria funds and for not fulfilling her administrative role, acting instead with political motivation. Their complaint was also motivated by the fact that students were not being taught in their indigenous Toba Qom language, which is the mother tongue of the whole student body. The local Toba Qom teachers who had completed teacher training long before and were trained in intercultural bilingual education had never been incorporated into the school staff.

The Minister of Education of Formosa Province came that day to the community to respond to their three requests.

He quickly agreed to the plea for Toba Qom teachers. Rafael Mansilla, the community chief, showed in his speech that he was very happy for the incorporation of three Toba Qom teachers, certified for intercultural bilingual education in this school. Rafael expressed his gratitude to God in his Toba Qom language in front of all those present. The parents felt they had won a battle against the system, since they realized that at least one part of the laws protecting and supporting indigenous rights was being put into effect.

Rafael clarified that what the community had requested and received was neither more nor less than was theirs by right. His voice trembled as he stressed that two of their three requests had still not received an official response: to remove the principal – a request made in the presence of the woman herself – and to implement a high school level program. To this day, students cannot complete their full primary education.

He explained that rumors against the community were unfounded, since they had never requested the removal of all non-indigenous teachers from that school. They only required that non-indigenous teachers treat their children well, teach them in an effective way and be committed to the well-being of the community. His words made it clear that the current teachers did not fulfill these requirements.

Last of all, and unexpectedly, Rafael presented a statement that had been composed beforehand. He asked the Minister of Education publicly to sign the document in recognition of the remaining unmet obligations to the community. The Minister signed it immediately without hesitating.

Mala' Lapel, San Carlos, 2005

I stopped at the junction of National Highway 11 and Provincial Highway 90, where the Toba Qom communities bordering the nearby town of La Leonesa have been blocking the highway for twelve days. Their goals are: (1) to urge the provincial government to move forward with the fulfillment of promises made long ago, (2) to demand the necessary budget for the Provincial Institute of Indigenous Peoples, and (3) to carry out specific political decisions for communities of the three ethnic groups living in the province.

Initially, they had blocked the road intermittently for two hours before allowing vehicles to pass. The National Guard helped control traffic in a reasonable manner. Later, since the governor continued to refuse to receive indigenous representatives, they began to allow cars to pass during only half an hour at noon each day.

The picketers and their families camp beside the highway. Several plastic and grass shelters protect them from the cold and frost at night. I found many members of different Toba Qom churches. Everyone is discouraged with the lack of attention from the government officials.

After five months of waiting, the governor still refuses to receive the Toba Qom leader, Orlando Charole, to dialogue. The indigenous people refuse the offer to talk with the Minister Matkovich, designated for the negotiation; they want the governor himself to receive them, not his Minister, who has a bad reputation among them.

Camino a Ltañi Lai', San Martín, 2006

Hospital and prison visits

The indigenous way of interpreting health problems differs from that of Western medicine. The indigenous worldview looks more at spiritual causes and indicates different treatments for illnesses. Consequently, seeking help in a hospital for a serious health problem is often quite frightening for them. They tend to turn to non-indigenous doctors only as a last resort, once their own native healers can no longer solve the problem, at which point patients are already in a desperate condition. Experience thus seems to confirm fears that the hospital is a place where one goes to die.

It is even harder for those who cannot communicate well in Spanish. They are simply labeled as ignorant and must wait long hours, often without an adequate explanation. Many rural patients, who are already seriously ill, come in alone, not knowing anyone. They do not understand what happens to them, nor the explanations doctors and nurses give. Limited visiting hours only serve to further separate them from their family group. Staff members may be inconsiderate or impatient. The indicated medical treatment – injections, surgeries, diets, medicines, etc. – creates distrust and fear of dying.

In such a distressing situation, indigenous patients are very grateful for a simple visit from one of us fraternal workers, even though sometimes we are strangers to them. During a visit, we listen carefully to their story and we pray together. When appropriate, we also contact the doctor in charge of the patient, in order to help us understand the whole condition, interpret if necessary and explain details in simple terms.

We also visit Toba Qom persons who have been arrested, and are being held at the police station for whatever just or unjust reasons. Sometimes relatives have requested a visit, or maybe because we have been involved with them previously, perhaps advocating for their rights. These visits may continue for as long as the detention lasts, sometimes years.

We may need to contact defense lawyers to safeguard proper treatment for prisoners or their citizens' rights before the law. We have at times intervened in cases of torture by the police, which unfortunately is quite common. As with all visits, these are opportunities to be with a person in a particularly difficult situation, showing through our simple presence that we have not forgotten or rejected them. We trust that love will open people up to God's grace and they will be empowered to follow the way of Jesus.

Intercultural Bilingual Education (IBE)

In the area of formal education, our team's accompaniment mainly involves encouraging indigenous teachers, providing them with materials, visiting their schools, thus strengthening their role as transmitters of language and culture. Through our trips and visits we serve as a link among teachers in different communities, which facilitates the exchange of experiences and materials.

Unfortunately, the school as an institution functions as a strong agent for disdaining what is uniquely indigenous, despite all the grandiloquence of education officials to the contrary. Indigenous culture is widely considered not only inferior, but entirely worthless. A commonly held notion is that in order to access power or participate in the economic benefits of non-indigenous society, "you must have an education." Such an understanding equates education with schooling and underestimates the traditional spaces and techniques for the acquisition of knowledge.[8] Indigenous people themselves come to accept the notion that only what we write down is truly

---

8. For more information, see Hannes Kalisch's work, included in the "Bibliography Part III."

important, that an illiterate person is certainly ignorant, that in order to become an important person one has to be able to read and write.

School is widely regarded as a non-indigenous place administered by non-indigenous people. Thus, participation means total submission to non-indigenous criteria and management. Educators practice a pedagogy based on cultural assumptions very different from those of indigenous students. Their ways of thinking, perceiving and storing information is diametrically opposed to that of people from an oral tradition. Indigenous children are subjected to many hours of required Spanish language classes, as well as to content, methods and testing alien to their way of perceiving the world, of feeling, thinking and speaking. The results are traumatic. Inferiority and the worthlessness of indigenous identity are simply confirmed.

For these reasons it is very important to value orally transmitted wisdom. For example, in the context of the church we practice and promote the Bible Circles. This unique space for learning is intentionally open to pre- and semiliterates. We are constantly amazed at the depth of their reflection and outstanding memory. Perception of the gospel clearly does not depend on literacy.

However, we are not opposed to the real need for literacy in the modern world. Indigenous children should be encouraged to acquire all the knowledge and skills possible for their meaningful participation in society. However, that goal should be pursued without destroying the pride and confidence in a genuine indigenous identity. Positive values of indigenous culture should be identified and strengthened. Only with a strong identity will ethnic groups make the best possible contribution in a diverse, multicultural society.

The reformation of the Argentine Constitution in 1994 guarantees the right to an intercultural bilingual education for all indigenous people. Prior to the reform, the Indigenous Ministries Team of the Catholic Church had already set up the first Research and Training Center for Indigenous Pedagogy (CIFMA, for its initials in Spanish). This community college located in the city of Sáenz Peña, Chaco, initially trained indigenous youth to be teachers' assistants and then intercultural bilingual teachers. In recent years, other significant steps have been taken toward the fulfillment of the legal certification for a valid intercultural bilingual education. Indigenous teachers are increasing in confidence and in awareness of the fact that they represent their people.

Nevertheless, to transform a school into a learning environment where indigenous students' education is based on their mother tongue and culture seems to be a long and difficult road ahead. Non-indigenous teachers still harbor doubt and prejudice against including IBE, as evidenced by these statements:

- "The kids get confused with two languages."
- "Is the Toba Qom language a complete one?"
- "They need to learn to adapt to our society!"

At the community colleges where non-indigenous teachers are trained, many topics dealing with IBE are still not included. Many indigenous children enter school speaking only their native language. This reality would call for a much needed strategy for teaching literacy in the students' mother tongue while simultaneously teaching Spanish as a second language. Since for this teaching approach it is necessary to use specialized methods, non-indigenous teachers would have to be trained to respond adequately to the linguistic needs of the school where they teach. Unfortunately, there is still very little teaching material in indigenous languages.

In recent years, another phenomenon has emerged which hinders the incorporation of future indigenous teachers into the IBE program: some indigenous students who are being trained to become teachers are no longer fluent speakers and, in some cases, have only a token knowledge of their parents' language. This is due to the breakdown in language transmission from one generation to the next among indigenous families living in urban or semi-urban surroundings.

Ute's report follows:

In a unique experience, I had the opportunity to collaborate in the final stage of formation of a group of indigenous teachers' assistants from the Pampa del Indio, Chaco area. I monitored the first student practice teaching (internship) in various rural schools composed mainly of children from their own ethnic group. These are some observations that emerged from that experience:

- Interns acted with a special grace and fluency when they told ancient tales of their own people. Storytelling was a natural, and easy for them to do.
- Their patience and respect toward students was remarkable.
- The fact that parents of students were able to talk with the indigenous teacher intern made a significant difference.
- Students practiced for several weeks at schools in indigenous communities, which had previously only worked with non-indigenous teachers. The students from those schools usually

enter first grade as monolingual speakers of their mother tongue. They are exposed to the traumatic experience of not being able to communicate with the teacher, learning with great difficulty. Learning is further complicated by the sense of subtle contempt which results from the teachers' ignoring or not incorporating the wisdom and knowledge the students bring from their own home and community.

- This new experience of allowing students to communicate freely in their own language with the Toba Qom intern, immediately created bonds of trust, increased freedom of expression and improved learning.
- It was somewhat difficult for the indigenous teacher interns to include more adequate strategies in order to apply the indigenous teaching approach to the school practice, such as having students sit in a circle, helping children discover for themselves, making use of outdoor spaces beyond the school building, etc.

It is possible that all these aspects were related to the teacher interns' own scholastic history and the non-indigenous educational model to which they were accustomed.

The challenge of urban migration

Between 15,000 and 23,000 Toba Qom and Mocoví people live in settlements near the cities of Buenos Aires, La Plata, Rosario and Santa Fe. Besides these, numerous semiurban ghettos skirt towns and cities in Chaco and Formosa provinces. Indigenous people move in search of seasonal work and to follow the dream of a brighter future. Life in the countryside offers little to retain them. Not much forested land remains accessible for hunting and gathering as was the lifestyle of their ancestors. Employment for farm workers is scarce, and when they do have a piece of land, few of them successfully farm the plot, due to a variety of factors, including adverse weather, lack of tools, or simply the way of life sometimes referred to as the "culture of poverty." In addition, it is known that in the cities more government aid is distributed.

But the migration to the cities also brings unfavorable consequences to indigenous people. Away from their natural environment, their children grow up without ever knowing the Chaco's thick thorn forest, the habitat that shaped their culture of origin. Besides losing their people's customs and culture, including language, they also lose the survival skills and crafts of the previous generation. The youth are thus very exposed to the influence of other identities. They adopt dehumanizing and destructive models of behavior and have little defense of their own against the offer of addictive drugs.

However, in the midst of the destructive effects of rapid urbanization, the church is not absent. The indigenous believers take the living church with them wherever migration leads. As many as thirty Toba Qom churches and several Mocoví churches exist in urban and semiurban settlements outside Chaco and Formosa provinces. All of these provide a refuge for their members, a space for maintaining identity in the midst of inhospitable contexts. The churches permit a sense of belonging to God and to an indigenous people. They are the only place where the indigenous language is habitually spoken in public. The experience of the worship service, including the dance with all its symbolic expressions of indigenous culture, helps youth rebuild a positive self-image.

As a team located in the north, we have not been able to visit these churches often enough due to the long distances separating us from them. Addressing the reality of urbanization is a challenge for the future.

Networking

Our ministry is simply one among many contributions. Numerous support groups, both church-related and secular, have been working for many years among indigenous peoples in the area and we have learned to value each one's efforts. Networking with others is important, since none of us can face all the challenges alone. We often need the expertise of others and consult with them for technical and legal advice. Sometimes we join in shared actions, such as working on land committees, supporting demonstrations against the provincial government or intervening in urgent situations like cases of police brutality. Our network of partners includes anthropologists, architects, lawyers, social activists, teachers, social workers, linguists, physicians, land surveyors. A good relationship is maintained by welcoming each other in our homes when we travel, sharing meals and conversation.

A truly valuable expression of team work has been the Inter-denominational Conference of [Christian] Missionaries serving in the Greater Chaco region (EIM, for the initials in Spanish). The EIM has met annually since 1979 for fellowship, reflection, and renewal. In these gatherings important decisions are reached which help set the foundation and convictions for our work with indigenous communities and our relationships among each other. Together we celebrate accomplishment and mourn injustice; we encourage each other and agree on future steps. The Missionary Conference is a genuine space for learning and interaction, a special jewel of God's kingdom that has led to a commitment to avoid sectarian proselytism and to question paternalistic action in all ministries among indigenous groups.[9]

Members of the EIM wrote and published *Memorias del Gran Chaco (1992-1995)* (Memories of the Greater Chaco region). This two-volume work is unique historical material narrating from the viewpoint of the invaded peoples the colonial invasion and the resulting suffering and survival of the Argentine Chaco peoples. Soon after publication, governmental education departments in the provinces of both Chaco and Formosa declared it to be valuable educational material, apt for official use in the public schools.

Accompaniment as affirmation

Response to accompaniment

At first, the indigenous people were surprised that these visitors acted so differently from the way other visitors related to them. They were puzzled by the respectful approach. What actually did they want, these outsiders, these *doqshi* (Toba Qom word for non-indigenous)? These "fraternal workers," as they came to be known, did not bring clothes or food to distribute, they did not urge changes in the local church life, they did not teach their own version of "the truth" and they did not pass out Bibles for free. Instead they sat down with them as guests. If offered something to eat, they ate thankfully. They drank from the same *maté* tea straws as their hosts. In church services, they listened patiently to the words of the speaker. Often they stayed overnight, or for several days, accepting whatever conditions their indigenous hosts offered.

With time this noninvasive, fraternal accompaniment earned a relationship of trust. It became clear that these visitors did not have ulterior motives. They did not try to proselytize for their own church, nor buy votes for political elections. They were not investigating for a scientific paper about indigenous culture. They made no promises with regard to projects. They honored and respected their indigenous hosts. At times, if it was made known that leaders of the community had a need for accompaniment in their interaction with government or other areas of non-indigenous society, the

---

9. See Bibliography, Part IV, Interdenominational Missionary Conferences, pp. 244.

fraternal workers joined them, but insisted that the indigenous leaders speak for themselves.

The style of accompaniment as guest practiced by the Mennonite Team has, without doubt, helped empower the Toba Qom church leaders to continue their chosen path of spirituality towards maturity in Christ, not only in the church but in broader society. To be affirmed as persons created in God's image, of infinite worth and with the capability to follow in Jesus' way is the most liberating and saving Good News anyone can receive. Surely it is the opposite of being conquered.

Some of the Mennonite Team workers spent more than half of their lifetime in the Chaco before returning to their country of origin. The indigenous communities and churches remember the testimony of their lives, extensive travels to visit in indigenous churches, their friendship, words and letters. Results are often not immediately obvious, but are, nonetheless, lasting.

One Mennonite missionary couple, Albert and Lois Buckwalter, are especially remembered. They lived more than forty years as guests in the Chaco. Albert is credited with defining the first alphabet for the three indigenous languages which he learned to speak well. He coordinated the translation of the New Testament into these languages working with indigenous translators. Together with Lois, Albert compiled and edited dictionaries in all three languages. One of them contains an introduction to the grammar of the Toba language. Upon reaching retirement age, Buckwalters returned to North America due to health problems. Nevertheless they continued their work and completed a synoptic dictionary for the three Chaco languages of the Guaycurú linguistic family. Albert died in 2004. In addition to gratitude for translation achievements, the Toba Qom people treasure the memory of the Buckwalters' sincere friendship and respectful accompaniment.[10]

Thus, the Mennonite missionaries who served in the Chaco long before us have left an unforgettable legacy of credibility, humility and respect. We were the second or third generation to join the Mennonite Team, but we gratefully received the heritage of their good reputation still felt after decades. The people trusted us without preconditions.

The following notes from Frank's travel diaries transmit glimpses of the indigenous' memory of earlier Mennonite fraternal workers:

---

10. The Buckwalters' attitude, which earned them this special place in the hearts of the Toba Qom, is beautifully expressed in their own words in their 1998 article, "The Inculturation of the Gospel," this volume, pp. 167ff.

At one point in the Mocoví service, when Pedro reminded the people of the former fraternal worker, Miguel Wigginton, all began to cry and to pray. Pedro then said: "Miguel suffered with us, ate with us and joined us on our path." His name was also mentioned in other conversations.

El Tabacal, 1997

All remembered the visit of Miguel and Marta Mast. Although it took place years ago, they still knew what had been taught in a Bible study on the parables of Jesus. They also remembered vividly a meeting of women which the Masts had led in the yard of the elderly pastor, Taboada.

Laguna Pato, 1998

The people were happy that after a long absence Marcelo Abel, visited them for the three-day celebration of their church anniversary. They had not forgotten him when he moved away. They appreciated him very much. In the service they also remembered the North American missionary, Juan Lagar. The celebration ended with a tasty beef barbeque.

Piguiñi Lai' – Pampa del Indio, 1999

Don Heriberto remembered the only meeting he had with Albert Buckwalter, in 1959, who arrived in the Jeep accompanied by Aurelio López. Albert lifted the hood of the motor and said in Toba: "dapaqa souaxat so naloxo" (It is so hot because it's in a hurry).

Pioq La'asat – Pampa Chica, 1998

The old pastor and his wife told me they remembered the visits of Albert Buckwalter in their house. At the time they were still young and did not know Spanish. Albert spoke Toba with them.

Makallé, 1999

I visited the local Foursquare Gospel Church here for the first time. The pastor welcomed me in the courtyard. I introduced myself and we spoke a bit in Toba. I sensed a bit of suspicion. A few girls who stood in the shade of the house giggled when they heard me speaking. It was quite obvious that so far no fraternal workers had visited here. Since the family could not imagine the cause of my visit they asked me many questions.

Tacai Lanaq – Diez de Mayo, 2001

The night service was small. The small gas lamp attracted lots of insects. They had never had a visit of a fraternal worker, so I was a bit unsure. Two of the little children of the Romero family chose my lap as a seat, which made me feel included.

Pioq La'asat – Pampa Chica, 1998

Here I was strongly aware of what it means to visit at a church where they had not known the Mennonite Team and, therefore, did not know what a fraternal worker is. I was present in the church service but wasn't recognized or given participation. I will need lots of patience.

Pioq La'asat – Pampa Chica, 1998

I spent a couple of hours with an older man at the fireside. He began to share intimate experiences of his pastoral ministry. This was an eye-opener and confirmed again the value of our role as fraternal workers who take the time to converse and share opinions in an unhurried setting, at their discretion.

Ltañi Lai' – San Martin, 1999

In the church service I was introduced as the one who "has come to us to eat with us in our homes."

Charadai, 1998

The morning service had already started when I arrived, but they had recognized me from a distance on account of my way of walking. They were happy that I came. The church leader called me "our companion" for the first time.

Tacai Lapa – Pampa del Indio, 1999

Pastor Ricardo used the same Bible text which I had read out loud in the service (1 Cor. 10:6-13). He took his time and did what I could not have done – he explained the ethical content of the text, appealing to the responsibility of the fathers and mothers present how they could use this text for the education of their children. He considered me to be his assistant, so to speak (*qadtaua* in Toba Qom).

Ltañi Lai' – San Martin, 2000

The pastor called me "*qadqaȳa* Frank *ȳataqta qantonaxaua*" (our brother Frank is a true companion in our joy).

Pioq La'asat – Pampa Chica, 2000

The elderly pastor Salustiano told me what the Tobas used to say, "We must take good care of our fraternal workers, Albert and Lois Buckwalter, since they are someone's children. Their parents live far away in another country. Since they were sent so far away, they probably think of their children all the time and weep. When we accept them here as our children then their old parents will be happy. We are grateful for our Mennonite brother and sister. They don't bring us money, but they come to visit us. They bring us the word of God and Bibles."

Quitilipi, 2003

God was there before us

In the words of missiologist Max Warren:

When we approach other peoples, cultures or religions, our first task is to "take off our shoes." for the place we are approaching is sacred. Otherwise, we would be stepping on the dreams of others. Even worse would be to not recognize that God was already present before we arrived.

The Chaco people clearly see that the Creator has always been present in their history and their culture. Throughout their dramatically tragic history they recognize the Creator's mercy. They consider the fact that they have survived the conquest as a people to be a sign of divine grace. God raised up brave and steadfast leaders to guide them, and even used the birds to warn them of danger.

The Creator gave the primeval forest to the indigenous people as a space to live in, but not to possess. Communal commitment was vital, with well-defined rules for those who would survive. All needed each other. They believe it is God's power of creation that generated all that was necessary for their former life. They often shared with us how they experienced God's guidance through dreams, visions, voices of birds, ecstasy, preaching, song, visitors and in church services. Considering their wisdom, useful customs, refined techniques of collecting and hunting, the signals of warning in dangerous situations, their knowledge of healing illness, Toba Qom believers do not doubt in attributing to the Creator all that served them in the past. The sum of all this is their "Old Testament."

As missionaries and guests, we sensed an ever deepening awe at the signs of God's presence in their culture.[11] We began to listen more and more carefully to not miss what *they* had to tell *us*. They view their situation similar to that of the Jewish believers as summarized in the book of Hebrews:

> Long ago God spoke to our ancestors in many and various ways by the prophets, but in these last days he has spoken to us by a Son, whom he appointed heir of all things, through whom he also created the worlds. (Heb. 1:1-2)

Many cultural concepts and values of the Chaco indigenous people seem to indicate how God the Creator might have envisioned a common life for humanity. Interpersonal relations are marked by a deep respect for each other, a refusal to violate the other's will. This is seen in the interaction between women and men, parents and children, young and old, indigenous persons and others. In conversation they listen patiently and allow the other person to finish speaking. They believe all things in life are meant to be shared. The one who is stingy or self-demanding endangers the survival of the collective entity, the clan. They do not accumulate property. One who becomes rich can only have accumulated that wealth at the cost of others.

Through keen attention and intuition they discern the signals of other living beings. Thus, birds and other animals or phenomena of nature can communicate to humans.

> The voice of birds warned our ancestors of the approach of soldiers . . . By flapping their wings and calling out they signaled that danger was near. The birds were the watchmen for the hunted indigenous people.[12]

No one can take God anywhere, nor is there any place one can go where God is not. We do not take God to others. We can, however, walk with them and discover God's presence together.[13]

---

11.   For a Mocoví testimony of this same truth see in this volume, Chapter 4, Albert and Lois Buckwalter, "The Inculturation of the Gospel," pp. 169ff.

12.   Oral testimonies of the Toba and Wichí in *Memorias del Gran Chaco*, Vol 1, p. 181 (translation by the authors).

13.   See in this volume Chapter 1, "The Image of God," pp. 12ff, and Chapter 5, Albert and Lois Buckwalter, "The Inculturation of the Gospel," p. 167.

God is present in and through the Spirit

Many indigenous believers bear witness that they have heard the voice of Jesus and been touched by a new spiritual power, which they identify as the Holy Spirit. Innumerable stories tell of the Spirit's transforming effect on their lives. The gospel movement has significantly influenced the thinking, feeling and acting of those involved. Sometimes this inner spiritual power becomes hindered by wrongly directed missionary activity. However, where it finds freedom, the Spirit is more often understood as a fulfillment of spiritual insights from the people's own past. Thus, the power of God's Spirit completes, rather than negates, their past. The Creator God, the Great Spirit, is now identified as the Spirit of Jesus.

For ages powerful indigenous healers knew that various treatments could be used to heal illness. Now Jesus is regarded as the mightiest healer. His authority, great enough to cope with all problems, transforms sorrows, as well as reveals invisible causes and modifies unfavorable effects of illness.

The novelty of their new religious experience is the direct communication with God available to all. In traditional spirituality, this is possible only for the shamans, the most spiritually powerful persons of their communities, who are accompanied by invisible companion spirit beings. Now, believers acknowledge the Holy Spirit as the best companion spirit, the supreme chief who guides and serves everyone who accepts.

Chaco indigenous believers express repeatedly how precious it is to know of a God who has created them, who cares for them as people, who lets them feel God's love and grace. During services people often sing with tears in their eyes: "It is wonderful that God loves me." God speaks the mother tongue of every human being, thus can be understood by everyone.

God knows what needs to be changed to bring life, freedom and trust to the people of every culture. We as foreigners and guests do not consider it our task to dictate these changes for the host culture. We trust God's Spirit will lead into a life of wholeness all those who seek. In intimate conversations indigenous believers tell us they have learned by the help of the Holy Spirit to better distinguish between those cultural features which produce harmony, freedom and life, and those which bring fear and death.

In a conference on indigenous spirituality an older believer in Jesus arose and said: "You anthropologists advise us to return to our roots and ancestral customs. You don't know what you are saying. You know nothing of the fears we have suffered. Our spirits had no words for us. The God we now know speaks to us and responds to our needs."

In practice, the indigenous churches demonstrate a wide variety of belief regarding traditional healers. In light of their faith in Jesus, many believers question the power and healing techniques used traditionally. Practices range from total rejection to limited acceptance. This topic profoundly relates to the Toba Qom worldview with its perception of the world and the community, as well as its particular understanding of the self and of illness. As an issue of debate it defies simplistic yes or no answers.[14]

In the words of North American theologian Richard Twiss, a member of the Dakota Sioux:

> There are two reasons unbelievers can create just laws, good music and sound education. First, they are created in God's image; therefore rays of light still shine through. Second, God's common grace, exercised through his providential sovereignty, restrains wickedness, vice and ignorance from taking us to the depths to which they could.[15]

Twiss goes on to say:

> Native culture, like all the cultures of man [sic], reflects to some degree the attributes of the Creator Himself. It is in Christ that we find the ultimate fulfillment of his holy and sovereign purpose for us as people. . . . When we come to Christ as First Nations people, Jesus does not ask us to abandon our sin-stained culture in order to embrace someone else's sin-stained culture . . . God wanted to set them free to express their love and devotion to their heavenly father through their unique cultural expressions of music, singing, dance, language and worship.[16]

The log in the missionary's eye

Living in close contact with the people of the Chaco has changed us. We continue a process of reevaluating our own culture which we now understand from a much different angle. The light shed by the strengths of the indigenous

---

14. For more on this subject see this volume Chapter 5, Albert and Lois Buckwalter, "The Inculturation of the Gospel," section: "The relationship of the gospel to the indigenous cultures . . . ," pp. 167ff.

15. Richard Twiss, *One Church, Many Tribes: Following Jesus the Way God Made You*, Ventura, CA: Regal Books, 2000, p. 78.

16. Richard Twiss, *One Church, Many Tribes*, pp. 78, 79, 81.

culture reveals more clearly the shadows within our own. The blindness and ethnocentrism of the dominant culture is exposed for what it is. When we think that we are the "civilized" and "highly developed," it is easy to believe that our own way is better and that others should become like us. With all our failings, however, we have found the way of accompaniment without conquest satisfying and fulfilling as an alternative missionary practice.

> A Toba Qom pastor asked me my opinion about the Lord´s Supper. At once I proceeded to give him a complete theological explanation with my smart arguments. The pastor listened with attention and then responded calmly. I realized immediately that he had simply wanted a conversation with me, but instead I had poured out on him my "superior" knowledge. I felt quite ashamed.
>
> *Yaicangui, Resistencia, 1997*

> Near the end of the service the leader invited a man to speak. He was elderly, unkempt, with worn out clothes and shoes. While he went slowly to the front, I wondered what he would have to say. But the old man began to speak clearly to the audience. To my amazement, he gave a brilliant theological exposition about God's revelation in sending Jesus, and the new filter that provides for understanding the Old Testament. I listened with rapt attention and felt ashamed that, based on his appearance, I had doubted his gifts.
>
> *Margarita Belén, 2003*

Jesus said, "Why do you see the speck in your neighbor's eye, but do not notice the log in your own eye? Or how can you say to your neighbor, 'Let me take the speck out of your eye,' while the log is in your own eye?" (Mt. 7:3-4)

We can identify a few of the logs in our blinded eyes which have hindered our sight:

- We feel smart and important if we have read many books and studied many courses.
- The person who has earned higher academic degrees or has obtained an influential position will be honored, respected and regarded as a person of authority, while the one who cannot read and write is thought to be unintelligent.
- We judge other people by their clothes and appearance.
- We are quick to make judgments, exclude others or become angry with them.

- It is hard for us to be patient.
- It is difficult for us to welcome a visitor if we have to change our plans.
- We aim at accumulating more and more goods to provide for our future.
- We are quick to present our opinions, proposals or advice.
- We think the newest is best.
- We consider that much in the world can be purchased.

Only an honest and critical attitude toward our own culture can enable us to accompany our indigenous brothers and sisters without belittling them. Recognizing cultural diversity helps overcome some of our own ethnocentrism. In a fraternal relationship free from the threat of conquest, the downtrodden are enabled to experience God's unconditional love. When we truly live among them as guests, vulnerable and weak, God's love empowers them to transform the world.

As we enjoyed the hospitality of the Toba Qom in their homes and churches, we also received them in our home as guests. We shared unhurried times of conversation, the common cup of *maté* tea, and the family table. Sometimes they also stayed to sleep. We hoped they would feel at home and want to return.

Guests, not conquerors

Not only is it important to recognize unhealthy attitudes in our own culture. We must constantly keep in mind that we are representatives of a society which continues to wound the weakest among us. We often take too lightly the ongoing harm done by discriminatory treatment of indigenous people today, as the following final diary entry reminds us.

> Throughout Latin America schools celebrate the "discovery of America" on October 12. A Toba Qom woman teacher told me that she cannot join the commemoration ceremony at her school. As she relives the suffering, powerlessness and pain afflicted upon her ancestors as a result of the conquest, she experiences such a profound sense of despondency and sadness that she finds it impossible to celebrate. In effect, the suffering inflicted by the Spanish continues today through the actions and attitudes of many Argentines.

The teacher remembered that once, during her training, a history professor spoke to his students about the events that had occurred during the military conquest of the Chaco. He spoke in such an insensitive way that all the indigenous students broke out in tears. "The memory of that pain," added the Toba Qom teacher, "has filled many of my people with hatred against all non-indigenous persons. But hate destroys us even more. It burns in us like fire. I have now chosen to go another way with the help of Jesus. I want to become healthy. I have asked Jesus to transform my pain into a power for action and love. That's why I became a teacher. I want our children to be proud to be Toba Qom. All non-indigenous people who want to help us should never forget our pain."

Fontana, 2006

Injustice and rejection of indigenous people by "Christians" is still common in the church and society. Even those of us sent as missionaries to share Jesus' love are sometimes inadvertently guilty of adding to the hurts, as Twiss expresses:

The Anglo expression of Christ and His kingdom has said to the Native expression of Christ and His kingdom: "I have no need of you. I don't need your customs, your arts, your society, your language, concepts or perspectives." . . .

Then, to add injury to the insult, the Euro-Americans have said to the Natives: "But you need us. You need our theology, our leadership, our traditions, our economic resources, education, sciences, Sunday Schools – ultimately, our civilization." . . .

The Native community is to this day primarily viewed by evangelicals as a needy but largely forgotten mission field.[17]

In our approach to indigenous people, we who claim to follow the way of Jesus must in repentance give up all action which continues any semblance of conquest. Only then will healing come to those who still harbor deep-seated resentment, anger, hatred and frustration about the conquest.

We, Ute and Frank, have learned much, yet still have a lot more to be taught. We offer this account of our unforgettable and rewarding years of service in the Chaco in the hope that it will inspire others to explore the way

17.   Richard Twiss, *One Church, Many Tribes*, pp. 79, 81.

of mission without conquest. Our expectation is that what we have shared in this chapter makes clear to readers that the alternative way of mission we learned in the Chaco is a viable and appropriate missionary stance for the indigenous context.

Part 2

4

Mission to the Indigenous Communities

Albert and Lois Buckwalter

Albert and Lois Buckwalter served in the Chaco mission program from 1950 to 1993, guiding the transition from mission compound to fraternal worker accompaniment and birth of the indigenous and independent *Iglesia Evangélica Unida* (United Evangelical Church). They coordinated linguistic work and Bible translation in Toba, Mocoví and Pilagá.

This chapter is a translation of a presentation given at the annual meeting of the *Encuentro Interconfesional de Misioneros* (Interconfessional Missionary Gathering), Resistencia, Chaco, in October 1987. An earlier version was presented to the *Equipo Nacional de Misiones* (National Missionary Team), Ypacaraí, Paraguay, in August 1979, and published in the *International Review of Missions*, v. 72, no. 287 (July 1983), pp. 464-466.

A Personal Testimony

We were born in English-speaking Mennonite homes in the United States. We studied in Mennonite Church colleges and then did theological studies in the Mennonite Biblical Seminary.

We arrived in Argentina in 1950, and in the Chaco area in 1951. The Mennonite Mission among the Toba had been founded in 1942, nine years before our arrival. It was a traditional mission-compound type: church, school, clinic, store, small farm, carpenter shop, houses for the missionaries.

We believed that our duty before God was to form a Mennonite Church, a common denominational goal. Our preparation for this task was the same that North American pastors received to work in North American churches. We had not received specialized training to relate to Native American peoples, not even linguistic studies, since the study and learning of the Toba language was not considered of importance. The assumption was that the Tobas needed to integrate themselves to the dominant society and therefore, it was not advisable to "waste time" with this unwritten language.

At no time was it suggested to us, nor did it occur to us, that we should begin our work assuming the stance of learning anything from the Tobas.

Consequently, our first years were full of many frustrations:
- We did not understand the Tobas.
- We saw the utter impossibility of transforming into Mennonites the Tobas of the three Mission churches.
- The work related to the administration of the Mission (education, agriculture, store, etc.) monopolized our time and energies, and left us exhausted and disgusted, without any enthusiasm remaining for the ministry of the Word, which in reality we considered the most important part.

We came to the extreme of doubting if we really should be a part of that mission. But the sustaining factor was our conviction that God had somehow called us to this place.

In 1954 God answered our prayers by sending us Dr. William Reyburn and his wife Marie (sponsored by the American Bible Society), a Christian couple, specialists in Anthropology and Linguistics and dedicated to mission. They did the initial study of the Toba language, identifying the sounds and suggesting an adequate alphabet for putting it into writing. They also prepared a brief analysis of some of the details of the grammar. Upon that base, we were able to begin the study of the language, and follow with the Scripture translation work that we have concentrated on to this date.

But their most important contribution was the anthropological orientation. They helped us to understand that every people has its history, its way of coping with reality, and that any new concept that comes to them is received and interpreted in terms of all the experience this people has had up to that moment, and that it is impossible that they respond to God in any other way that is not their own.

They challenged us to have faith in God, the creator of all reality, to believe that his Spirit was able to illuminate the new believers, so that they might hear God's voice through the Scriptures and might understand what he wants of them in their lives and in their situation.

They opened our eyes to the reality that:

- There already existed an incipient Christian movement which included more than twenty-five churches in isolated indigenous communities organized by the people themselves.
- They had heard the gospel for the first time from non-Indian Pentecostal preachers and others, in the main cities of the Chaco province, or who had come to their communities to visit.
- The government, by a 1948 law, required that all non-Catholic churches be registered in the Department of Non-Catholic Religions, which required a bureaucratic process in the distant capital city of Buenos Aires. So some of the indigenous churches, in order to continue functioning, had registered under the registration number of a non-Indian church.

Along with Reyburn, we visited in many Toba churches where we had already been invited, and the leaders always insisted that we participate in the services. In these churches we observed:

- A preoccupation with and fear about their precarious legal status, because they felt abandoned by the non-Indian pastors who visited them very infrequently.

- A remarkable spontaneity and spiritual vigor which were absent in the three "Mennonite" churches, even though we visited them several times a week.

- A joyfulness that did not exist among the mission residents, even though the latter received many economic benefits.

We discovered that one of the "Mennonite" churches would meet when we weren't present, to have Pentecostal type services, and only when we were present would they adapt themselves to the worship form imposed by the missionary.

Reyburns helped us see that this adapted Pentecostal form of Christianity was authentic and very logical, and in accord with the Toba cosmology. This was most difficult for us to accept and believe at this time.

A very important decision

When we accepted at face value the Interpretive Report of the Reyburns, we in fact experienced a profound conversion. Consequently:

- We decided to stop thinking of ourselves as the owners of the indigenous church.

- We based this decision on the conviction that God was able to form his church among the Toba through the Holy Spirit.

- The Toba believers themselves would know better than we how to live out the gospel among their own people.

- We called ourselves simply *fraternal workers,* but they call us *counselors.* They desire our occasional visit and our participation in the preaching of the Word in their services.

- We decided to devote ourselves exclusively to the church, and particularly to the translation of the Scriptures in the languages of the indigenous peoples that make up their churches.

- We dissolved the traditionally established Mission, to be able to dedicate ourselves exclusively to the church, recognizing the categories into which the Tobas classify community activities: *spiritual and material,* and that there is not to be duplicity of functions. He who is in charge of one, must not be in charge of the other.

After several years, and sensing there existed a strong desire to strengthen tribal unity, we encouraged the indigenous Christians themselves to form their own legal church organization, independent from the non-Indian churches. They called it: United Evangelical Church (*Iglesia Evangélica Unida/IEU*).

- In 1958 the first Consultation Conference was held, in which twenty-nine congregations decided to unite to form their own independent organization.

- In 1961 the Department of Non-Catholic Religions granted them their own registration number in the National Registry.

- In 1974 they affiliated with the Argentine Federation of Evangelical Churches.

Characteristics of the IEU

- It is an autonomous church.

- They elect their own pastors and leaders in their own way.

- They plan their own organization and activities.

- During the first twenty years they provided their own finances. At present the majority receive a monthly stipend from a European mission.

- In the beginning they also built their own churches.

- They are thoroughly evangelistic.

- They carry out all the work of the church (baptism, communion, etc.).

- Their theology is authentically their own, since it arises from their own life vis-a-vis the Scriptures.

- The churches affiliated with the IEU reach about 120, scattered all the way from Buenos Aires to Embarcación, Salta, and including Toba, Mocoví, Pilagá and Wichí, besides some groups of non-indigenous peoples.

Strong Points of the IEU

- It is a deeply evangelistic church, needing no one from outside to show them how to carry out evangelism among their own people.

- They call denominationalism the "work of politicians."

- They have a capacity to confront problems that are very difficult to resolve and the ability to handle them with true wisdom from God. They themselves make specific applications based on the Scriptures.

- The church is the center of the life, activity, and interest of the community.

- Christian education is done in the church, without separating the children and the young people from the adults, and in the home

– a practical learning, non-theoretical, following their traditional teaching forms.

Weak points of the IEU

- The temptation to reject their own legacy (language, traditions, legends, customs, values, etc.)

- Because they are in an inferior position in relation to the dominant culture, they are tempted to try to imitate the ways of non-Indian people, which really do not fit their life, as though this would prove that they are no longer Indian, looked down on by the non-Indian.

- The overwhelming urge to receive outside funds, which in the long range sabotage the true motives of the church, threaten the unity of the believers and divert an inordinate amount of time to their management.

Lessons for us

- Not to call unclean what God has cleansed, and to accept as valid the expression of faith of other traditions, recognizing that God is the judge of us all. (See Peter's experience in Acts 10.)

- To be able to see ourselves through others' eyes as invaders and intruders.

- Not to usurp the responsibilities that belong to and are the privilege of the indigenous believers themselves.

- It is a challenge to our own Christianity, because it illumines our own faults and limitations.

Concerns

- How to free ourselves of everything that stands in the way of our sharing the gospel, from our world to a very different world, without distorting the message?

- How to enter the indigenous community without distorting their life because of our presence?

- How to relate to the indigenous peoples without creating dependence?

An unwritten language

If we should want to have a New Testament in an unwritten language, where would we begin? This is the question we asked ourselves in 1951.

Almost from the very beginning, we were deeply frustrated because we realized that in order to communicate adequately with the people, we would need to learn their language. Most of the sounds we were hearing were similar to those in Spanish, but others seemed to get lost in the people's throats. We made an initial effort to write down the language, but the problems we encountered seemed insurmountable.

We are grateful to God for the modern science of linguistics which came to our rescue through the Reyburns and their specialization in Anthropology and Linguistics. Little by little, we began to fill notebooks with words, paragraphs, speeches, while discovering the rules of the grammatical structure of the sophisticated Toba language.

How are we to learn to speak a language when there are no books, nor grammars, nor dictionaries in that language? We know that children learn their mother tongue by prolonged contact with their family. But we adults need exercises and lessons and grammatical notes to help us in our oral practice. So we prepared our own lessons and our learning progressed until the time came when we could begin with the translation of the Scriptures.

Bible translation

The first book that was translated was the Gospel of Mark, this work being the result of close cooperation between my Indian informant and me. I helped him to understand the meaning of the biblical text and he helped me to put this meaning into the most natural speech of the Indians. The United Bible Societies only published translations done by native speakers in consultation with the missionaries.

Perhaps it would appear that to translate scriptures into a language that has no written literary tradition would be even more difficult but that is not the case. The translator must study the same basic questions that all translators of the Bible need to resolve.

- What is the original text? The translation must be faithful to the meaning of the original.

- What does the original text mean? The translation must contain the same message contained in the original language.

- What must be said in this translation so that it expresses the same meaning as the original text? The translation must be in natural, idiomatic language that does not appear to be a translation by using the normal language of the people.

In our case, we allowed biblical scholars to resolve the first two questions, but the third, what must be said in this translation, we needed to resolve.

The translation of the Scriptures that we are doing in three Indian languages is the one called "dynamic equivalence." In Toba we used as our basic text the Good News Bible in Spanish ("*Versión Popular*"), while in Pilagá and Mocoví we are using the Toba New Testament as our basic text. The Indian translators consult various modern translations of the Bible, as well as commentaries in Spanish, while I do the same in Spanish and English.

For those of us who prepare popular versions in Indian languages, the commentaries in English that are provided by United Bible Societies are especially useful. These commentaries anticipate many of the problems that will confront the translator and give him guidelines to follow to find a satisfactory resolution to each case.

Erroneous ideas exist about indigenous languages. They are not merely dialects, but rather languages, and they are not inferior in their grammatical structure and in their capacity to adequately contemplate reality and faithfully express it. All human beings are the creation of the same God, and he has enabled us to communicate satisfactorily with the other human beings in our linguistic communities.

We all know that the Bible translator has the inescapable duty to faithfully translate the original, even though he may dislike what it says, nor must he introduce any of his own ideas or personal interpretations.

However, in these indigenous languages, as well as in other languages in the world, at times the translator inevitably has to resort to an interpretation in order to translate.

Due to the sophisticated system of obligatory articles in these languages, we must be specific and not ambiguous, for example in the translation of the word **Lord** as found in 1 Corinthians 4:19. Some scholars say that **Lord** here refers to God, and others say it refers to Jesus. Others say it is undetermined.

In these languages we must decide whether to use God or Jesus. We decided to say Jesus in this instance, *so qadataxala'*, which means our *chief that was on earth before,* instead of God, *ñi qadataxala', our chief seated in heaven.*

Other issues may have to do with concepts of singular and plural. In these languages there are two categories of plurals: a few, or many. Every time we translate the phrase *the disciples of Jesus,* we must determine who they are: the twelve, several, or his disciples in general, who would be many. The text must indicate one or the other.

There are also special terms from the biblical way of life, foreign to peoples of the Chaco, like *prophets, synagogue, priests, apostles,* and which require a phrase to describe their function:

priest	he who speaks to God for the people
prophet	he who speaks for God
synagogue	meetinghouse of the Jews
apostle	Jesus' sent one

Other problems relate to the differences of culture and environment. In Acts 20, Paul compares false teachers among the believers to wolves among sheep. In the Chaco there are no wolves. Instead the phrase "*ravenous beasts*" was used.

The responsibility of the Bible translator is tremendous. In this task the presence of the Holy Spirit is a determining factor. We continually trust the Lord's promise in James 1:5 that states: *If any of you need wisdom, you should ask God, and it will be given to you. God is generous, and won't correct you for asking* (CEV).

In conclusion, neither the many challenges, nor the weariness of many years of tedious work, nor the criticisms against the translation of the Scriptures into indigenous languages, nor the confusion caused among the people by those who claim that the Spanish Reina Valera version of the Bible (comparable to the English King James version) is the only valid translation . . . nothing can obscure the value of the work taking place in the hearts of those who are reading or hearing these scriptures read.

Hebrews 4:12: *What God has said isn't only alive and active! It is sharper than any double-edged sword. His word can cut through our spirits and souls, and through our joints and marrow, until it discovers the desires and thoughts of our hearts.* (CEV)

In Toba: *Cha'ayi da l'aqtac ñi Dios ÿataqta nca'altauec, qataq huo'o da l'añacac. Qataq nallaxa napactalec ca ÿilonec mayi dos naua ala'pi. Qataq damayi ishit da ividau'a cam ÿataqta pa'auo saq cha'a nachaalataxac ca shiÿaxaua qataq som capegue' lqui'i, qataq ishit da ÿaateec naq'en ca lhuennataxac qataq da lavilÿaxac.*

The Toba translation says: *Because the spoken word of God really lives and has power. And its sharpness surpasses that of a knife with a double mouth. The word can reach into the secret inner life of a person, and into his spirit, and can put in sight his thoughts and intentions.*

5

The Inculturation of the Gospel

Albert and Lois Buckwalter

The original Spanish version of this article was commissioned by the *Encuentro Interconfesional de Misioneros* (Interconfessional Missionary Gathering) and read at its September 1998 meeting in Resistencia, Chaco.

The presence of God in the indigenous cultures of the Gran Chaco before the arrival of the gospel.

What signs of LIFE in the cultures are traces of the presence of God?

- Throughout the centuries, the indigenous peoples of the Argentine Chaco have continued to wrestle for survival with an often extremely inhospitable environment. They trusted in benign spirits that supported them in their struggle, and kept them safe and sound.
- A Mocoví pastor related to us that his mother, as a child, was taken captive by the white invaders. However, she was able to escape during the night, crossing fields, swamps, and forests, because she was constantly praying to *qota'olec, our universal father.*
- In the Toba myths there are references to *ñim qad'ot, he who created us.*
- There are many facets of the indigenous daily life that challenge our cultural norms. For example, their strong compulsion to share food; the priority they assign to social obligations; their practice of giving away rather than accumulating possessions.

What elements of DEATH may suggest doubts of the presence of God?'
The same human weaknesses present in the so-called civilized cultures, manifest themselves in the indigenous cultures, as well.

- Given their world vision, they were terrified at natural phenomena, considering them punishment for not having kept the rules of life, or for disobeying a taboo.
- Illness or death gave occasion for revenge by means of magic or sorcery.

How does the Bible shed light on this subject?

- The human story of God's interaction, found in the Bible, is an illustration of what we observed among the indigenous peoples of the Chaco. There was a deep sense of the correct behavior that should rule, and there was punishment for the one who did not reach that goal.

The inculturation of the gospel among the indigenous peoples of the Gran Chaco

What do we understand by inculturation of the gospel?

- When the native peoples recognize that their practices as believers in the gospel are according to their own consciences, without considering the forms of other ethnic groups, then there has truly been an inculturation of the gospel. They are aware if their daily actions do not conform to the model shown in the New Testament, while their consciences encourage them in their efforts to reach that ideal.

What forms of inculturation have been observed among the indigenous peoples of the Gran Chaco?

- Probably the most obvious form is the ritual of the *danza*, the dance outdoors around the church, that takes place as part of the dedication ceremony of this space to the worship and praise of God. But even more powerful and profound is the fact that believers continue to regularly celebrate public worship, and that to that end they build structures that are simple but generally more elaborate than their home dwellings.
- Their frequent prayers are directed to God with great fervor.

What does the Bible say in this respect?
- The Gospel narratives describe human activities and clearly indicate what does or does not please God. The indigenous peoples recognize that distinction without any outsider having to tell them. Their own consciences condemn or approve them.

The relationship between the gospel and the indigenous cultures of the Gran Chaco

In what way does the gospel mean a continuity of the culture?
- The gospel doesn't indicate what culture we should own, but rather clearly states that we must believe in God and seek to do what pleases God. As believers in the gospel, the people feel strengthened to follow the good in the teaching of their ancestors, now enlightened by their reading of the Word. In the character of Jesus they see the clearest example of God's will.
- The traditional festivals have been totally transformed into zonal meetings to celebrate and share their faith, and thus promote the work of the church.

In what way is the gospel newness of life in the indigenous communities?
- The first indigenous persons in the Chaco to become believers always gave this testimony: "I was sick. I surrendered to the gospel, I was healed, and my life was changed."
- The native peoples themselves testify that the believer now lives with less suspicion and distrust of his neighbor, and therefore, is more friendly and eager to share his newfound faith.
- On a certain opportunity a Toba leader declared, during a church conference, that his father had always cautioned him never to spend the night among people who were not his relatives, since he would be at risk of being killed. With great satisfaction he pointed out that he had been spending several days in this place, far from his own people, with full confidence and no fears.
- A Mocoví leader told us that when he is in town he likes to spend time at the bus terminal, meeting and greeting any indigenous persons that pass through, even though he many not know them. He observed that if the strangers are believers, they are always pleased to respond. Not so, if they are not believers!

- A Toba leader related that he and some other young people, already believers, wanted to test if it was really dangerous to walk across the cemetery at night. They tried it, proving that such a belief, as he put it, was "superstition," an unfounded fear, now that they believe in Jesus.
- An elderly Toba, on his death bed, told his son: "I know who is killing me, but I won't disclose his name, because now we are believers, and do not take revenge on our enemies."
- A Toba woman, very active in her church, was now facing death. She shared this with her congregation, and then named the women who should assume her responsibilities. They did, as though responding to a call from God himself.
- A young girl had stolen an earring. In the church service the next morning, the grandmother brought the child forward and presented her to the congregation. The leader said, "Now that we are believers, we don't steal anymore." Then he called for special prayer for the child, that the demon of stealing would go out of her.
- A Mocoví man, after his conversion, decided to rid himself of his firearms. His friends urged him to sell them, for no small gain. But as he thought about it, he decided that to do that would be tantamount to encouraging someone else to become a scoundrel. Secretly one night, he took his weapons and ammunition to a secluded spot and buried them deep.

What does the Bible teach us about the relationship between cultures and the gospel?

- The description that we find in the Bible of the human being with no faith, is of a person who is lost, without a guide, without light, without life. We find no reference to a change of culture, unless it be a total change in life's focus and in the purposes that drive life.

In what way should this debate affect our missionary presence?

- We should recognize that our main work among the indigenous peoples has to do with inspiring a new life perspective, a new focus, and nothing to do with the basic form of their culture, be it "civilized" or "primitive." As we see it, nowhere in the Bible do we read that one culture is more acceptable to God than another. However, we read much about a change of attitude, about recognizing that we are God's creation, that we are totally dependent on God, and that our happiness is found in our complete surrender to God's will in our lives.

- All missionary activity should have as its focus strengthening the religious-spiritual movement among the indigenous peoples. This is what they themselves consider most important in their lives. Any activity that may not contribute to that end, or that distracts from it, or that makes difficult a clear vision of the gospel, or that pushes them to expend their energies looking for non-attainable goals, must be avoided at all cost. We have observed that when they discuss what they call "material matters" and "spiritual matters," they always prefer the spiritual. This contributes to the unity, peace, harmony, and well being of the community.

- To suffer hunger or thirst, heat or cold, or intense weariness, always gave them the opportunity to demonstrate their strength of character. We missionaries are constantly in danger of distracting them from these values, which are inculcated in them by their parents. The missionary who appears with a lot of baggage is a distraction that sabotages the gospel itself, the gospel that appeals to the indigenous people because of the clarity and simplicity of its teaching.

- A missionary said he was tired of all the requests that were always dominating his visits to the indigenous communities, making it impossible to converse about more fundamental matters. He was trapped in a development program that had monopolized the relationship between him and the people from the beginning. A Toba pastor related this incident: A missionary openly complained that the people were wearing him out by asking for material aid. The Toba said, "The missionary himself is to blame. He came here and asked us what we needed, and we simply told him. So he just stepped into the trap!"

- The cultural focus of the indigenous people contrasts with our Western materialistic culture and is a constant challenge to our own forms of understanding and applying Jesus' teachings to our own lives.

This is why we should examine our own inculturation of the gospel so that we ourselves do not become fateful and subtly treacherous obstacles in the people's spiritual pilgrimage.

Our personal testimony

As we have walked with the Chaco native peoples for more than 40 years, it has cemented into our souls the reality of a God with far greater power and love than we would have known without having experienced it among the indigenous Christians of the Argentine Chaco.

It helped us understand that every people has its own history, its own way of coping with reality, and that any new concept has to be received and reinterpreted in light of its own experience. It is impossible for people to respond authentically in any way other than their own. When we are too easily convinced that we have superior knowledge of how the Christian faith should be expressed, we rob ourselves – ourselves, mind you – of seeing the glory of God in its fullness.

6

Why We Didn't Plant a "Mennonite" Church in Argentina

How God Changed our Minds

Albert and Lois Buckwalter

This article appeared originally in *Mission Now* (Summer 1998), p. 7, as part of an issue on "A Declaration for Independents." *Mission Now* was a publication of the Mennonite Board of Missions, Elkhart, IN. A Spanish version was read at *Encuentro Interconfesional de Misioneros* (Interconfessional Missionary Gathering), Resistencia, Chaco in September 2002.

We went to the Chaco region of northern Argentina in 1950, never imagining the profound change awaiting us in our first term with MBM (Mennonite Board of Missions). We dutifully followed the traditional patterns of Mennonite mission already established: to form a church clearly identifiable as Mennonite using a traditional mission compound – church building, school, clinic, carpenter shop, store, farmland and dwellings – established nine years before our arrival.

But as we worked among the indigenous, semi-nomadic Toba tribe, which lived off the uncultivated products of their subtropical environment, we increasingly sensed that the Toba people weren't really interested in hearing us. In fact, it seemed they would not become Mennonite in even 200 years. So, how could it possibly be God's will for them?

In our deep frustration, we turned to a Christian anthropologist-linguist couple, who were invited to help us with the previously unwritten Toba language. They introduced us to scientific language analysis and, far more significantly, they opened our eyes to what was happening, a reality we had flatly rejected. The Toba people were themselves developing their own culturally appropriate response to the Christian gospel, but were hiding it from us lest we be offended and leave (a too typical missionary response). They knew rejection.

We remember how threatened we initially felt the time it was pointed out to us that the Toba were holding unauthorized meetings in their own language in one of the "Mennonite" churches. Several times a week, they were worshiping in their own fashion with their own chosen leaders. When we arrived on Sundays, they conformed to the "Mennonite way" with worship in Spanish.

It was a momentous decision for us to announce that we were no longer in charge of their churches. Initially, they assumed we were abandoning them. At that point, we promised we would continue to visit their churches and bring the word of God – a promise that soon included Bible translation. In practice this meant that, despite biting criticisms from non-indigenous Christians, we would stand by the Toba as we responded to their invitations.

With faith in God's ability to raise up a church, we watched the Toba people turn to Jesus Christ to heal them – body and soul. They were losing their faith in their native healers, the traditional taboo system and in the spirits they believed had healed them in the past.

The United Evangelical Church, which they formed, became the principal integrating factor in indigenous life in the Chaco region. They elect their own leaders in their own way. They are deeply evangelistic. Their theology is authentically their own. They have the capacity to confront problems that are very difficult to resolve, and to handle them with true wisdom from God.

Because of that, the Toba Christians drew many into their Bible-centered fellowship, where they could authentically hear and respond to God's voice. Who would dare to rob a people of their God-given privileges and responsibilities by interfering?

As we have walked with them for more than 40 years, it has cemented into our souls the reality of a God with far greater power and love than we could have known without having experienced it among the indigenous Christians of the Argentine Chaco. It helped us understand that every people has its own history, its own way of coping with reality, and that any new concept has to be received and reinterpreted in light of its own experience. It is impossible for people to respond to God authentically in any way other than their own. When we are too easily convinced of our superior knowledge of how the Christian faith should be expressed, we rob ourselves – ourselves, mind you – of seeing the glory of God in its fullness.

Albert and Lois Buckwalter

7

Important Considerations for Preaching the Gospel to the Toba Indians

Albert Buckwalter

In July 1963, at the end of a year of study at the Kennedy School of Missions in Hartford, CN, Buckwalter wrote this essay for a presentation to the Bible Society and non-Indigenous church audiences in Argentina and Uruguay.

The purpose of this essay is to describe the setting in which the Toba Indians of northern Argentina receive the gospel and interpret the will of God for themselves. Also we propose to make some points about the literature that is needed to assist the development of the Christian church among the Tobas.

Before the colonization of the Chaco

The extensive zone called the Chaco comprises the current provinces of Chaco and Formosa in Argentina and the entire region west of the city of Asuncion in Paraguay. This zone was the last to experience the permanent influx of Europeans and there are still some corners where land is being colonized that the Chaco tribes had used for their migrations.

The land that remains for the Indians continues diminishing slowly, making ever more difficult their integration into national life in a dignified manner.

The tribes that occupied the Chaco had a fairly rudimentary life. They circulated in groups of extended families, each one under the guidance of the man who was most capable of finding food and defending his family members from enemy attacks. In practice, these people lived from hunting and from gathering wild food products, such as honey, roots, fruits, etc. Cultivation of squash, melons and corn was a sporadic diversion rather than a secure method of obtaining food.

One could say that in their technological development, these tribes lived in the Stone Age, with the exception that, since they completely lacked stone, they used bones and pieces of the hardwoods that are abundant in the region. Their arrows were made of cane, their nets and bags from the fibers of the *caraguata*, their coats from the fur of tigers and deer, and their camps from branches planted in the form of domes, covered with grasses.

When they were not occupied in hunting for food or in manufacturing arms or tools for daily life, they occupied themselves in social endeavors. For the Chaco Indians, to spend hours chatting with family is a social obligation.

Periodically, several groups would gather for feasts. In these reunions, the men drank large quantities of chicha and the young people passed hours dancing and playing, while the women prepared the chicha and served as arbiters if quarrels arose among the drinkers. Daily life was hard; their motto might well have been: let us eat and drink for tomorrow we die.

The explorers observed the general poverty of the Chaco Indians and in particular, that the chief was always the poorest of them all. This poverty was logical, an integral component of the Tobas' interpersonal relationships and of their concepts of economic realities: generosity is a most important virtue among the Tobas, in reality it is obligatory. Social superiority is maintained through generosity. If the chief wanted to maintain his leadership position, he had to satisfy the desires of his people. If anyone wanted his leather jacket, for example, he gave it to him. The person who gave away the most was the person with the most prestige.

For survival it was necessary, to a certain degree, to share food and shelter. The person who did not have what he needed, simply asked for it. In those circumstances, the person who refused to share was labeled as selfish and abominable and would always be at risk of suffering retaliation.

As to their religion, the Tobas were animists. For them, there were spirits in all things and all places. In addition, mythological beings could confer blessings or punishments on people according to their behavior; the spirits of deceased human beings sometimes also stayed nearby to bother survivors. The elderly would take responsibility for placating these spirits and maintaining the tranquility and security of the family.

If anyone became ill it was necessary to call a native doctor who by means of his healing techniques would remove the object that caused the discomfort, whether an insect, snake, twig or any other alien object. Possibly the illness was the direct result of the sorcerer's work paid by an enemy to take revenge for a prior wrong.

The conquistadors and colonists arrive

When the conquistadors arrived in the sixteenth century, many of the Chaco Indians stole their horses, and mounted on horseback rode out in defense or assault. Although they became transformed into a fearsome force, difficult to conquer, in the long run their resistance meant their end. The Indian groups that became warriors no longer exist; little by little they were totally destroyed. The rest of the Indians, who largely remained on foot, awaited colonization.

Shortly after the beginning of the twentieth century, Argentine soldiers opened the way for colonists to enter the Chaco. In those years, killing an Indian was not a serious matter. The Tobas who survived that time remember clearly when the invaders would hunt them like animals. As recently as 1947, a group of soldiers with machine guns opened fire against supposed rebels in Formosa province. Many Indians submitted to government authority. But many others did not, and they remained outside the stronger influence of the dominant culture.

The situation today

The most numerous tribe in the Argentine Chaco and in many senses the most dominant, are the Tobas. The Mocoví and Pilagá Indians, together with the Tobas, form the Guaycurú linguistic family. The Wichís, also misnamed Matacos, are from another linguistic family, and live in the far western regions of the Chaco and Formosa provinces, and in the far north of Salta province. The Toba population averages between 10,000 and 20,000 inhabitants (currently they total some 80,000) who live in small colonies scattered across an area of approximately 40,000 square miles. Almost all the arable land between these small colonies is already occupied by colonists of European descent who primarily grow cotton.

In the last ten years the Argentine government has made an effort to provide opportunities to the Toba Indians to adapt themselves to the new environment, by granting them generous credits as well as technical advice for cultivating cotton on their farms. This program has been successful in only minimal cases. Many Indians have failed for one reason or another.

One of the main reasons would seem to be Toba philosophy. One elderly man expressed it this way: "In the beginning, when material goods were distributed to all the earth's inhabitants, the Tobas in their ignorance, were very stupid and rejected almost everything." The whites, this is to say all non-Indians, accepted these offers. Given this Toba explanation for the current economic situation, they would now seem to be waiting for a new distribution in which they would accept the portion that rightly belongs to them. This attitude is confirmed when one observes that a Toba will spend his last pesos to travel somewhere if he hears rumors that something will be distributed there.

In the presence of the white man, the Toba appears to feel crushed, without hope or value.

His vision of reality has been overturned. What was virtue before, has now become a vice. The white person says: you should save your money, not spend it. But Toba morality says: You shouldn't be selfish; you should share what you have. Which view is right? The result is a condition of psychological trauma. A common Toba expression is: "The Indian isn't worth anything."

Besides, the Tobas fall victim to illnesses for which they have no resistance, for example tuberculosis. Many die at an early age. Free medical attention is available in almost all parts of the Chaco, but most Tobas mistrust it. Little by little, this resistance has been giving way and a growing number of sick Indians now seeks help at medical centers.

Toba adults sometimes remember past times, when current conditions had not yet taken hold. They talk of that time with pride, saying that the Toba then was strong, healthy, and brave, and knew how to defend himself from everything. But when they leave behind those memories of a past age that perhaps has the glow of glory, they return to the sad contemporary reality with an almost totally passive attitude: they consider themselves of little worth, poor, of little social importance, lacking the strength to defend themselves, and that they can be helped only by others. In their souls they feel an emptyness that they believe must be filled with everything that the world around them offers. Therefore they have stayed prisoners of all types of vices and evil.

Whites in general despise the Tobas, due to their poverty and to customs that keep them removed from the dominant society. Other whites, with humanist and Christian sentiments, treat the Tobas as though they are children instead of adults, and consider them mentally inferior.

On the other hand, it is a fact that the standard of living of some non-indigenous neighbors is very similar to that of Tobas. In the proximity of Indian colonies some non-indigenous have married Indian women. Although the man is never able to become psychologically part of the Indian group, the children in these households generally are, especially those in homes established within the Indian colony.

The arrival of the gospel

In that crucial historical moment when the Tobas experienced almost total defeat, they were reached with the message of Jesus Christ, through the love and providence of God.

The pastors and missionaries who worked among the Toba used two methods of evangelization. The first method was to establish a colony. Already in the sixteenth century the Jesuits tried to establish themselves among the Chaco Indians. Most of these missions were totally destroyed by the Indians. Several remain today, but they have failed almost completely to plant the Christian faith in Toba life. It is highly interesting to observe that in the "Catholic" colonies, evangelical churches abound.

The method of establishing a religious colony (mission compound)was also used by the Emmanuel Mission, from England, and by the Mennonites. The purpose of the colony, besides teaching Indians the gospel, was to educate them in the ways of the white man's world, in a word, to civilize them according to the missionaries' conceptions.

With this method it was possible to work at one time with only a few families who ended up becoming economically dependent on the missionaries, but otherwise continued their own intellectual and spiritual paths. As a consequence, the relationship between Tobas and missionaries frequently was not one of harmony and understanding.

The other evangelization method began among the Tobas themselves. Some of them heard news of a preacher who healed the sick through prayer, in Resistencia, the capital of the Chaco. A few Tobas walked for an entire week to get there. One related that he barely could get there due to his illness. But what an indescribable experience for a Toba! He related that he was received in the house of the preacher, who read the Bible to him, laid his hand on his head, and prayed for him. He was healed and converted in that very moment. The preacher gave the Indians Bibles and hymnals in Spanish, taught them Bible verses and choruses, and they returned home happy.

Without delay the Tobas organized meetings to sing, testify, read the Bible if they could, and pray. Some discovered that they also could heal the sick through prayer: a movement had been born. In a short time, dozens of churches had been formed, affiliated with two opposing Pentecostal groups. Hardly an Indian colony remained that did not have a church.

The Mennonite Mission continued its established course, while the Emmanuel Mission was closed by the Argentine government in 1947. After 1950, dissatisfaction was growing because the Tobas in the Mission's colony had become increasingly frustrated. In 1954, we communicated with Dr Eugene Nida, of the American Bible Society, and through this contact we received the help of the anthropologist and linguist William Reyburn, who currently works in Africa as a translations consultant for the Society.

The advice that Reyburn gave us transformed completely our stance and as a result our work among the Tobas.

The United Evangelical Church

As a direct result of this transformation, the United Evangelical Church (UEC) was established. It was legally constituted as number 819 in the Argentine government's register of religious organizations. UEC congregations are free to establish relations with any church, pastor, or worker who is interested in cooperating with them. In reality, they maintain psychologically close links with the Mennonite missionaries. Twenty-nine churches are already affiliated and at least twenty or more are requesting affiliation from the Indian Church Convention.[1]

Until now, we three Mennonite missionary families are perhaps the only missionaries who have tried to value the Toba environment and the ideals that mold their lives. We are the only ones who have devoted ourselves exclusively to working among the Indians. Although other denominations

---

1. In 1963, the date of this writing. Currently there are many more.

work among the Tobas, their work is secondary to their churches among white people and therefore they cannot dedicate to it the attention required to satisfy the Indians.

Also, it is difficult for those workers to detach themselves from the problems that are common to their own churches, in order to identify with the distinct problems of the Indian parishioners and be of real help to them. Frequently, their advice is very useful to their own congregations but impractical for Indian congregations. Lamentably, this results in unnecessary frustrations and undesirable sentiments that impede the spiritual growth of the church.

Although not all problems have disappeared, the relationship between the Mennonite Mission and the UEC is fruitful: the churches are free but not abandoned, and receive advice but are not dominated.

In consultation with the Toba believers we have prepared a handbook that serves as a guide in the faith and practice of Toba church life. Each congregation chooses its own leaders who take charge of managing all the work of the church. In general no conflict exists between the chief of the community and the church leaders, unless he feels that his authority is weakened. In these occasions, he will assume responsibilities in the congregation that do not correspond to him, altering the tranquility and unity of the church and the community.

Preaching is mostly in the Toba language, but almost all preachers can read Spanish. Some have never attended school; others have taken two or three grades although with very irregular attendance. Naturally, reading and comprehending the Bible in Spanish is very difficult for them. Currently they receive the simplified popular version with much enthusiasm.

As to the preparation of church leaders, we have observed that it has been most beneficial for the missionary to visit each congregation personally, accompanied frequently by three or four preachers from other colonies. During the visit, as well as during the trip itself, there are many opportunities to get to know each other intimately as we study the Bible, share testimonies of the blessings of God, and seek the help of the Lord to carry out the work of the church. In practice, the trip becomes a Bible institute on wheels. Periodically we send each leader copies of Bible studies that will provide background material for his sermons.

We calculate that about half of all Tobas profess the Christian faith. Some colonies are composed of just a few families, while others have a hundred members or more, representing many families. In all the colonies, the church has come to be the principal integrating factor in the social life of the Tobas. Evangelization has followed the social lines that predominate among the Toba, that is to say, kinship lines. In some cases the church is composed of an extended family which includes the chief together with his wife and sons and their families. They are united by strong family ties as well as by language.

Most Toba men are bilingual, but when they express their intimate sentiments in Spanish they do so with great difficulty. Women and children speak Toba almost exclusively, because it is the language of the home. Children have the opportunity to attend public schools where they learn Spanish. However, at times of heavy farm work, attendance declines.

Toba believers, when they give their testimonies, thank God for giving them the desire and courage to confront their problems of daily life. They feel released from their illnesses and their vices, and they have gained renewed strength to face their tasks as responsible adults. They give themselves to evangelizing their own people and take numerous trips to visit those who are in remote colonies.

Now then, since the Mennonite missionaries are in a very strategic position to influence the development of the Christian church among the Tobas, what can we do and what must we do, particularly about Christian education? Frankly, we have searched everywhere for materials fit for the Tobas, but with fragmentary results.

Materials currently used by the Tobas

What does the Toba believer currently buy?
- A pocket New Testament or a Bible. The New Testament is preferred because it is a pocket edition.
- Several books of the Bible in the Popular Version that is used as a commentary on the Reina-Valera version.
- Hymnals. Tobas sing hymns from the "Gloria" and "Zion" hymnals. Another hymnal they use is "Hymns and Songs of the gospel." Also, they always request new choruses. They sing so much that everyone knows all the songs by heart and can identify them by number and hymnal.
- Any book or pamphlet with Bible pictures or illustrations. The most popular has been the illustrated "The Life of Christ," because it is full of pictures. Unfortunately, it is so expensive.

- Dictionaries. They want dictionaries of the Spanish language to decipher what they read. The truth is that the dictionaries confuse them more than they help them. Some preachers have become accustomed to preaching sermons based on dictionary definitions. The phrases "this means" or "this signifies" are repeated time and again. I heard a certain preacher say, with a little paper in his hand: "Glory means the apostles, the apostles mean the Holy Spirit, the Holy Spirit means the word of God," etc. People marveled at his erudition. Fortunately, this is an extreme case and most preaching is more relevant.

Dr Nida's suggestions

In 1960, Eugene Nida honored us with a week-long visit, a time during which he gave us some very valuable suggestions for Christian education in our work among the Toba believers. Below, we quote from his Interpretive Report of March 1960:

1. Publication of a monthly magazine or periodical with articles in simple Spanish as well as Toba, on:

   a. Topics of permanent or ongoing interest; for example: material for Sunday school lessons, translations of various parts of the Bible, articles on health and illness, explanations of natural phenomena such as earthquakes, eclipses, meteorites;

   b. Topics of immediate interest, for example events in the churches, plans for conventions, the start of new projects, news, etc.

      Section "a" of the magazine could be prepared in advance and section "b" could be a mimeographed insert page. Sunday school material could be published later in the form of a pamphlet for more permanent use.

2. Preparation of a series of books to provide orientation on the Old Testament. The Tobas have rejected their own mythology and history and speak of it with shame, but they do not having anything to replace it. Without doubt if they had a keen sense of history, their sense of responsibility for their current

situation would increase. In a certain sense, Jesus Christ is a cultural hero, a mythological person.

What the Tobas need desperately is a sense of the plan and purpose of God in the world, His creation, His call to His chosen people, His relation to them throughout the years, the preparation for His anointed and the coming of the Lord. The Tobas must understand that God has a purpose and a destiny for them, and therefore they have a great responsibility for the redemption of the world for God. Until now they have learned to answer the call of God, but they are not yet very convinced, nor do they know clearly for what end He has called them.

1. Translation of the following books of the Bible: Mark, Acts of the Apostles, and Romans. It is recommended that these books be translated into Toba, to give the Indians the base or the core of the truth of the New Testament. Mark is clearly the best first book for these Indian people who have so recently converted from paganism. Acts is most important to give them the history of the church. John gives a different and significant view of Jesus. Romans offers an excellent synthesis of the basic doctrines of the New Testament. For certain special problems, such as for example the tendency of the Tobas to become dependent on others, the Second Epistle to the Thessalonians would be very useful. As the teaching program develops, it will become clear what would be good to translate.

2. Preparation of materials for Sunday school. Sunday school materials should cover general areas of the content and doctrines of the Bible. It is possible that some of the materials could be written in simple Spanish, but at the beginning it would be good to introduce the essential materials in Toba, especially for children. Otherwise, people will not understand how to communicate adequately the information and knowledge received.

   There should be three categories or levels of materials:

   a. For children,

b. For young people,

c. For adults.

We have moved forward with some of the cited suggestions. Thus, we have completed a preliminary translation of the Gospel of Mark which should be reviewed before publication, when we have greater facility in the use of the Toba language. Periodically and through correspondence we have sent preachers a mimeographed sheet with a Bible study and commentary, together with a pastoral letter.

Conclusion

The following summarizes some of our important considerations as we work among the Tobas:

1. A recognition that the Toba's response to the call of God is just as valid as that of any other person. The reality is that many Toba believers have been rejected by Pentecostal brethren themselves because of their excessive shows of emotion and the ritual dances that sometimes occur in their worship services. Toba preachers affirm that it is not that easy to distinguish between sincere and false individual expressions, but they intend to patiently await the fruit, before judging precipitately.

2. A deep understanding, on the part of the missionaries, of the intellectual, economic, social, and spiritual environment in which the Tobas live. The missionary must try to adapt as much as possible to this world, to avoid irrelevancies in what is said and done. Experience has taught us that many of the things we did in the beginning, and even some of the teachings we thought were necessary doctrines, were completely incomprehensible and only caused hypocrisy and confusion.

   The message of reconciliation of God in Jesus Christ must be adapted and molded to the Toba's world of experience and translated into the words of his daily language.

27 July 1963

8

"Why Do Doqshi Always Tell Lies?"

Elmer S. Miller

Elmer S. Miller and wife, Lois (Longenecker) Miller, lived in Sáenz Peña, Chaco Province, where they served under the Mennonite Board of Missions from 1958 to 1963, during the time of the beginnings of the United Evangelical Church of the Toba. This chapter is a slightly revised version of a paper presented in Spanish at the I Congreso Internacional de Etnohistoria at the Instituto de Ciencias Antropológicas, Universidad de Buenos Aires July 17-21, 1989. It was also presented at the 13th South American Indian Conference a month later at Bennington College, Vermont.

A fundamental flaw in the literature on interethnic relationships between indigenous people and Indo-European populations who have settled, and formed nation-states, in the new world is the one-sided nature of discourse. The concept of ethnicity and inter-ethnic conflict is not an aboriginal construct, nor does it address matters of primary concern among indigenous Gran Chaco populations. This is not to suggest they have no opinion on the subject, but rather that their individual and social identity is essentially structured around kinship. While the Toba may be curious about the social life of their European intruders, they never raised the subject in our social interactions.[1] Failure to identify a genuine aboriginal opinion on inter-ethnic relationships has produced a body of literature that has not addressed well the genuine concerns of the people whose lot is universally deplored, even while their most serious preoccupations tend to be persistently neglected. Books and articles on the plight of indigenous people's loss of land and access to resources serve to document serious social problems, but they seldom generate the required action that might transform the subordinate position in which they find themselves as they continue to cling to kinship as a means of social identity.

The notion of systemic conflict and incongruity does not appear to intrigue, nor arouse genuine interest among the Gran Chaco Toba.[2] For the most part it is not the systemic character of social systems that attracts Toba attention, but rather the loss of access to land and resources over which they once had control. As the Chaco became increasingly colonized by European populations it was the loss of access to game, and confinement to increasingly smaller territorial domains, that generated suspicion and resentment toward the European intruders. After failing to defend their territory against these invaders, they became increasingly isolated in increasingly smaller territorial spaces. Loss of access to game led them to eventually work as laborers in cotton fields, as axmen in the forests to cut down trees for lumber, and in more recent years at urban odd jobs where their interaction with the white intruders is consistently in a subordinate position. A Toba once acknowledged to me that tree-cutting work created a moral dilemma for him, since trees are sacred creations. White neighbors, job bosses, the provincial governor, even the national president, are all evaluated and judged by the manner in which they interact with the environment, as well as the respect, or lack thereof, shown toward Toba individuals and families. The fundamental basis for Toba evaluation of an interpersonal relationship, their judge of character, is trustworthiness. The most essential ingredient of human interaction for the Toba is the extent to which one can rely on what another person says and

---

1. In 1988 my family and I spent eight months in the urban settlements of Sáenz Peña, Resistencia, Rosario, and Buenos Aires, where I became aware of greater inter-ethnic awareness among the younger Toba population.
2. The Toba, together with the Mataco, constitute the two major indigenous populations still found in the Chaco region of northeastern Argentina. Two smaller groups, the Mocoví and Pilagá, are closely related culturally to the Toba. The former, located in the southern portion of the region, are more articulated with Argentine society, while the latter, to the north and northwest, remain more isolated and less acculturated. For more information on the relationships between these groups, see Miller 1979, 1980b, Braunstein 1983.

does. Thus, the primary basis for evaluating interethnic relationships for the Toba is the same as that for maintaining good interpersonal relationships among themselves – the degree to which commitments are made and fulfilled. This observation held true for on my personal interactions with the Toba, from my initial encounter in 1959 until the last one in 1988. While my most extensive and intimate relationship were established during the five years Lois and I lived with them from 1959-63, subsequent visits and research in 1966, 1974, 1979, and 1988 have continued to confirm and reinforce this original perception.

The title of this essay poses a question the Toba have raised with me repeatedly over the years when the subject of inter-personal relationships between Toba and non-indigenous people, *doqshi*, was addressed. It constitutes an example of the closest they have come in my experience to generalize about their interactions with white people. This observation had faded from memory until my return to the Chaco in 1988, when I encountered the inquiry on almost every new encounter. It came as a surprise to hear it from several major Toba leaders who have been spokesmen for their people with various governing agencies in recent decades. Since the question was raised seriously at their initiative, it merits serious consideration. Why it is raised, what it means and has meant for Gran Chaco interethnic relationships over the centuries, is the subject to be explored here.

The term *doqshi* is an old Toba word for identifying non-indigenous people with roots in the initial years of colonial contact. It appears, for example, in the oldest recorded documentation of Toba vocabulary. The Toba themselves have translated the term consistently throughout the ages as "white people," or "Christians," much as North American Indians have referred to the European as "Pale Face."[3] The semantic load carried with its etymology, however, is difficult to ascertain. Clearly it is associated with the color white per se. It may also have an association with the word *ndoxotteec*, which connotes abandonment, i.e. leaving one's family and companions to move to a different location, which was how the European immigrant appeared to the Toba during the first four centuries of contact. It could also be linked, with less probability, to another Toba term *doqo*, which means lacking in luster and genuine character. Whatever the root meanings, both the referential and emotive connotations have changed significantly throughout the centuries as

---

3. *Doqshi* is the plural form of the word. The single term is *doqshil'ec* for a white male, and *doqshilashi* for a white female.

the Toba came to know the European settlers more intimately. It is possible that the term *doqshi* may be taking on more new meanings at the present time than it has at any previous period in the history of contact.

It is also important to keep in mind that Toba encounters and interactions with Europeans were highly sporadic and superficial from initial contacts in the early 1500s until the mid-twentieth century. Apart from the exceptional isolated case, sustained personal relationships between Toba (*Qom*) and Europeans (*Doqshi*) have been established only in recent decades. Even today, such relationships are the exception rather than the norm. The Toba also have a word *ndoqshishaxaic*, which refers to a person who imitates whites because he/she is ashamed to be identified as *qom*, i.e. an aborigine. As can be imagined, the term is not a compliment! The degree of stigma attached to its usage, however, depends upon the extent to which an individual fulfills or abandons personal obligations to the extended family unit. Another term of interest is *doqshagui*, which signifies a person of mixed blood; i.e., a Toba with a white parent. It would be interesting to investigate the precise understanding associated with this term at the present time. I have never heard either term used in address, only referentially when speaking about an individual outside the extended family unit.

In my doctoral dissertation entitled *Pentecostalism among the Argentine Toba*, 1967, and again in *Armonía y Disonancia*, 1979, I have argued that this extended period of superficial contact had a profound effect upon the nature of Toba relations with those who came to govern and settle the Chaco region. There is no need to repeat here arguments already established, except to note that the extended confrontational nature of Toba interaction with Spanish conquerors and explorers produced a sense of resentment toward the intruding Europeans. Furthermore, the disillusionment associated with what the Toba consider broken contracts, beginning with the Ferre Agreement of 1864 and continuing through subsequent agreements during the period of colonization, resulted in the loss of autonomy and territorial control. This produced skepticism and distrust on the part of the Toba comparable to that found characteristically among North American Indians toward governmental policies in the United States.[4] The deep-seated mistrust lingering from these memories may well underpin the accusation implicit in the title of this essay.

While there can be little doubt that deception and fraud occurred in the process of appropriating land once under the control of the Toba, it would be misleading to conceptualize mistrust as entirely one-sided. Many Chaco settlers also have come to distrust the Toba, with the assertion they are not consistently reliable employees, having learned to depend too heavily upon governmental programs for their subsistence needs rather than rely on their own demonstrable initiatives. Toba women who walk the streets looking for handouts in urban environs also give the impression of the Toba as beggars, rather than people who work for a living. The significant point here is that a great deal of mutual distrust boils down to cultural differences, to differing expectations, and to a lack of cross-cultural understanding.

The generation of Toba elders who provided leadership in dealing with *doqshi* during my stay with the Toba in the early 1960s was unanimous in the assertion that land and other natural resources had been misappropriated from them, and what they received and continue to receive in gifts and credit represented inadequate compensation. Their great admiration for President Peron was based on the Toba procurement of land security and other resources he facilitated at a critical time when land tenure appeared to be in jeopardy. Furthermore, access to land rights, and handouts from governmental agencies, were not viewed as special favors, but rather as fulfillment of a promise, as simply doing what was right – however inadequately and belatedly! Subsequent provisions, such as seeds, equipment, and credit made available through the Direccion del Aborigen (the Office of Indian Affairs) were generally viewed in the same light. Thus, what administrators considered governmental generosity, the Toba tended to view as inadequate compensation for the loss of land, and failure on the part of the European to teach them how to manage the new economy. A related problem that generated considerable consternation was the fact that those who failed to pay their debts to the Colonial Administration continued to

---

4. Governor Ferre made an agreement with the Toba in which both Toba and Vilela guides led a group of governmental personnel on a trek through the heart of the southern Chaco region from April 29 through May 24 of 1864. Most of the place names associated with the stopovers, currently the names of towns in the southern Chaco, are of Toba origin. The *doqshi* residents who have settled the region are unaware of the Toba etymology and may be surprised to learn of it.

receive practically the same amount of credit the subsequent year as those who had paid back their loan. This gave the impression the families who had faithfully fulfilled their obligation had been stupid rather than responsible.

The new generation of Toba has not lived through a similar period of land loss and uncertainty. Consequently, while they appear to have inherited some of the suspicion and apprehension toward dealings with *doqshi* from ancestors, they are better informed about white traditions and have a clearer understanding of the multiple forces at work which shape their mutual relationship and eventual destiny. Furthermore, the term *doqshi* itself has taken on greater diversity as this generation establishes closer ties with white neighbors in the city as well as in the country. The traditional distinction between *gringo* and *crioillo*, formerly more class-like in nature, owing to the position of Toba laborers in cotton fields (*gringo*-boss; *criollo*-fellow worker), has come to take on a different content as younger Toba men develop agricultural skills and compete with *gringo* neighbors for labor and markets. In the city, Toba interactions with a variety of rural migrants, as well as with more permanent residents, also have given the term broader meaning.

The ethnic identity issues affirmed above persist despite changing relations with doqshi at the present time. Part of the difficulty in mutual understanding is a presumption on the part of the dominant society that effective communication is taking place when, in fact, it is not. What *los blancos* sometimes express as intentions or desires tend to be interpreted by the Toba as commitments. When such intentions/commitments fail to become realized, white folk tend to be inclined to accept the failure as fate, or the system at work, thus considering the matter an annoyance rather than a moral outrage. The Toba, however, particularly those raised in rural traditional families, perceive such results as failed promises, leaving them with a sense of frustration and futility. It is an essential component of the same cultural processes of making and fulfilling commitments documented in the opening paragraphs. Several examples from personal experience should serve to clarify this affirmation.

Land constitutes the number one priority on any Toba want list. The desire for land supersedes any other desire capable of generating envy toward white neighbors. Yet, access to land continues to constitute an enigma for the Toba. How it is allocated, both in the country and in the city, appears problematic and inconsistent. With the establishment of the Instituto del Aborigen Chaqueño (IDACH) in the Chaco province in October of 1988, an organization designed to place decision-making and planning in the hands of the Toba and Mocoví themselves, expectations were raised sky high with regard to what might be accomplished to restore land and other resources to the indigenous populations. The institute was established to replace the Office of Indian Affairs. Its officers were chosen by ballot, two each from the Toba, Mataco, and Mocoví, with the President named by the Executive office of the provincial government at the recommendation of the various individual communities. Six replacements were also elected. In addition, a white Executive Counsel was named to work with the elected body of Aborigenes. While the stated intention was to hand over all decision-making and financial operations to the elected members, all indications suggest that the aborigenes merely serve as fronts for the same white administrators who functioned previously. Understandably, it will take time for the new officers to learn how to manage their affairs, but there is a serious question whether such learning is effectively taking place.

At one point a rumor proclaimed that land would be bought near Colonia Aborigen in the Chaco province for the purpose of facilitating the return of families who had migrated to Rosario and Buenos Aires. When I inquired into this rumor in the administrative office of the provincial government in 1988, I was informed such an idea had been initially proposed, but serious problems arose that precluded the possibility of successfully completing such a transaction. Meanwhile several family heads in Rosario and Buenos Aires, who had been there for considerable time, made tentative plans to return to the Chaco based on the promise of land to be provided. When I suggested caution to a related family member in Resistencia in order to avoid future disillusionment, he stated this would likely be one more false hope dangled before indigenous people with no intention of fulfillment. My attempt to distinguish between genuine intention and potential unforeseen problems proved unconvincing to the disillusioned relative.

What might constitute a reasonable resolution to the dilemma delineated here? How might the more blatant misperceptions on both sides be remedied? Here are a few suggestions. Invite Toba individuals to sessions such as this one in Buenos Aires in 1988. Listen to what they have to say. Ask what agenda items they would like to see addressed before the final agenda is decided. What do they see as the major themes and topics to be addressed? This will not be easily done, but we **must** try. Perhaps our major problem is the paternalistic notion that we know best what needs to be done to change the unequal status. We should lose the notion that we know what projects are needed, and that our offer of serious input is magnanimous. We do **not** necessarily know what the best policies are for the Toba. They may come up with an idea that would blow us away! It is worth the attempt, certainly. The formation of IDACH is an excellent example of what is being suggested here. La Iglesia Evangelica Unida is another one, where the entire leadership and planning is done by the Toba themselves. It is no coincidence that the current aboriginal leadership in the Chaco and Formosa provinces has come through the ranks of church leadership. The new president of IDACH was the President of Iglesia Evangelica Unida for many years.

Certainly what is being proposed here is more easily said than done. Last year while visiting in the Castelli region I was invited to spend a day in dialogue with Toba and *doqshi* at the Rural Educational Center of El Colchon. The project, sponsored by Junta Unida de Misiones, was dedicated to dialogue between Toba and *doqshi* on an agenda proposed jointly. Teachers, agricultural advisors, mission representatives all sat with Toba leaders and students to learn new skills and dialogue about creative ways to integrate Toba traditions into the contemporary world as we find it. For me the most difficult part was patiently listening to the topics of concern among the Toba participants, and not rushing to another topic until everyone was satisfied that the original one had been fully discussed.

A further recommendation would be to exhibit more caution in making what appear to be commitments until we are in a position to carry them out. A classic example involves cameras. The Toba generally prefer not to be photographed, but when they are, it is absolutely essential that a copy be given to them when available. Do not assume they will forget – they will not! Better to pass up an opportunity to record an exotic moment than to make a promise you cannot keep.

Above all, the main conclusion to be drawn here is that *doqshi* must make far greater effort to understand the cultural differences that divide us. Whites tend to be the ones making plans and developing programs intended to serve the Toba. Thus, it behooves us to make the greater attempt to bridge the cultural gap, rather than vice versa. We should recognize that Toba readings of our intentions may not be what we may imagine, and that their sensitivities can profitably be read as a mirror of our own actions. When we acquire the patience and the courage to acknowledge this, the insight we gain into our own comprehension and pronouncements may prove surprisingly rewarding.

9

Perspectives on Accompaniment Style Mission: Responding to Queries

Keith Kingsley

Kingsley ministered among the Toba Qom from 1997 to 2011. Midway through his tenure he was asked by the Mennonite Mission Network, his sending mission, to respond to a series of questions about the missional understanding and way of working of the Mennonite Team in the Argentine Chaco.

What, to you, is mission?

Mission in the Christian context is the work of God, through Christ, reconciling the world to God's self (2 Cor. 5:19). This work of God seeks to restore the world to its wholeness: the harmonious interrelatedness of its grand diversity, and its acknowledgement of God as its loving creator and parent. In creating the universe, God manifested God's own blessed diversity and community through the created order, one evidence of which is the wondrous variety among the "families, languages, lands, and nations" of the earth (Gen. 10:31-32). In some manner and measure, God is present to and reveals God's self in every people, through their particular history and culture. There are no peoples unreached or untouched by the God of all creation. (Rom. 1:19-20; Acts 17:24-28)

God's mission seeks the redemption of all peoples, which means the preservation and healing of their distinctive cultures, but not their homogenization. It depends, in part, on the presence of God's people and their willingness to be faithful "ambassadors" of God's reign in every culture. This people delights in and witnesses to every hint of God's presence, whether explicitly evident in Christian worship and discipleship, or implicitly manifest, anywhere, in expressions of compassion, wisdom, beauty, justice, and integrity.

The church of Jesus is the movement among peoples of the earth who are

- willingly being reconciled to God through the death and resurrection of Jesus;
- being liberated from powers of death, division, addiction, and domination; and
- formed to live and celebrate the hope of all creation set free from its bondage to decay.

Their mission belongs to God and the church belongs to Jesus as his "body"; neither belongs to us (1 Cor. 15:28, Col. 1:20, Rev. 5:9, 7:9).

The authenticity of God's mission in human practice depends on the willingness of its messengers and witnesses to live as "exiles" in the empires of the day. This implies a commitment

- to live in society without being in charge;
- to nurture community that is alternative and voluntary, marginal but inclusive, noncoercive but resilient, honoring the authority of the Word of God communally discerned;
- to be oriented toward the local, the weak, and the peripheral;
- to work in hope despite failure and suffering.

With whom do you work?

The "people with whom we walk" are three ethnic groups whose languages are related: Toba, Pilagá, and Mocoví. Of these peoples a contemporary author has written with good reason: "There no longer exists the land, nor economic relations, nor footprints through the forest, nor rivers abundant with fish, nor tattoos that reveal the tribal lineage, nothing . . . The world that existed before the arrival of the white man has been destroyed. All has been destroyed."[1]

---

1. Carlos A. Duarte, "Pentecostalismo y Cultura Aborigen," *Cuadernos No. 5.* Centro de Estudio Cristianos, Buenos Aires, Argentina, (1990), p. 26.

After centuries of explicit conquest – including ravaging diseases brought by the conquerors – followed by decades of cultural disdain by the surrounding society, sometimes subtle, sometimes not, many indigenous peoples in northern Argentina tended toward attitudes of low ethnic esteem, victimization, dependency, and/or belligerence toward white society. These factors helped to prompt the eager acceptance of the Christian gospel by these peoples in the 30's, 40's, and 50's. This happened largely through grass-roots movements that found nurture in several traditional, evangelical missionary efforts (one of which was Mennonite), but even more in pentecostal preaching-healing campaigns among the surrounding non-indigenous population. As a result of this history, our accompaniment is among people who now largely identify themselves as believers in Jesus.

Why do you do what you do?

The Mennonite team is present among indigenous peoples not to solve problems or promote development, but rather to encourage and witness to the vindicating, liberating, reconciling intentions and work of God. We believe this work of God can be undermined or prolonged not only by ill-intentioned, but also well-intentioned, attitudes and actions of others. Actions motivated by the outlook that indigenous peoples don't have the necessary capacities or resources to sustain themselves or to adjust to today's world tend to subvert God's work of building up these peoples and cultures.

In our accompaniment style of mission among indigenous peoples, we begin as *guests* and *learners*, and become, when invited, *accompaniers, interlocutors, witnesses,* and *brothers and sisters.* We work this way because it respects the prior presence of God among the people with whom we walk. It recognizes that elements of God's truth were here long before we came, and that this wisdom is for our liberation and wholeness as much as our "truth" is for their restoration. It is a way that contributes to the renewal of dignity and self-esteem that will increasingly liberate a victimized people to contribute the peculiar gifts that God has given to them, as a culture and as individuals.

For our accompaniment to be respectful of the prior presence and work of God among the Mocoví, Pilagá, and Toba, for it to value the wisdom that God has given these groups, for it to hope for the restoration of ethnic dignity and self-respect, we follow these guidelines:

- Building relationships with indigenous persons, churches and communities, without establishing churches of our denomination.

- Affirming the use of indigenous languages, and making an effort to learn the language.
- Respecting group, family and individual capacities to provide for basic living needs (food, clothing, shelter), and so responding to requests for material assistance only when the need is unusual or urgent.
- Refusing roles of leadership in indigenous contexts, but rather affirming indigenous leadership and initiative in all those settings which are rightfully theirs.
- Participating in contexts of dialogue and mutual exchange in indigenous settings, avoiding the creation of dependency or false expectations (e.g. of employment or role).
- Valuing indigenous oral culture (wisdom, histories, legends, myths) that relates to recent history and that reaches behind the Christianized experience of recent history.

"Guests" and "witnesses": those are our preferred ways of describing our presence among the Toba people. As **guests**, we are respectful of and dependent on our hosts, eating the food they serve us, taking our cues from them. As **witnesses**, we testify when invited about what we have seen and heard and touched of the Word that is life, and receive with gratitude the testimonies of our hosts, to share with others.

Why is this approach successful?

It's hard to know when a finding of "success" could reasonably be made; maybe in 50 to 100 years? In fact, one might propose that the evidence of the "success" of our style would be that no one would identify either us or our style as the reason for their transformation. Success would rather be measured by the discipleship that happens largely by and among indigenous people, churches, and efforts, without adverting to accompaniers who might have encouraged such indigenization. We believe this is, in fact, largely the reality. There certainly are indigenous persons who, over the years, have deeply appreciated the friendship, the companionship, the spirituality of various Mennonite workers, and who have been influenced by them. As with all personal relationships, the influence has probably been more a factor of particular qualities and gifts than of a peculiar method of ministry.

How have folks been transformed because of your way of working?

A few testimonials from indigenous believers:

"You folks [of the Mennonite Team] can enter the door of any (Indian) church without any problem, because you don't offer anything. You don't bring things that may cause us to fight (i.e. create competition)." – Dionisio Moreno, Toba pastor

"We don't want you to come and teach us the Bible. We want you to come so that we can read the Bible together." – Hugo Díaz, Toba zonal pastor

"You don't bring clothes (used clothing to distribute). You bring the Word of God, and nothing more." – Luis Mendoza, Toba pastor

"Missionaries ought to come to stay. I'm not in agreement with the 'trans-cultural experience' model (i.e. short-term visits). It doesn't matter much to us what you do; what matters is that you stay." – Orlando Charole, Toba civic leader

Keith Kingsley, July 2011

10

The Bible Circle

Community Bible Study in the Indigenous Setting

Willis Horst and Frank Paul

How the Bible Circle was born

Bible teaching had always been one of the primary ministries of Mennonite missionaries in the Argentine Chaco. However, even though they used a variety of methods and formats, during the 1970s and 80s they sensed they had not yet discovered the most suitable method. Something didn't quite fit!

The missionaries became frustrated with the scholastic educational model: the professor up front (the missionary in this case), and the students seated in rows taking notes. They searched for methods more appropriate for oral cultures. The quest was for a method of studying the Bible that better fit the context, a method that is:

- community centered. Faith issues are not a private affair.
- participative. In oral cultures learning takes place by doing.
- inclusive. Open to all, including non-readers, women, and the elderly.
- transferable. Easily imitated by persons with little or no formal education, who had scarce access to formal teaching materials.

In addition, the content needed to be:
- simple, but not simplistic.
- relevant for daily life.
- culturally adapted, formulated in dialogue with the indigenous participants themselves.

During a personal retreat while reflecting on the profound centrality of the Circle in indigenous cultures, Willis was inspired to create the Bible Circle format. While not meeting the expectations of those who wanted to "know more about the Bible" in the style of a Bible Institute or of a more formal systematized study program, the Bible Circle responded to the grassroots hunger for spiritual guidance. For many indigenous participants the Bible Circle became a means of encountering Jesus as a transforming power.

The goal of the Bible Circle

Rather than the transmission of intellectual knowledge about the Bible, the purpose of the Bible Circle is to create a context for a spiritual experience of being in the presence of Jesus. In the circle we seek a communal encounter with God, a consciousness of the presence of the Spirit, an awakening of the desire to be together in our diversity, to join in a common commitment to follow the way of Jesus. A focus on the communitarian nature of discerning God's message strengthens group solidarity and encourages the search for unity in diversity. In a circle, participants tell their experiences from daily life and hear selected Bible texts relating to their stories. This personal participation becomes transforming.

The Bible Circle embodies several important aspects that directly influence biblical interpretation:

- The **symbolic importance of the circle** in indigenous culture and spirituality throughout the world can hardly be overestimated. The circle represents equality, unity, fullness, inclusion, sharing, and much more. Spatially, the circle symbolizes the four directions, the four winds of the Spirit of the Creator, as well as community life. Functionally, the circle serves as the organizing principle of the corporate life of the hunting-gathering communities in their search for life in times of crisis or celebration. To be in the circle means to feel "at home."

- The **communal character** of decision making is part of the sociological reality of life in small clan-based, face-to-face societies. Individuals change lifestyles and thought patterns on the basis of group pressure. This aspect remains strong in current Toba Qom culture.

- In **oral cultures**, discernment of the sacred is not an intellectual exercise. The sacred is perceived through other senses – visual, tactile, audio – as well as dreams, visions, and the spoken word. A person becomes convinced of the reality of a spiritual power because of seeing the miracle happen, not through intellectual argument. The written word seems foreign to the reality of the Word living among the people (as the *logos* expressed in John 1:1).

- Toba Qom worldview considers **everything to be interconnected**. It is important to keep Bible study closely joined to life. The daily life situation and the Word of God have the same source; both are rooted in the life of the Creator. Thus, the Word of God in Scripture is discerned by approaching from the reality of experience – from life to the Word and back to life, a method of reading the Bible commonly known throughout Latin America as the "hermeneutical circle."

What the Bible Circle is not

- a school classroom where one person (teacher) transmits knowledge to the rest.
- an exercise aimed at increasing or verifying knowledge about the Bible.
- a conversation designed to achieve uniformity in interpretation of a Bible text.

Additional advantages of the Bible Circle

- It strengthens the self-esteem of those who too often have become accustomed to remain quiet and submissively listen to the "expert." It is informal, which encourages participation.
- Participation does not require previous Bible knowledge.
- It calls attention to the community process and away from using the Bible as a sacred object with "magical" power.

- It gives practice in reading the indigenous languages as well as Spanish.
- Almost any person with a sincere desire and love for the Word of God can coordinate the Bible Circle. The coordinator does not need to be a theologian or professor, although it is very helpful if he/she has skills in group dynamics.

Description of the Bible Circle process

A. Preparation

The arrangement of the physical space communicates symbolically. Chairs, benches, or stools are arranged in a circle. The face-to-face position makes communication more natural. All are seated to show equality in the presence of the Word: women and men, elderly and young, oral and literate, etc. An open Bible in one of the local languages is placed on a small table, stool, or box in the middle of the circle. The Bible is an open book; that is, it "wants" to share a message we can understand, in contrast to an object: a closed, foreign, unintelligible, magical power object. Everyone is equally close to the Bible to show that God is no more distant from one than from the rest. We all have the same access to the Spirit who is our teacher and speaks to us through the Word in the language we understand best. The Spirit also speaks to us through others in the circle.

B. Materials

There are no requirements as to what the participants bring to the meeting. If they want to take notes, sheets of paper and pencils may be provided. If they are readers they are encouraged to bring Bibles or notebooks. Those who are totally oral are encouraged to participate with their own gifts. The coordinator may want to use a chalkboard (or markers and paper on the wall or floor) for a graphic representation, to make a special emphasis, to note Bible references used, or to draw attention to someone's input. Writing should also be as much as possible in the language of the group.

The coordinator selects portions of the Bible ahead of time, usually based on a theme chosen by the inviting group. When possible, the coordinator prepares photocopies of the main text. This facilitates the reading process and gives participants a copy to take home to share with family.

C. Procedure

1. The local pastor (or the person responsible for scheduling the Bible Circle) guides the opening moments with prayer and songs.

2. The coordinator then begins the group discussion process.

a. The coordinator seeks to maintain an **atmosphere of prayer** throughout the meeting anticipating prayers at any moment, whenever someone senses the need. Thus, participants experience a consciousness of the presence of the Spirit of God.

b. The coordinator makes a clear and specific **invitation for all to speak.** Those accustomed to the classroom format and those who have been programmed to feel inferior need strong encouragement to participate. The gathering must be a safe place. Because of the uniqueness of each person in the eyes of God, we each know something which we alone have received – an experience, a learning, a suffering, a story, a dream. That "something" which we alone "know" is to be valued as a gift from the Spirit to the group. When shared with the group, it takes on a communal nature. If not shared, no one will "hear" or learn about it and the group will miss the opportunity to experience that part of the abundance of diversity which is God's gift to the human community. Therefore, each contribution blesses those assembled; each input becomes sacred, a "revelation" of the Spirit.

c. The coordinator **introduces the Bible Circle** with a simple oral explanation, possibly accompanied by distribution of a written description for those who read. If the experience is new to the group, a longer time may be needed for clarification. Aspects deserving special attention are:

- the symbolic importance of the circle,

- the value of hearing from each participant, and

- the emphasis on hearing the Spirit of God through the community.

3. Hearing the Bible texts.

The Bible texts chosen for study are normally read verse by verse in the circle. Additional texts are suggested by participants as the discussion progresses and are included. All those who can and desire to read have opportunity.

Those who are just learning are encouraged to practice their reading skills; the more fluent can help the learners. The same verses are read several times and in as many versions as are present. The repetition helps those who are totally oral hear and learn the text well. The coordinator has at hand a copy in the simplest version available and includes it for comparison and better comprehension.

Reading the text in the indigenous languages demonstrates their value and increases comprehension. In this way the meaning of the text penetrates the heart. Therefore, the text should be read in as many languages as are represented by the participants.

The coordinator can use inductive Bible study techniques to determine textual meanings. However, (s)he must be ready to allow for other ways of getting at the significance of the text – memory, story, analogy, cross referencing, even free association – without rejecting any person's honest contribution. The completely oral and unschooled contributor sometimes gives the most surprising and relevant interpretation of meaning. Participants are also encouraged to freely suggest alternative or parallel texts on the subject under consideration.

4. The discussion time
The coordinator's planning includes preparation of several suggestions or questions to invite sharing and reflection on the texts chosen. These should meet the following criteria:
- be expressed in the local language,
- not answerable with a yes or no,
- allow for a variety of responses: there is not one "correct" answer,
- be related to life situations.

The discussion time is divided roughly into the following:

a. The period of time preceding the hearing of the texts, is a space for participants to tell a personal story or testimony; this encourages sharing since it is something familiar. This time might also serve for identifying aspects of the local cultural context which may either coincide or contrast with the biblical wisdom or teaching to be identified in the texts that have been chosen for reading. For example, for a conversation around the theme of true blessedness in Matthew 5:1-12, one might ask, "According to what we hear on radio and TV, what do people today need to have or do in order to find true happiness?"

b. The reading and hearing the Bible texts as described in C.3. above.

c. The next suggestion/question for discussion follows the repeated readings. It solicits each participant's reflection on the biblical text. Responses should focus on relating the Bible texts to experiences from their own lives and those of the community. For example, on the text about peacemakers in Matthew 5:9 one might ask, "Who are the peacemakers we know today and what have they done to be considered such?"

d. The final suggestion/question should point toward practical application. For example, "What does this text encourage me to do or practice in my life this week?

D. Group dynamics

The coordinator will need all the skills of group dynamics at his or her disposal.

1. Before any discussion, remind the participants of the rules of the circle: to give everyone in the circle a chance to share. speak and then to wait for others before they speak again. Encourage those who are shy or hesitant to express their thoughts. Suggest that no one speak twice until all have spoken once. A "talking stick" may be a helpful tool. This object can be passed to one person at a time, who then has freedom to speak while all listen.

2. No one should be interrupted while talking, unless of course, they are obviously abusing the privilege to speak. Neither should anyone's contribution be corrected. Rather, if necessary, the comments can be balanced out with additional or alternative points of view. Indigenous logic is not dualistic by nature, so one does not have to be proven wrong for another to be right.

3. Oral cultures may not be accustomed to the question and answer method of learning. A more effective technique to stimulate sharing is often the suggestion: "Tell us about a time when . . ." Allow sufficient time for a response following a question/suggestion. Some participants will need more time (even as much as 5 or 10 minutes of waiting in silence!) to think, formulate their responses, and take the courage to share in the circle. The coordinator should never bombard the group with additional questions or rephrasing, especially while they are preparing their responses.

E. Written memory

A final function of the coordinator is to prepare, from his or her notes, a summary of the most significant teachings and contributions shared during the Circle (which may include those noted on the chalkboard, paper or notebook). The coordinator sends this summary to the participants as a way of valuing their involvement. It also serves as a recorded history of the event which they can share.

11

The Mystique of the Earth

Mocoví Movement (Movimiento Moqoit), Chaco

Juan Carlos Martínez

The following chapter is translated from *La Educación en nuestras manos*, No 77, December, 2006. Juan Carlos Martínez is a Mocoví community organizer, educator, religious and political leader. He heads a Mocoví organization in the struggle for indigenous land rights.

We, the Mocoví people, number 10,000. We are survivors of the conquest of the Americas. Many of us, myself included, don't have a single hectare of land, so we've had to rent nearby fields just to have a piece of land to live on. Our struggle for the land is very strong; it has taken us to the deepest level of cultural pain that remains in our peoples' collective memory.

Our white brothers often do not seem to understand the spiritual nature of our relationship to the earth. Our way of connecting with the earth has to do with the spiritual, with feeling, with the freedom to be able to live in a "place." When we speak of "place," we refer to the space in which we move and develop, where we have a much more direct contact with creation, a greater sense of life, where life expresses itself – life that we experience among us. Without a place, without land enough to really live, we feel like we are drowning, we are suffocating.

Oftentimes we Mocovís, when we encounter an indigenous brother from the south or whatever place in the country, we sense that we are struggling for the same cause. In that same moment, without communicating, and without personal conversation, we feel drawn together in this effort. This may be new for the white brother. Among us indigenous, there is a spiritual communication, a feeling, that *this* year *this* issue will be our struggle; another year it may be another. Without directly speaking together, without meeting or knowing each other, we understand. This is a part of the worldview we share.

To illustrate how place affects our experience and development, we feel lost and disoriented when we are in a space that has been "squared off," where reality is rigidly structured. An example of this is the measuring of land into hectares, when for us land is a spatial reality without boundaries, a natural space, a place where we sense intimacy with the universe in which we are journeying, a place we circulate in freely.

We know that everything revolves around the sun although our grandparents say that not only the earth revolves, but the sun revolves as well. And not only the sun, but also the stars. And really, in some way, we all revolve together in space. And that movement is circular, we might say, like a spiral.

There is a traditional story from our grandparents that speaks of the creation of humans and of the tree that reaches to the sky. That tree which reaches to the sky is like a whirlwind; it is hollow, a cavity which begins within the earth and moves outward, toward other planets. So then, we might say, that's how we human beings came to be on the earth.

Possibly, many would think that the story has nothing to do with this matter of the earth, but in our culture it certainly does; it is deeply related. Through that tree people came down, persons just like any of the indigenous peoples, but they liked the earth so much that they stayed in order to possess it. Because of their desire to become owners of the earth, the tree was chopped down, and now that tree is fallen.

Since I am one who does not believe everything I hear, I go to my grandfather and ask him, "What does this have to do with what science teaches us?", because it seems unrelated.

He tells me, "Science has not yet determined what we believe."

So I ask him another question, "Does that tree grow upward or downward?"

"No," he says, "That tree doesn't grow either upward or downward. That tree is growing towards us in this present time." Because in our way of thinking there is no up or down, no big nor little; it is simply a necessary space.

So he says to me, "What is not yet known is what kind of beings will arrive by that same tree, when that tree reaches the earth."

This may be a bit complicated, but our worldview believes that there is a moment when the Mocovís, with deep feeling, perceive that in this year the struggle will be for the land. This is the year when the Mocoví people join together with their Wichí kindred in the Chaco to say, "We are being strangled by so much lying, by so much oppression, by so much lack of human respect."

And there is another message which many of us have learned from our elders. In addition to asking for land for ourselves – that it be returned to us – we are asking our white brothers and sisters – even those who privatize the land and have a lot of it – to take care of the land. I don't know how, but my grandparents are aware of something: that because of the mistreatment of the earth, we are all reduced. Therefore, we ask those who have much land that they care for the earth, because they do not really know her. Today many come to possess the land, yet they do not know the secret of the earth, and the power she holds.

Our fight for the land in the Chaco is unwavering. Years ago we did not have the courage to undertake this kind of struggle. However, we finally realized that if we indigenous people did not get out there and take up the fight ourselves, no one else would do it for us. It's a struggle of many years. It will only end when the majority of the white [non-indigenous] brothers and sisters that run the Government understand the significance of the land for us. It cannot have a monetary value. The land is worth more than life itself.

12

Holistic Mission – Toba Qom Style

Willis Horst

In 2007, writes Horst, a growing youth movement among Toba Qom churches became the vehicle of holistic ministry: healing, re-education, and witness to the surrounding urban society. His long-time friend, Qom Pastor Luis Mendoza, offers a perspective, both poignant and profound, on indigenous experience and the apprehension of God's power.

We from lands other than the Chaco, who have been formed spiritually in differing "Christian" environments, sometimes find it a huge stretch to understand certain elements of Toba Qom church practices. They seem not to fit with our understanding of Christian ethical standards. I refer to such practices as infant baptism, common law marriage, praise dancing and healing techniques, among others. However, I am challenged by some expressions of faith and practice in the Toba Qom church that seem to grow directly out of their traditional spirituality and are confirmed or enhanced by their turning to Jesus.

We have long observed the strong values of hospitality and sharing in Toba Qom culture. The Creator has led them to develop a way of life which does not depend on material possessions for a sense of wellbeing. Thus a spirit of generosity is nurtured naturally. This cultural norm grows out of God's revelation at a deep level – a whole worldview – which shapes Toba Qom understanding of creation and human relationship to her, as well as

God's role in it all. If the Creator's Spirit is present in all of creation, then mission is by nature holistic – no dimension of life is excluded.

I share the following rather long story to illustrate how holistic mission is happening recently in a local indigenous community.

The Toba Qom settlement on the outskirts of Formosa City started over 30 years ago. Earlier identified by its geographical designation as Rural Lot 68, it is now known as Nam Qom, taking its name from the tribal name of the Toba Qom people. The few original families who migrated from the countryside to find work and school opportunities have grown to a semi-urbanized neighborhood of over 5,000. The presence of a few families of other ethnic groups complicates the picture since they traditionally did not live in proximity. With the increase in growth and urbanization have come the common maladies of dislocated rural populations: disoriented adolescents, disillusioned parents, abject poverty, delinquency, alcoholism, disease, drugs and violence. The resulting mistrust leads to an overwhelmingly dysfunctional conglomeration of families, who often demonstrate a high level of frustration, resignation, and hopelessness. A whole range of community services provided by the sometimes-benevolent provincial government, struggles to alleviate these conditions.

In the midst of this seeming chaos, however, the gospel is alive. Presently seven congregations of believers in Jesus struggle to make the gospel a viable option for life. These congregations, some of which have been present since the beginning of the settlement, function with differing degrees of effectiveness. Toba Qom leaders have learned a version of the Christian gospel that is expressed in Pentecostal language, oriented towards securing a happy afterlife, while enduring untold suffering in the present life. Church life is focused on praise and worship, rather than on intellectual content and growth. All seek in one way or another to apply the gospel message of love and forgiveness in the changing Toba Qom context. Most see the only answer to alcohol abuse in a radical conversion to Jesus. Preaching, however, brings few results. How could the gospel bring about real change in this community?

In our role as visitors, encouragers, and sometimes-Bible-teachers, we from outside often discuss possibilities with Toba Qom pastors about what can be done. As western-oriented believers, we are inclined to consider it our task to "change the course of human history." We look for ways to intervene. Our analytical minds isolate factors which seem "manageable." But recent developments in Barrio Nam Qom, under the guidance of the Spirit of God, are pointing a new way toward holistic mission, Toba Qom style. Truly God moves in mysterious ways to bring about wonders.

Persons shaped within an indigenous spirituality often feel a need to dance their emotions. At a deep level, this is a form of prayer, built on an innate impulse to express truth in physical, concrete manners. An elderly believer recently confided to me that when he began dancing his joy during a thanksgiving prayer in church for gifts received, the visiting non-indigenous pastor obliged him to stop. With tears in his eyes, and circular gestures to his chest area, he lamented to me, "I hurt all through here."

In the last perhaps five years a new dance movement among the youth has emerged throughout the Toba Qom church. This is a more organized, controlled and deliberate movement than the traditional ecstasy-oriented, spontaneous dancing. Small groups of up to ten or so, usually girls, organize dance ensembles. They choose a leader, a name (taken from the Bible), a color (for their dance outfits), and rehearse carefully coordinated choreographies. During worship, the praise leader (male or female) calls on different groups to lead the dancing, each ensemble with its own steps and movements, or invites another dancer to lead everyone in a group dance. Music ensembles consist of youth (more often male than female) playing a variety of instruments. They are also called upon by turn to present prepared "special" musical numbers.

As this new movement began several years ago, criticism common to new trends in worship soon arose: "not appropriate," a "temptation," or even "of evil spirits," since it provided space for various kinds of new and strange behavior, albeit within the worship context. It also reduced the time given to preaching. However, it attracted the youth in large numbers. The churches that permitted or encouraged the movement began to fill with enthusiastic young persons. In addition, those who became part of the dance movement came into the church and began to overcome their addictions.

The question the pastors now face is not whether to allow worship dancing, but how to guide these youth in transforming their lives. A common complaint of those in opposition is that the dancers get tired and do not stay for the preaching which usually follows the worship time of music and dancing. How to include teaching and discipling for these enthusiastic youth?

A local pastor, Luis Mendoza, has followed the Spirit's leading in a creative approach to holistic mission. Instead of discouraging the dancers, he welcomes them. He even gives out credentials signed by the United Evangelical Church president, that recognize each dance group or music ensemble as being authorized by the church! This brought an influx of youth into his church. A large group of young men and boys found such peace and happiness in the church activities that they began to stay all night at the church singing and sharing. The insecurity on the streets and in their homes was such that they preferred living in the church building! Luis responded with typical Toba Qom-style hospitality. Let them stay in the church, work out rules for acceptable behavior, and at the same time disciple them. He considered, "They are better off in the church, dancing and singing, than on the streets drinking and carousing. The community is better off as well." What Luis didn't count on was the demands this new commitment would mean for the church!

Luis and a few of the church elders spend time with the young men. They organize the boys to clean up the church yard, paint, sweep, fetch firewood, and do their own cooking – although Luis and his wife, Delfina, provide most of the staples. "We want them to learn how to live, how to follow Jesus," Luis explained. Presently there is a group of about 20 living in the church while several more live in Luis and Delfina's home, along with others of the pastor's own extended family. Eight more have moved into the home of one of the congregation's teachers. On Saturdays, or whenever one of the church elders is available, he or she leads the youth groups in Bible studies for new believers. Nightly church services are open to all and provide for testimonies and other ways of demonstrating Christian commitment. The dancing is a wholesome activity which burns up a lot of youthful energy under the guidance of trusted adults.

This is Toba Qom therapy at its best! Traditional Toba Qom values are enhanced through coming to know Jesus – hospitality, sharing, group identity and support, dancing, singing, praying and serving. We learn to follow Jesus by doing it together. Luis spells out his understanding of holistic mission by telling stories of what is happening. "Living together helps them not to fall back into drinking. Filling their minds with Bible texts strengthens them against temptation. Learning to pray keeps them in touch with the power of the Spirit of God."

This movement is a new step in the dance of sacred history of the Toba Qom people. Part of the challenge is to guide the movement from becoming a show, of turning the activity into a sample of indigenous folklore. The provincial government tries to do just that, pressuring Luis into bringing his group into the city on stage. The following incident demonstrates the seriousness and sacredness with which this movement is embraced.

April 19 is a continent-wide Day of the American Indigenous People, declared as such in Mexico in 1945. Each year the government of Formosa Province organizes special activities, using the occasion to make obvious the multi-ethnic diversity of Formosa culture, and to proclaim their benevolence toward the Indigenous peoples. This year the special celebration was scheduled at a time and place designed to detract from an anti-government demonstration sponsored by the teachers' unions. Pastor Luis, who has a secular government job, was invited (obligated) to bring his church group in to the city to "perform." At first he refused, but later accepted the invitation with the clarification that his group would only conduct a regular church service – "nothing outside of the Bible," as he put it.

Luis brought his congregation. They prayed, danced, sang, and preached intermittently for two days and nights on the street downtown. His message to the gathered group of non-indigenous spectators was a clear call to trust in the power of God, and to accept Jesus' way of life. As a result of the indigenous presence, the protest demonstration largely dispersed. However, what reporters and government officials publicized was that the indigenous population from Barrio Nam Qom had provided a demonstration of their traditional indigenous culture in dance and song. From their point of view this was pure folklore, one more sample of cultural diversity. There was no recognition of the group as a church, of the activity as a church service, of the power of prayer nor any mention of God. Luis was hurt. He felt profoundly manipulated. Several days later he confided to me, "The government, the politicians, use us like a spare tire. When they need us they get us out and use us. When we have served for what they want, they discard us till the next time we are needed. When they call on us for prayer, we pray and God answers, but they don't even realize what the power of God is."

Luis' indigenous spirituality does not allow him to separate spiritual activity from historical processes. Seen from his viewpoint, mission is holistic by nature because all of creation is spiritual. Our western difficulty in grasping the meaning of holistic mission is due to our traditional separation of spiritual and material. I am witness to an expression of holistic mission as understood from a Toba Qom worldview. I marvel at God's strategy of changing the course of human history – one life at a time.

Formosa, Argentina
24 April, 2007

Appendices

1. Chronology of the Evangelization of the Toba Qom

Argentine Political Events	Other Missions and Churches	Mennonite Presence	Indigenous Events	Description of Events
1492				Columbus arrives on indigenous soil
1520				First contact of Toba Qom with European invaders.
1585				Alonso de Vera y Aragón founds the first Spanish city, Concepción del Bermejo, in Toba Qom territory. (Destroyed in 1632 by hostile indigenous)
1587	Jesuits			Jesuit missionaries arrive in the Chaco region
1711 to 1765	Jesuits			Jesuits establish eighteen missions
1767				Spanish colonies expel Jesuits
1774				Peace treaty recognizes sovereignty of indigenous peoples of the Argentine Chaco
1810				May Revolution in Argentina
1816				Argentina declares independence from Spain and recognizes the liberty of the Chaco indigenous
1853				Argentine citizens approve Article 67, section 15 of the national constitution. (later considered racist)[1]

---

1. Section 15: "In the Argentine Nation there are no slaves: the few who still exist shall become free as from the swearing of his Constitution; and a special law shall regulate whatever compensation this declaration may give rise to. Any contract for the purchase and sale of persons is a crime for which the parties shall be liable, as well as the notary or officer authorizing it. And slaves who by any means enter the nation shall be free by the mere fact of entering the territory of the Republic."

Argentine Political Events	Other Missions and Churches	Mennonite Presence	Indigenous Events	Description of Events
1884				Argentine military campaign in the Chaco to "subdue" indigenous; considered "completely successful."
1900	Franciscans			Franciscans establish reservations in Chaco and Formosa Provinces
1911				Argentine government establishes reservations in Chaco and Formosa provinces
	1914			Anglicans establish mission in Formosa Province
			1919	Hostile indigenous destroy Fortín Yunká Formosa military outpost. Argentine National Guard massacres Pilagás in retaliation
			1924	Starving Toba Qom and Mocoví of Napalpí reservation in Chaco Province walk to town seeking food. Military fear an attack and massacre in retaliation
	1932			Emmanuel Mission begins work among the Toba Qom in Chaco and Formosa provinces; later handed over to Church of the Nazarene and the Grace and Glory mission
			1940	Toba Qom contact with John Lagar of Go Ye Mission (from the United States) in Resistencia, Chaco Province
			1941	Massive people movement of conversions to Jesus begins among indigenous...within ten years about 10,000 accept *el evangelio*, (the gospel).

Argentine Political Events	Other Missions and Churches	Mennonite Presence	Indigenous Events	Description of Events
		1943		Mennonites establish a mission at Pampa Aguará, Chaco Province
			1944	Luciano Córdoba (Pilagá) begins *Corona* (Crown) religious movement in Formosa Province
	1946			Baptists establish Toba Mission in Chaco Province
1947				Argentine military massacre of over 750 Pilagas in Las Lomitas, Formosa Province
		1953		Three Toba Qom Mennonite congregations total 100 members
		1956		Mennonite missionaries evaluate program, decide to close the mission compound. Toba Qom now in charge of the three churches.
		1956		Mennonite missionaries, now called fraternal workers, begin distributing quarterly pastoral letter, *Qadaqtaxanaxanec* (Our Messenger).
			1958	United Evangelical Church organizes, with 17 Toba Qom congregations, with Mennonite fraternal workers' accompaniment
	1961			International Foursquare Gospel Church begins in Pampa del Indio, Chaco Province
			1961	United Evangelical Church receives its own legal registration number in the Argentine National Register of Non-Catholic Religions.

Argentine Political Events	Other Missions and Churches	Mennonite Presence	Indigenous Events	Description of Events
	1964			United Board of Missions (JUM) establishes a medical mission in J. J. Castelli, Chaco Province
			1967	Pilagá and Mocoví congregations begin to join the UEC
			1968	UEC has 2000 members in 40 congregations in Chaco and Formosa provinces
			1974	UEC joins the Argentine Federation of Churches, (headquarters in Buenos Aires)
			1976	Toba congregation near Asuncion, Paraguay, joins the UEC
	1977			Swedish Mission establishes The Good Shepherd Foundation in Sáenz Peña, Chaco Province
			1983	Orlando Sánchez, president of the UEC, establishes relations with South American movements promoting indigenous rights
	1984			Argentine Catholic Church organizes National Board for Indigenous Ministries (ENDEPA)
1984				Formosa Province approves first provincial law of indigenous rights in Argentina, No. 126
1985				Chaco Province approves provincial law of indigenous rights
			1987	UEC becomes a member of the Latin American Council of Churches

Argentine Political Events	Other Missions and Churches	Mennonite Presence	Indigenous Events	Description of Events
			1988	UEC totals about 4,500 active members in 120 congregations in five provinces of Argentina, and Paraguay
			1992	UEC totals about 140 congregations
		1993		Mennonite Team members begin to accompany the struggle for indigenous land rights
1994				Argentine legislature approves revision of National Constitution to recognize indigenous rights (Article 75, section 17 replaces Article 67).[2]
1996				Process of Participation of Indigenous Peoples (PPI) compiles indigenous opinion (two-year process).[3]
			1999	Indigenous win back 140,000 hectares of land in northwestern Chaco Province, with fraternal workers' accompaniment

---

2. (1994) Article 17 - To recognize the ethnic and cultural pre-existence of indigenous peoples of Argentina.

3. (1996) PPI extensive consultation conducted by the National Institute of Indigenous Affairs and the National Board for Indigenous Ministries on issues of land, health, education, etc.

2. Visits to Indigenous Communities

A. Guidelines for visitors on service assignments[1]

1. Keep in mind that we are entering a different culture, neither better nor worse than our own. Therefore, the first requirement is respect for the habits, customs and values of the local people. It is possible that some aspects will seem strange but remember that *we* are the strangers.

2. Upon arrival as a group, we should not spread out to explore. Wait to be introduced to our hosts. Generally we will be offered chairs or logs for sitting in a circle. Accept willingly if we are offered *maté* tea; listen with attention to the conversation. Our first task is to "take off our shoes." Don't forget that God was already there before our visit.

3. The indigenous are hospitable and congenial whether they live in urban neighborhoods or in rural forested areas. We can be sure they are happy for our visit, although they may not talk much nor express their emotions freely with strangers. Respect their timing and to move according to their rhythms. Times of silence, which to us may seem uncomfortable, can be more positive than fast talking or immediate action. A good custom is to be silent until those we visit sense the time is right to share something or ask us about our visit. A worthwhile practice is to remain silent except to respond.

4. Before carrying out any initiative or action, either as a group or individually, we consult those with more experience and with local leaders. The temptation to carry out or complete *our* project, or what we bring to offer, should be laid aside. What we *do* look for is mutual dialogue in order to discover with the people what might be *their* dreams and projects.

---

1. Based on recommendations prepared in 2001 for groups from the La Lucila Baptist Church in Buenos Aires in preparation for trips to the remote areas of Chaco Province where they carried out brief service assignments among indigenous communities.

5. It is not enough to recognize that we do not know the context and the history of the place and of its inhabitants. We must be willing to be vulnerable and ask for help and/or counsel of the local people. If we allow people to help us, perhaps they will also allow us to be of help to them.

6. Never, never, make a promise. Before deciding on any future plan of action it is necessary, without exception, to first consult with the local leaders, those who know the local situation and can decide the appropriate time to act. We should avoid paternalism, handouts or charity, which destroy local responsibility. It may be appropriate that our hands help others to fly, but may we never take the place of *their* wings.

7. Remember that what for us may be a necessity, may be an unnecessary comfort for them (for example, a mattress for sleeping). Try not to create needs where they do not exist. Their reality is not necessarily the same as ours.

8. We should be more ready to receive than to give, to learn than to teach, and to recognize our limitations. We must give up whatever sense of superior power or the illusion that we can "save" others that our technology or urban wisdom might lead us to claim.

9. Remember that a trip to an indigenous community is not a safari. Let us leave adventures aside. We should not put ourselves in situations of unnecessary risk, for example, go alone into the forest, explore an unknown place, get into a river, or stick our hand into a hole.

10. If we must travel far, we might need to spend the night on the road because of a vehicle breakdown, or we may have to wait somewhere for several days until the rain stops. We will be patient, helpful and flexible, willing to change our travel plans.

11. We will take mineral water along for drinking during our stay, or drink local water only if boiled.

12. The indigenous people are in charge of their own lives and, like us, are capable of deciding their own way. If we desire to accompany them, we may, with their permission. But the decisions made must be theirs. They know better than anyone else what are the problems and the right solutions for them.

13. The visit can be a special time in which God may want to speak to us. Therefore, Be attentive to the Holy Spirit and the Word of God, ready to hear.

B. Suggestions for visits to indigenous churches[2]

First of all, congratulations on your desire to visit the Pilagá people. As well as being true sisters and brothers in Christ, the Pilagá we will meet are persons who live as foreigners in their own land, marginalized and neglected. We want to be a blessing and share God's love with them. We communicate God's love better through who we are than through what we say.

Before we enter into direct contact with members of an indigenous culture unknown to us, we should prepare thoroughly. This includes not only the physical details for the trip itself, but also psychological and spiritual preparation. We need to find out the best way to interact with them that will dignify them.

We recognize with humility that many times the simple act of giving things, even with the best of intentions and with all good purposes, can easily communicate an attitude of technological, economic or religious superiority. Perhaps the best gift is our time, an attentive listening ear, or a sincere prayer. We should be aware that even the recordings of the Audio Scriptures or the printed Bible are simply tools; they are not a miraculous cure to change living conditions or situations of discrimination.

Whatever the gift to persons of other cultures, whether material or spiritual, it can be an ambiguous gesture. For any gift to be a blessing to the recipient(s), it must, without fail, be given to and received by the local people in a culturally appropriate manner. The conditions must be agreed upon beforehand. Whatever is given should be received and incorporated into the community in a way which the receiving group considers suitable. Respect for local customs and local leadership is crucial.

For all those considering the visit we suggest that you closely read Chapter 8 as well as Appendix 3. Here you will find important principles to study and discuss before arrival in the indigenous communities.

In addition, we invite you to consider in all seriousness what Lila Watson, an aborigine woman from Australia, once said:

> "If you have come to help me, you are wasting your time. But if you have come because you truly believe your salvation is tied to mine, then come, and we will walk together."

---

2. Guidelines suggested by Willis and Byrdalene Horst for those accompanying personnel of the Argentine Bible Society for distribution of recorded Audio Scriptures to Pilagá church leaders in April, 2011.

Of course, it is not possible to fulfill this commitment in one brief visit, since it would demand a long-term connection. It really implies a lifetime relationship. However, the visit can awaken within us the desire to commit ourselves to a lifestyle of service with the oppressed. Jesus invites us to meet him in the marginalized persons around us wherever we are.

As spiritual preparation we might take a good dose of prayer and contemplation reflecting on the truth that we do not save anyone nor do we solve anyone's problems for them. Jesus' attitude teaches us that the best help we can offer someone is to serve them as if they were Christ himself; that is, recognize Christ in the other as well as in us, and show them that we are in solidarity with them, as we both search for life in its fullness. Ask God for humility to accompany them without judging, condemning, or dominating. We need the patience to not interfere where uninvited, grace to wonder at the new, and wisdom to value that which is different.

As a final precaution, be aware that visits from outside the communities are usually made by persons who come with their own egocentric needs, be they political, economic, or religious, and with very little understanding of what it means for the indigenous community. A visit loaded with selfish purposes turns the hosts into objects: something to investigate, a goal to conquer, a target for marketing, or a candidate for converting. Or, perhaps simply the object of well-intentioned "help." The truth is that none of these goals dignifies the host. Take into account that we are simply one more of the many who arrive from outside and that for the local residents we are intruding. Even worse, if we arrive in more than two vehicles we are a *caravan* of intruders!

We have tried to prepare some of the Pilagá people ahead of time for the upcoming visit. They understand that we are not going to conquer them, to solve their problems, or to pass out candy. They understand that the reason of our visit will be to begin the distribution of the Audio Scriptures in their language, parts of the Bible in spoken form. It is understood that we are also followers of Jesus and that we want to visit them as equals. We pray that through God's Spirit they will be able to guide others to understand the purpose of our visit.

Also remember that the Pilagá believers are happy to meet followers of Jesus from the non-indigenous world. They quickly sense that we belong to the same family of faith. When they realize that we come simply as brothers and sisters in Christ, they feel blessed. It really isn't necessary to share anything more than God's work in our lives. They are always glad to hear of the long trip one has made to arrive at their community. The simple greeting *"Paz del Señor"* (The peace of the Lord) along with a gentle handshake is usually enough to break the ice, while a *"Jéga, yaqáya"* (Hello, my brother/my sister) shows respect for their ethnic identity.

We trust these suggestions will be useful to you. May they help your visit be one that will dignify and bless the Pilagá people. May your visit also be a blessing for all of you, their guests!

3. Comparative List of Cultural Traits

Indigenous societies	Technological societies
Cooperation	Competition
Sharing	Saving
Patience	Action
Harmony with nature	Conquest over nature
Inclusive	Exclusive
Live one day at a time	Plan for the future
Lack of time consciousness	Acute time consciousness
Group identity	Individualism
Respect for the elderly	Emphasis on youth
Smallness	Greatness
Seek tranquility	Seek success
Avoid confrontation	Provoke confrontation
Tradition	Novelty
Concrete	Abstract
Spoken word	Written word
Silence	Verbosity
Intuition, mystical	Reason, empirical
Unity of religion and life	Religion as a segment of life
Reality undivided, unity of all creation	Reality divided into opposites: clean, dirty; work, play

Compiled and adapted from lists prepared by Lawrence Hart, 1991; and from Little Rock Reed, in *Journal of Prisoners on Prison*, Vol. 3 No 1, 1990.

4. Graphic of Chaco Mennonite Mission Transition

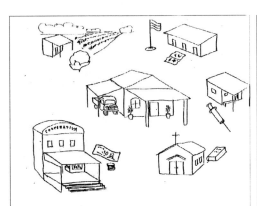

1. Mission compound:
Model of missionary practice of Mennonite Mission 1943–1955

2. Traditional Mennonite Mission: had to die so that the authentic indigenous church could be born

3. Accompaniment: fraternal workers of Mennonite Team walk together with Toba Qom believers

Bibliographies

Part I: Works by indigenous authors

Arce, Alfredo, *El ministerio que Dios da: seis reflexiones bíblicas* (The God-given ministry: six biblical reflections).

Castro, Ceferino J., *Da llicỹaxac qataq da chigoqta'ague nam i'otpi* (biographical stories). J. J. Castelli, 2006.

Chico, Juan, *Napalpi. La voz de la sangre* [Oral histories of the massacre in Napalpi Reservation in 1924] Subsecretaría de la Cultura de la Provincia del Chaco, Resistencia, 2009.

Francia, Ambrosio, *Testimonio de la vida y de la familia de Ambrosio Francia* (Testimony of the Life and Family of Ambrosio Francia.), Equipo Menonita, 2007.

López, Salustiano, *Escritos de Toxoỹaxayii: El llamado misionero; Principios del aprendizaje de la lengua y cultura; Pueblos no alcanzados; Cómo establecer iglesias autóctonas; y otros.* (Toxoỹaxayii's writings: The missionary calling; Principles of language and culture learning; Unreached peoples; How to establish autochthonous churches, and others.)

Sánchez, Orlando, *Rasgos culturales de los tobas* (Cultural features of the Toba people), ISEDET Instituto Superior de Estudios Teológicos, Buenos Aires, 2006.

Sánchez, Orlando, *Da na'aqtaguec nam Qompi Toba mayi lma' na lta'adaic Chaco, nam ỹi'axat som lquedoxonecpi namayipi, Historias de los aborígenes tobas del Gran Chaco contadas por sus ancianos."* (Oral histories of the Toba Qom people from the Gran Chaco told by their elders), bilingual edition, Librería de la Paz, Resistencia 2009.

———, *Cronología de la formación y del crecimiento de la Iglesia Evangélica Unida en el norte de la Argentina* (Chronology of the creation and growth of the United Evangelical Church in Northern Argentina. Equipo Menonita, 2005.

———, *Lengua Qom-Glosario Toba: Curso de apoyo para aprender para recuperar la lengua materna y la cultura.* Librería de la Paz, Resistencia 2009.

Suárez, Valentín: *Sobre la historia de los Qom de Da'añaalec Lachiugue* [*Riacho de Oro*]. Equipo Menonita, 2007.

Part II: Publications edited by Mennonite Team

Dictionaries, bilingual. Albert Buckwalter and Lois Buckwalter (compilers and editors), Mennonite Team, Formosa, Argentina.

Vocabulario Toba   Revised Edition 2001

Vocabulario Mocoví   First Edition 2001

Vocabulario Pilagá   First Edition 2000

VocabularioGuaycurú-Castellano First Edition 2004

New Testament (in partnership with United Bible Societies)

Toba   1981

Mocoví   1988

Pilagá   1993

Short Old Testament (two-thirds of O.T. text) (with United Bible Societies)

Mocoví   1991

Toba   1993

Collection of Old Testament Stories

Toba – Orlando Sánchez, translator (1974)

Mocoví – Roberto Ruiz, translator (1976)

Pilagá – Ramón Tapiceno, translator (1976)

Pastoral Bulletin/Periodical, *Qad'aqtaxanaxanec* (Our Messenger) published by Mennonite mission workers since 1955. Index for 1956-2006 available from Frank Paul.

Histories of Indigenous Churches, Transcriptions of oral histories and memories of four communities, Eric Kurtz (ed), Equipo Menonita, Formosa, Argentina, 1998.

-Barrio NamQom, Lote 68, Formosa

-Colonia Chicá Dawaxán, Pozo Navagán, Formosa

-Colonia Bartolomé de las Casas, Formosa

-Villa Margarita, Las Palmas, Chaco

Ministers' Manual for Indigenous Churches *Ntaunaqte na Nataxala'pi, Manual para Ministros Indígenas,* bilingual Toba Qom-Spanish, Willis Horst (ed.), Equipo Menonita, Formosa. 2007.

Collection of Toba Qom stories published in previous issues of *Qad'aqtaxanaxanec. Cochoc, Milec, Lotaxañi y otros.* Equipo Menonita, 2006.

Literacy Aids and Bible Studies, José Oyanguren Netoqqui (ed) and Cornelio Castro.

Bilingual Literacy Manual *Manual de Lecto-escritura na Qom La'aqtac,* Castelli 2006.

Toba Qom Primer *Soʼonataxanaxa na nedaquecpi naua qom laʼaqtaqa,*
   Castelli 2007.
Introductory Courses to Old Testament and New Testament in Toba Qom,
   Castelli 2007.
Illustrated (comic book format) **Stories of Bible Characters** in Toba Qom
   translated from Spanish, Equipo Menonita, Resistencia, Chaco.
   Som Yaʼacoxoic – Da naʼaqtaguec so Pedro. (The Life of Peter, the
   Fisherman), 2006.
   Som ỹale mayi huoʼo da namaxasoxonaguec – Da naʼqtaguec so Pablo. (The
   Life of Paul, the Apostle), 2007.

Part III: General works

Bergallo, Graciela Elizabet. 2004. *Danza en el viento: Ntonaxac - Memoria
   y resistencia qom* (Dance in the Wind: Ecstasy – Toba Memory and
   Resistance). Resistencia: Subsecretaría de Cultura.
Boff, Leonardo. 1986. *Desde el lugar del pobre* (From the standpoint of the poor).
   Buenos Aires: Ediciones Paulinas.
Braunstein, José and Elmer S. Miller. 1999. "Ethnohistorical introduction." In
   Peoples of the Gran Chaco, edited by Elmer S. Miller, 1–22. Westport: Bergin
   & Garvey.
Bremer, Margot. 1993. *La autogestión del pueblo de Israel* (Self-determination of the
   people of Israel). Paper presented in the XXI Jornada Anual de Misioneros
   Indigenistas (XXI Annual workshop of indigenist missionaries), Asunción.
Buckwalter, Albert S. 1975. "Brothers, not Lords." In *Being God's Missionary
   Community: Reflections on Mennonite Missions, 1945-1975, 39–45.* Elkhart:
   Mennonite Board of Missions.
Cook, Guillermo. 1994? *La Revelación de Dios en las Culturas: pistas misionológicas.*
   Photocopied material of anabaptist orientation from workshop in Central
   America. Semilla.
CONAPI (Coordinación Nacional de Pastoral Indígena). 1992. *Tierra, Autonomía,
   Cultura, síntesis teológico del IV Encuentro Nacional de Pastoral Indígena.*
   (Panamá, 13–18 September).
De Mello, Antonio. 1995. *El Canto del Pájaro.* Santander: Editorial Sal Terrae.
Drumm, Paul. 2002. *Codependency in Development and Social Work.* Occasional
   Paper No 30. Akron PA: Mennonite Central Committee.
Duarte, Carlos A. 1990. "Pentecostalismo y cultura aborigen." *Cuadernos No. 5.*
   Buenos Aires Argentina: Centro de Estudio Cristianos.

FUNCOOPA (Fundación Coordinadora de Pastoral Indígena). 1997. *Iglesias Indígenas de Abia Yala Frente al Desafío del Nuevo Milenio.* Memory of annual workshop with participation of Jaime Prieto. (August 1997). Higuito, Costa Rica.

Hernández, Isabel. 1992. "Quinientos Años . . . : el duelo más largo de la historia" (Five hundred years . . . : the longest period of mourning in history). *Suplemento Antropológico,* Vol. XXVII, No 1, (June 1992): 297–308 (Anthropological Supplement, bulletin of the Center of Anthropological Studies of the Catholic University), Asunción.

Hiebert, Paul G., R. Daniel Shaw, and Tite Tienou. 1999. *Understanding Folk Religions: A Christian Response to Popular Beliefs and Practices.* Grand Rapids: Baker Books.

Horst, Willis G. 1996. "The Use of the Bible in Mennonite Mission Strategy in the Argentine Chaco." Unpublished manuscript.

Kalisch, Hannes. 2000. *Hacia el protagonismo propio (base conceptual para el relacionamiento con comunidades indígenas.* (http://www.enlhet.org).

Lind, Timothy C. 1977. "Biblical obedience and the church's involvement in development." *Development Monograph Series,* No. 6, (revised March 1978). Akron PA: Mennonite Central Committee.

———. n. d. "Service and servanthood." Akron PA: Mennonite Central Committee.

———. 1989. "Service as a form of learning: The world church and the universal God." *African Newsletter* 4 (2). Akron PA: Mennonite Central Committee.

———. 1990. "Church goals at odds with God of all creation." *Mennonite Reporter* 20 (4). February.

Little, Christopher R. 2010. "The Economics of Partnership: Partnerships in Pauline Perspective." *International Journal of Frontier Missiology* 27 (2): 61–68.

Loewen, Jacob A., Albert Buckwalter, and James Kratz. 1965. "Shamanism, Illness and Power in Toba Church Life." *Practical Anthropology* 10 (6): 250–280.

Mast, Michael. 1972. "An Approach to Theological Training Among the Tobas of Argentina." Unpublished master's thesis, Fuller Theological Seminary, Pasadena.

Miller, Elmer S. 1970. "The Christian Missionary – Agent of Secularization." *Anthropological Quarterly* 43 (1): 14–22.

———. 1975. "Shamans, Power Symbols and Change in Argentine Toba Culture." *American Ethnologist* 2 (3): 477–496.

———. 1979. *Los tobas argentinos, armonía y disonancia en una sociedad.* Mexico: Siglo Veintiuno Editores, S.A.

———. 1980a. *Harmony and Dissonance in Argentine Toba Society.* New Haven: Human Relations Area Files. HRAFlex No. SI12-001.

———. 1980b. *A Critically Annotated Bibliography of the Gran Chaco Toba.* 2 Vols. New Haven: Human Relations Area Files. HRAFlex No. SI12-002.

———. 2005. "Transformations of the 'Missionary Mandate' – An Example from the Argentine Chaco." *Studia Missionalia.* Svecana.

Missions NOW. 1998. "A declaration for independents." *Mennonite Board of Missions quarterly magazine,* Summer 1998. Elkhart.

Oyanguren, José. 2010. *"Los conceptos de Espíritu Santo y carismas en 1 Corintios y su relación con la pneumatología indígena toba/qom."* Equipo Menonita, unpublished manuscript, J. J. Castelli, Chaco.

Regehr, Walter. 1981. "Movimientos Mesiánicos entre los grupos étnicos del Chaco Paraguayo." *Suplemento Antropológico* 16 (2): 105–117. Asunción, Paraguay: Universidad Católica.

Reyburn, William. 1954. *The Toba Indians of the Argentine Chaco: An Interpretive report.* Elkhart: Mennonite Board of Missions and Charities.

Richardson, Don. 1981. *Eternity in their Hearts.* Ventura: Regal Books.

Rooy, Sidney. 1992. "La tercera conversión de Pedro: el encuentro de dos culturas" (The third conversion of Peter: the meeting of two cultures) presented in *CLADE III: Tercer Congreso Latinoamericano de Evangelización,* (Third Latin American Congress on Evangelism) Quito, 1992. Presentations edited and published by the Fraternidad Teológica Latinoamericana (Latin American Theological Fraternity), 1993, 49–54.

Sánchez Cetina, Edesio. 1990. "La traducción de la Biblia y las teologías latinoamericanas" (The translation of the Bible and Latin American theologies). In *¡Que toda lengua proclame!* (Let every tongue proclaim!), edited by Ivan Balarezo and Mary De La Torre, 113–119. Quito: Puente.

Shenk, Wilbert R. *1999.* "New Religious Movements and Mission Initiative: Two Case Studies." In *Changing Frontiers of Mission.* Maryknoll, NY: Orbis Books. Chapter 5: 59–68.

Silva, Mercedes, ed. *1998. Memorias del Gran Chaco,* 2 vols. Resistencia, Argentina: Encuentro Interconfesional de Misioneros.

Stahl, Wilmer. 1994. "Chaco Native Economies and Mennonite Development Cooperation." Unpublished. Filadelfia, Paraguay: Asociación de Servicios de Cooperación Indígena-Menonita.

Suess, Paulo. 1995. "O Evangelho nas culturas: caminho de vida e esperanca" (The gospel in cultures: way of life and hope). Notes for the V Congreso Misionero

Latinoamericano (V Latin American Missionary Congress), Belo Horizonte, July 18–23.

Swartley, Willard M. 1994. *Israel's Scripture Traditions and the Synoptic Gospels: Story Shaping Story*. Peabody: Hendrickson Publishers.

Tamagno, Liliana Ester. 2001. *Nam Qom hueta'a na doqshi lma' (Los tobas en la casa del hombre blanco: identidad, memoria y utopía)*, (Tobas in the White Man's House: Identity, Memory and Utopia). La Plata: Ediciones Al Margen.

Turner, Harold W. 1981. "New Vistas, Missionary and Ecumenical: Religious Movements in Primal (or Tribal) Societies." *Mission Focus* 9 (3): 45–55.

Twiss, Richard. 2000. *One Church, Many Tribes: Following Jesus the Way God Made You*. Ventura: Regal Books.

Wessels, Anton. 1990. *Images of Jesus: How Jesus is Perceived and Portrayed in Non-European Culture*. Grand Rapids: Eerdmans.

Wright, Pablo. 1987. "Iglesia Evangélica Unida: Tradición y Aculturación en una Organización Socio-Religiosa Toba Contemporánea." *Cristianismo y Sociedad* 95, 71–87.

———. 1994. "Dream, Shamanism and Power Among the Toba of Formosa Province." In *Portals of Power: Shamanism in South America,* edited by E. Jean Matteson and Gerhard Baer, 149–172. Albuquerque: University of New Mexico Press.

———. 1997. *"Being-in-the-dream," Postcolonial Explorations in Toba Ontology*. Ph.D. dissertation. Philadelphia: Temple University.

Part IV: Indexes

For those interested, indexes of the following publications are available upon request from Frank Paul or other members of the Mennonite Team.

Qad'aqtaxanaxanec *(Our Messenger)* Index of contents for issues 1956-2006. See Chapter 3 section 6 d "Publications" for fuller description of this bulletin published periodically by the Mennonite Team from 1956 to the present.

Bible Circle summaries 1989-2006, Index of topics, times and locations where held. See Chapter 8 "The Bible Circle" for fuller description of this contextualized method of Bible study.

Interdenominational Missionary Conferences (known in Argentina as EIM for its name in Spanish: *Encuentro Interconfesional de Misioneros del Gran Chaco*). Available listing of annual meetings 1980-2005, including presenters invited, and themes offered and discussed. See Chapter 3 section "Networking" for fuller description of this organization.

Notes on Contributors

Willis Horst and Byrdalene Wyse Horst

WILLIS (1939-2013) and BYRDALENE HORST served with Mennonite Mission Network from 1971 to 2010, accompanying indigenous churches in the Argentine Chaco. Willis developed the Bible Circle, in which participants explore their spirituality and the values of Jesus within their own culture. Willis cared passionately for creation, and distributed hundreds of tree saplings among congregations they visited. They retired to the USA and their four children and seven grandchildren live in Argentina and the USA.

Ute and Frank Paul

UTE and FRANK PAUL lived with their children in Buenos Aires and in Resistencia, Chaco from 1990 to 2007. They were part of the Mennonite team, collaborating in the accompaniment of the Toba Qom churches with visits, Bible circles, exegetical counseling in the Bible translation project and bilingual teachers' training. Frank, a theologian, and Ute, a teacher, have three adult children and are members of the ecumenical Reichelsheim Fellowship Community (ojc.de) in Germany. Deeply enriched by implementing vulnerable mission in ministry, they advocate this approach to worldwide mission at conferences, seminars and in speeches (see vulnerablemission.org).

Albert S. Buckwalter and Lois Litwiller Buckwalter

ALBERT and LOIS BUCKWALTER served in the Chaco mission program from 1950 to 1993, guiding the transition from mission compound to fraternal worker accompaniment and birth of the indigenous and independent *Iglesia Evangélica Unida* (United Evangelical Church). They coordinated linguistic work and translation of the entire New Testament into the Toba, Mocoví and Pilagá languages, as well as the Short Old Testament into Toba and Mocoví, dictionaries in each of the three indigenous languages, and a quadrilingual dictionary of the three languages with Spanish. Albert died in 2004; Lois resides in Goshen, IN.

Elmer S. Miller and A. Lois Longenecker Miller

Lois and Elmer served in the Chaco mission program 1958-1963 followed by anthropological studies. He published numerous works on the Toba Qom people during his career as anthropologist and ethnologist as head of the Anthropology Dept. of Temple University, in Philadelphia, PA, where they currently reside.

Keith Kingsley and Gretchen Neuenschwander Kingsley

Gretchen and Keith served in the Chaco mission program 1997-2011. They worked primarily in the north and eastern region of Formosa Province among the Tacshic and Shiu'lec dialects of the Toba Qom in church accompaniment, empowerment of women, and Bible studies. Keith coordinated the Mennonite Team 2004-2011. They reside in Elkhart, IN.

Juan Carlos Martínez

Juan Carlos Martínez is a Mocoví community organizer, educator, religious and political leader. He heads a Mocoví organization in the struggle for indigenous land rights. Juan resides with his family at San Bernardo, Chaco Province, Argentina.

Fraternal Workers of the Mennonite Team (2008)

At the time of publication, of the remaining members of the 2008 team, only the Oyanguren family still reside in the Argentine Chaco.

	Acosta, Mónica and Luis Pedro Zanni 763 PB "A" (5000) Córdoba, Argentina Tel. +54 351 488 6096 luisacosta.chaco@gmail.com Coordination of translation team of Toba Qom Old Testament; consultant for recuperation of indigenous lands.
	Friesen, Ruth Anne and Richard (deceased 2010) The Clearing, 722 Monroe St. Evanston IL 60202 USA Tel. +1 847 3280796 rabfriesen@gmail.com Visitation of indigenous hospital patients, coordination of revision team of Toba Qom New Testament.
	González Zugasti, Susana and Esteban, Paloma and Bernabé Ayacucho 3446 (7600) Mar del Plata Pcia de Buenos Aires, Argentina Tel. +54 223 475 0405 egzugasti@gmail.com Visits to Mocoví churches in Chaco and Santa Fe provinces; consultant for recuperation of Mocoví lands.

Horst, Byrdalene and Willis (deceased 09/2013)
1502 S 16th St, Apt 2
Goshen, IN 46526 USA
Tel. +1 574 5349641
willyberta70@yahoo.com
Coordination of production of Pilagá Audio Scriptures; Bible Circles; visits to Pilagá churches in Formosa Province; intercultural theological study group.

Kingsley, Gretchen and Keith
1619 Benham Ave
Elkhart IN 46516 USA
Tel. +1 574 2945190
quitoana@gmail.com
Visits to Toba Qom churches in Formosa Province; Bible circles, preparation of bilingual Bible story books, coordination of Mennonite Team.

Oyanguren, Alfonsina and José (Emilia and Felipe)
Calle Alejandro Huespe c/Salta
Bo. Cichetti, Mz 1
3705 J. J. Castelli, Chaco
Cel. +54 364 447 1317
joseoyanguren@hotmail.com
joseyalfon@yahoo.com.ar
Visits to Toba Qom churches in Chaco Province; bilingual Bible studies and literacy materials.

Paul, Ute and Frank
Reichelsheim Fellowship (OJC)
Helene-Göttmann-Str. 5
64385 Reichelsheim (Odenwald) / Germany
Home +49 6164 5167005
Cel. +49 151 509 13 816
www.ojc.de / chacofrank@gmx.net
utepaul@gmx.net
Visits, Bible and bilingual training in indigenous churches; coordination of readers' feedback for the Toba Qom Bible translation team; accompaniment of Toba Qom prisoners and teachers.

Scenes from the Life and Context of the Mennonite Team Accompaniment Ministries

For the indigenous peoples the dense vegetation of the Argentine Chaco has always been their territory for hunting and gathering.

Chaco pond, source of water for Chaco inhabitants. During several months of the year, safe and sufficient drinking water is a serious problem for persons and animals.

Espina corona, common native tree of the Chaco forest.

Cattle arrived in the Chaco with colonization. Grazing inhibits the natural reforestation of the native forest.

Common rural dwelling. The forest provides all necessary materials: wood, grass and mud.

Urban Toba Qom neighborhood in Fontana, near the capital city of Resistencia, Chaco Province. Many years after hundreds of Toba Qom families settled in this urban locality, the neighborhood successfully obtained government housing with electricity and running water.

Surrounded by part of his family clan, patriarch Heriberto Romero observes a globe. This wonderful family hosted Frank Paul for years during his visits while he learned Toba Qom language and culture.

Group of Pilagá believers, c. 1970.

Toba Qom boys at *Mala' Lapel*, San Carlos Reservation, Formosa Province. As a protest against discriminatory treatment in the reservation school, parents kept their children out of classes. Following months of protest, the Minister of Education of the province finally intervened and appointed the requested Toba Qom teachers.

Open air church service in shade and sunshine.

Prayer at a baptismal service.

Sharing the table.

Anniversary of the founding of the United Evangelical Church at Quitilipi, Chaco Province. Believers of the host congregation donated cows for feeding the guests. Caring for guests and generosity are two of the most valued traits of the Toba Qom.

Celebration of United Evangelical Church of Quitilipi, Chaco Province. The children wait for the barbecue.

Logo of the United Evangelical Church displayed above the door of a church building. This denomination is the first truly autochthonous church in Argentina and now consists of approximately 200 local congregations.

A church dance instructor practices with youth in preparation for the service. The Toba Qom consider the dance to be an authentic indigenous expression of praise to God which unites forms of traditional culture with their new experience of faith in Jesus.

Following classes at the Indigenous Bible Institute in J.J.Castelli, participants share a meal.

Adolescents of various ages revitalize their identity through dance. Participation gives them a healthy pride in being indigenous and also in serving an important function in church life.

Ismael Castro, José Oyanguren Netoqqui, Cornelio Castro, Juan Carlos Pellegrini, teaching staff of the Indigenous Bible Institute, J.J.Castelli, Chaco Province. They are recognized for preparing their own materials and for teaching in the Toba Qom language. In addition, the Toba Qom team members make a significant contribution to literacy in their mother tongue among youth and adults in the region

The struggle for sufficient land for the indigenous population continues to be long and difficult. Here, a group with José Luis Leiva, Jerónimo Rodríguez and Julio Leiva, in Piyo' Lauac, Fortín Lavalle, Chaco Province, show a boundary marker left from a survey of 10,000 hectares (24,700 acres), an area ceded to the Toba Qom in 1924 by then Argentine president, Marcelo T. de Alvear, land which still has not been recuperated.

Evangelist Pablo Benítez and Alfredo Arce, missionary pastor of the United Evangelical Church, are close friends of Frank Paul. Their frequent visits are always an encouragement and inspiration.

Rafael Mansilla, Toba Qom chief of *Mala' Lapel*, San Carlos Reservation, Formosa Province, pastor and Bible translator. Rafael is known for claiming his indigenous identity, for the depth and clarity of his spirituality and for courageous community leadership.

Rosenda Diarte, Rubén Álvarez and Rafael Mansilla, revision team for the Toba Qom New Testament at work in Formosa City. Richard Friesen, fraternal worker of the Mennonite Team, coordinated this team that completed the revision in 2009.

Mennonite Team, 2006

Mennonite Team with visit of Pastor Jorge Galli, team counselor from Buenos Aires, 2007.

Mennonite Team members (incomplete) during a meal at family retreat. From left to right: Esteban González Zugasti, Gretchen Kingsley, José Luis Oyanguren, Ruth Anne Friesen, Richard Friesen, Ute Paul, Frank Paul, Willis Horst, Byrdalene Horst, Alfonsina Finger Oyanguren, Emilia y Felipe Oyanguren and Keith Kingsley

Ute and Frank Paul, content and grateful for shared experiences.

Mennonite Mission Network

The mission agency of
Mennonite Church USA

Mennonite Mission Network serves 21 area conferences of Mennonite Church USA in all their diversity—rural and urban congregations, younger and older populations, long-standing and new immigrant communities, speaking multiple languages, and many with varying convictions about how to be God's faithful people in today's world. We embrace this calling with a commitment to serve the whole church in all of its parts. We seek to engage challenges that we face as a diverse body of Christ with understanding and reconciliation. The following nine beliefs inform and guide our approach to ministry within the United States and in 57 other countries around the world:

The mission and glory belong to God.

- God's redemptive reign sets the agenda for our mission.
- Mission is rooted in God's love, focused on Jesus, and empowered by the Holy Spirit.
- Our mission is a joyful response to God's abundant grace.

The church is the primary model and messenger of God's love.

- The church is a sign of God's redemptive reign.
- Faithful congregations extend and reproduce themselves.
- The church expects opposition and is willing to suffer.

Reconciliation and transformation are possible.

- The gospel reconciles and transforms creation.
- Jesus' earthly ministry shows that the gospel must be adapted to cultural context.
- The final victory already belongs to God through Christ.

Mennonite Mission Network
PO Box 370, Elkhart IN 46515-0370 USA
www.MennoniteMission.net
Toll-free (USA): 1-866-866-2872

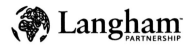

Langham Literature and its imprints are a ministry of Langham Partnership.

Langham Partnership is a global fellowship working in pursuit of the vision God entrusted to its founder John Stott –

to facilitate the growth of the church in maturity and Christ-likeness through raising the standards of biblical preaching and teaching.

Our vision is to see churches in the majority world equipped for mission and growing to maturity in Christ through the ministry of pastors and leaders who believe, teach and live by the Word of God.

Our mission is to strengthen the ministry of the Word of God through:
- nurturing national movements for biblical preaching
- fostering the creation and distribution of evangelical literature
- enhancing evangelical theological education

especially in countries where churches are under-resourced.

Our ministry

Langham Preaching partners with national leaders to nurture indigenous biblical preaching movements for pastors and lay preachers all around the world. With the support of a team of trainers from many countries, a multi-level programme of seminars provides practical training, and is followed by a programme for training local facilitators. Local preachers' groups and national and regional networks ensure continuity and ongoing development, seeking to build vigorous movements committed to Bible exposition.

Langham Literature provides majority world pastors, scholars and seminary libraries with evangelical books and electronic resources through grants, discounts and distribution. The programme also fosters the creation of indigenous evangelical books for pastors in many languages, through training workshops for writers and editors, sponsored writing, translation, strengthening local evangelical publishing houses, and investment in major regional literature projects, such as one volume Bible commentaries like *The Africa Bible Commentary*.

Langham Scholars provides financial support for evangelical doctoral students from the majority world so that, when they return home, they may train pastors and other Christian leaders with sound, biblical and theological teaching. This programme equips those who equip others. Langham Scholars also works in partnership with majority world seminaries in strengthening evangelical theological education. A growing number of Langham Scholars study in high quality doctoral programmes in the majority world itself. As well as teaching the next generation of pastors, graduated Langham Scholars exercise significant influence through their writing and leadership.

To learn more about Langham Partnership and the work we do visit **langham.org**

CPSIA information can be obtained
at www.ICGtesting.com
Printed in the USA
FFOW04n1632071015
17513FF